MOMENTS

365 DEVOTIONS

MOMENTS

3 Minutes Meditation

Daily Walk With God

Satiating Spiritual Nourishment

365 DEVOTIONS

IMOLE FOLAMI

ISBN: 978-1-7356003-0-7
Printed in the United States of America

Cover and book design by 7th Day Notion

MOMENTS

TO

FROM

DATE

To

Tolulope,

Jason and Jesse

Contents

Acknowledgements

As far as acknowledgements for this devotional go, I have a long list. Still, I dare not begin giving my thank you's without first adoring my Lord and Savior, Jesus. It's all about You, Lord—everything in this book is about You. You alone deserve all the glory.

To my beloved husband, Tolulope Folami, no one has ever believed in me and supported my dreams like you have. We spent months going over the details in this book. I remember all the sleepless nights you pulled just to get Moments ready for publishing. I love you...thank you.

To my younger brother, Temiloluwa Temola, ever since we were little, you have always been there for me. Thank you for your sacrifices for this book. Thanks for being my very first editor.

To my mom, Mojisola Temola, you are a major part of Moments story. Your selfless and exemplary life over the years has taught me so much. And to my father, Evangelist Ayorinde Temola, thank you for always being my cheerleader and for being one of the editors of Moments. To my mom-in-law, Remi Folami, thank you for being such a beautiful soul. Mr. and Mrs. Toyosi Temola, Mr. and Mrs. Tunde Temola, Mr. and Mrs. Tayo Folami, Mr. Oladele Osisami and Fiyinfoluwa Temola, you all are just too kind.

To the entire team of Moments, I am grateful to you. Rev. Yemi Adedeji, Pastor and Mrs. Charles Folami, Pastor Gabriel Eziashi, Andrew Adeshina, Danielle Westfall, and Heather Owen, thank you for being such terrific reviewers. Paul Akadi, you played a major role in the success of this project.

I appreciate your selfless service. Kemi Adeniyi, Adedeji Adedayo and Clement Dapo Olayiwola, thank you all for your support in the promotion of this project. To my chief editor, Daphne Parsekian, I appreciate and enjoyed working with you.

To my springtime family, I owe you all a debt of gratitude. I am thankful to everyone of you for your constant love and support.

Temidayo Akintoye, we have come a long way. You are exceptional, and your creativity has no bounds. I am blessed to have you on this team.

To my spiritual parents, Pastor and Mrs. Ropo Tusin, you have been a big inspiration to my family—thank you. To the pastors, ministers, and members of my church, Household of Faith in Arlington, Texas, I am grateful to you all. Thank you for being by my side through this journey.

I must also express huge gratitude to everyone who has in some way been a part of this book. If I were to mention all the names, I could fill the whole book. Thank you all for your encouragement and feedback. It is because of you that Moments has been successful. Finally, for you who have picked up this book and have decided to make it your companion for one year, I appreciate you. God had you in mind when this book was written.

A Note from the Author

Although I am the author of this devotional, if I am being honest, this book has very little to do with my human knowledge. I am only the instrument God chose to pass His message through. This book is a journey that took me six years to complete. During those years, God took me through various processes that made me ready for His work. *Moments* is built on the gospel and it also cuts across every sphere of Christian living. For everyone who will read this devotional, God had them in mind during writing the process of the book.

I know you may have some questions. Here are answers to a few:

Who is this devotional for?

It is for everyone—Christians and non-Christians, young and old, male and female.

How can I use it?

It is a daily companion, so you can use it however you please. It is available in both written and audio versions. You may read or listen to it any time of the day you desire—in the morning, while driving, or at night before you fall sleep.

What makes this devotional unique?

Moments is divided into nineteen series. Each series contains daily messages that align in flow and thoughts. With each series, you will be taken on a special walk with God. During the walk, God will reveal His heart to you in ways you can relate to. Each devotion is precise and begins with a scripture, followed by the message and a confession at the end. With *Moments*, you can fellowship with God within three minutes or spend longer if you so desire.

What should I expect?

As a reader, please note that this devotional is specifically for you. It is undiluted nourishment from God to you. This book will expose you to transforming revelations that will turn your life around. Also note that this devotion encourages you to be yourself and be real with your God. Readers need not worry about being judged as this book does not do that. Rather, Moments encourages you to be yourself and approach God as you are.

How can I contact the author?

I would love to meet you. I would also love to know what your journey with this book has been like. You can tag me with a picture of yourself reading *Moments* using the handle ***instagram.com/imolefolami*** on social media. You can also send me an email at ***info@imolefolami.com***. Thank you for choosing *Moments*. I'm excited to meet God with you.

GOD'S LOVE

JANUARY 1

BEAUTIFUL NAMES OF GOD AND THEIR MEANINGS

God knows us all by our names. Today, let us take time to study some of the names by which He is known and learn what they mean.

- El Shaddai – Lord God Almighty (Genesis 17:1)
- El Elyon – The Lord Most High (Genesis 14:19)
- Adonai – Almighty Ruler (Genesis 18:2)
- Yahweh – Unchanging God (Exodus 6:3)
- Jehovah Elohim – The Lord Strong and Mighty (Genesis 1:1)
- Jehovah Jireh – The Lord Our Provider (Genesis 22:14)
- Jehovah Mekoddishkem – The Lord Who Sanctifies (Exodus 31:13)
- Jehovah Nissi – The Lord Our Banner (Exodus 17:15)
- Jehovah Rapha – The Lord Our Healer (Exodus 15:26)
- Jehovah Shalom – The Lord Is Peace (Judges 6:24)
- Jehovah Shammah – The Lord Is Present (Ezekiel 48:35)
- Jehovah Sabaoth – The Lord of Hosts (1 Samuel 1:3)
- Jehovah Tsidkenu – The Lord Our Righteousness (Jeremiah 23:6)

God's names have distinct meanings, and the origins of these names are specific to situations in which God manifested Himself. As Christians, we should make a habit of declaring these names in our daily lives. Today, call God by His beautiful names and confess their meanings to your situations.

Confession: *Dear God, I declare that You are good. Your names are marvelous. I confess these names to my circumstances today. I believe with all my heart that You will manifest Yourself. Amen*

JANUARY 2

GOD'S LOVE

This is how God showed his love among us: He sent his one and only Son into the world that we might live through him.
1 John 4:9, NIV

The story of Jacob and Esau often raises questions. Why would God say that one of the twin brothers (Jacob) He loves and the other (Esau) He hates (Romans 9:13)? For this reason, some wonder if God loves everyone equally, like the scripture seems to state in Romans 2:11. Some theologians say the word "hatred," as used by God, does not connote "hatred" as defined in the dictionary. Still, I say God is God. His ways are not our ways. There are some things we cannot understand through human knowledge.

What God needs us to understand, always, is that He loves us dearly. He demonstrated this by providing His only Son as a sacrificial lamb for our sake. Such an ultimate sacrifice! God also shows us how much He loves us by blessing us daily. Whenever we call to Him, His listening ears are ever attentive to our needs. He favors us with that which we do not even deserve. Unless we close our eyes to it, God's love for us is evident, glaring, and immeasurable. His love for us is greater than all the grains of sand on the seashore. His love for us is unfathomable. If you have not believed in the past, please do so now. God loves you. But how can one fully key into this love? We'll explore this and much more in this new series, "God's Love."

Confession: *Dear God, You are good. Your mercies are overwhelming. You love me and make it obvious. Thank You for who You are. Thank You for all You do. I love You.*

JANUARY 3

CHRIST'S AFFECTION DEMONSTRATED

This is how we know what love is:
Jesus Christ laid down his life for us.
1 John 3:16a, NIV

Christ died on Calvary, and there could have been only one reason for Him to do all He did: love. Today we'll take an imaginary trip to that fateful day on the cross. Let's recount some events that transpired.

First, Jesus was betrayed by one of His own disciples, Judas Iscariot. Afterward, He was deserted by those who claimed to love Him. Peter, one of Jesus's closest friends, even denied knowing Him three times only hours after he swore he never would. Jesus then went on to be tried by Pilate, where He was falsely accused by the religious leaders. These same leaders were behind the coup that brought about the release of Barabbas, a known criminal originally condemned to be crucified before Jesus took his place.

After Jesus received His death sentence, He faced fiercer torment. He was beaten, mocked, taunted, made to carry His cross, and then placed between two criminals. Finally, Jesus was crucified—a cruel death that involved the driving of nails of five to seven inches long into His wrists and feet. How painful! How agonizing! How unedifying that day must have been for Jesus. He had so many reasons to choose not to go through all He did, but He did it out of love. His love for us eventually saw Him through His ordeal.

Confession: *Lord Jesus, I'm thankful for Your death on the cross. Despite how awful that day must have been for You, You thought of me above yourself. You gave up Your life for me. What a sacrifice! I appreciate Your love.*

JANUARY 4

COME TO HIM AS YOU ARE

Who will bring any charge against those whom God has chosen? It is God who justifies.
Romans 8:33, NIV

Why do we feel there is a certain way, where, and when we need to approach God? Why do we have to go, pretending or acting, to the One who made us? Is it our doctrines and places of worship that have placed such demands on us? Perhaps, is it our parents' teachings that have convinced us of certain traditions that we must follow to be right with God? Well, here is what Romans 8:38a says: "And I am convinced that nothing can ever separate us from God's love."

Religion may demand doctrines and traditions, but our God does not. We do not have to act like a saint to impress God. God knows us down to our souls, so why the ceremony? Why the formality? No wonder the Pharisees never embraced Christ. They were just too fake!

An inventor understands the ins and outs of a designed product. He or she also understands its shortcomings. The same goes for our God, who made us all. So be yourself! Bare your soul to Him the way it is. Bring your pain, guilt, and scars to the One who made you. He knows about them anyway. Come plain, transparent, and naked. Appear to your Maker as you are. He loves you regardless.

Confession: *Dear God, thank You for the grace to always be "me" in Your presence. Today I come to You spiritually naked and unashamed. I receive Your love wholeheartedly. Amen.*

JANUARY 5

HOW SOME BIBLE CHARACTERS SAW GOD

This is how we know what love is:
Jesus Christ laid down his life for us.
1 John 3:16a, NIV

The Bible recorded Esther as the Jewish girl who later became the Queen of Persia (Esther 4). During her reign, one of the king's high officials, Haman, plotted to execute her Countrymen, the Jews. Esther knew she needed to act quickly to stop the plot. The law of the land at the time stipulated that no one could dare enter the king's presence without being summoned. But Esther understood precisely what her God meant to her, so she went in to see her husband, the king. Before she did, she said, "I will go into the King, though against the law, and if I perish, I perish" (Esther 4:16). This statement gives us a clue about what this brave lady must have perceived about her God. According to Esther, God is One who favors His children.

David was up against a giant of over nine feet tall named Goliath. Despite this, David could not stop boasting about how big his God was compared to the mere mortal in front of him. First Samuel 17:46 says, "Today the LORD will conquer you, and I will kill you and cut off your head. And then I will give the dead bodies of your men to the birds and wild animals, and the whole world will know that there is a God in Israel!" Imagine such powerful words coming from the mouth of a young man. David saw God as his Deliverer.

In addition to Esther and David, other Bible characters saw their God in specific ways. Some of them include Abraham, Daniel, and Jesus' disciples. Interestingly enough, God responded and revealed Himself to them in the same manner in which they saw Him. The question now is "Who is God to you and me?" This and more are what we will discuss next.

Confession: *Dear God, You are good. You are my all in all.*
You are all-sufficient. This day, please reveal Yourself more to me.
Let me experience Your grace in all I do. Amen.

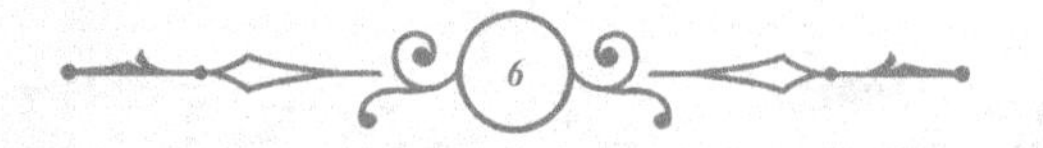

JANUARY 6

HOW DO YOU SEE GOD?

Have you not known? Have you not heard? The LORD is the everlasting God, the Creator of the ends of the earth. He does not faint or grow weary; his understanding is unsearchable.
Isaiah 40:28

Who is God to you? This is a question different people have different responses to. How we perceive God matters because this affects our perception of life. Some see God as a highly authoritative figure ready to punish anybody that crosses the line. Some perceive Him as The Consuming Fire, who is on standby, ready to burn the enemies of His covenant children. Some say He is a lenient God who only looks through the eyes of mercy. Many believe He is an all-sufficient God who always provides for His children. Many also agree that He is a benevolent God, who is gracious to those who turn to Him.

None of these perceptions of God is wrong. In the Old and New Testaments, God revealed His likeness in various manners. However, it is imperative that we do not view God just from one perspective. God is not just one of these earlier discussed characteristics. Instead, He is all of these and more. Our God is all in all. He is the beginning and the end. He is all-encompassing.

Confession: *Dear God, how do I even begin to describe You? Words are not enough to qualify Your graciousness. You are everything to me. The more I know You, the more I long to know You. I'm grateful for all You are. You are God. Amen.*

JANUARY 7

GOD CARES ABOUT THE LEAST TOO

And the very hairs on your head are all numbered. So don't be afraid; you are more valuable to God than a whole flock of sparrows.
Luke 12:7, NLT

Many of us are aware of God's love for us, but deep in our minds, we believe He only cares about the "significant" things. We attempt to deal with the insignificant things ourselves. Unconsciously, a lot of us are in the habit of trying not to bother God with the little stuff because we feel He has many "big things" to attend to.

God knows the number of hairs on our heads. This means He is interested in everything—both the significant and the seemingly insignificant things. He is keen on every aspect of our lives. So whatever you need, go ahead and tell Him. Is it cooking a delicious meal, buying quality things at the store, pimples disappearing from your face, or looking elegant for work? You just name it, and God is listening. Yes, it may sound bizarre to us but not to Him. He is ready to help with both the big and the little things if we let Him. In our continual walk with God, we will find Him drawing us into a more intimate relationship. We will also find ourselves communicating freely with God wherever we are. This may be on our knees, in our car, or in the bathroom. God loves us dearly. Because of this, all our concerns also concern Him.

Confession: *Dear Lord, thank You for your unconditional love. Teach me to understand that You care about every detail of my life—big and small. I choose henceforth to let You in on every one of my concerns. Thank You for Your ever-present, listening ears. Amen.*

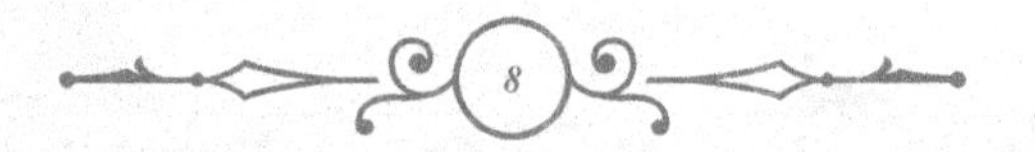

JANUARY 8

GOD UNDERSTANDS BETTER THAN WE THINK

Not that I have already obtained this or am already perfect, but I press on to make it my own because Christ Jesus has made me his own.
Philippians 3:12

We think we have blown it and have done the unpardonable! Yet all God is doing in heaven is smiling at how seriously we take ourselves. A lot of times we humans forget that we are human. We expect from ourselves only what God has: perfection. According to today's scripture reference, perfection is a work in progress and not something that happens overnight.

Sometimes we will not get it right, and when we don't, forgiveness is just a step away. God loves us. Even if we sometimes feel undeserving of His love, it still doesn't change the fact that He does. Yes, the constant thoughts in our heads may be about how much God is upset with us for doing that which we should not have. But are our thoughts God's thoughts? No.

I remember one time when I messed up. I asked for forgiveness but still could not get over the idea that God was mad at me. So I asked the Holy Spirit for help. When the Holy Spirit showed me a picture of God, it was that which portrayed Him with His arms stretched out. He was waiting for me to run into His embrace. All God required from me at that point was for me to not beat myself up. He wanted me to accept His forgiveness and have a repentant heart. God never wants His children to wallow in guilt. He wants us to always be in His peace. God understands us and our shortcomings better than we think. All He requires is our honesty.

Confession: *Dear Lord, You know everything. You see me inside and out. I'm sorry for all my past transgressions. Today I accept Your love as I run into Your embrace. I surrender it all to You, God. Amen.*

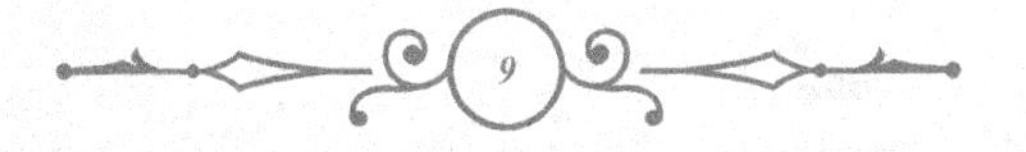

JANUARY 9

WHEN OTHERS TURN THEIR BACKS

Father to the fatherless and protector of the widows
is God in his holy habitation.
Psalm 68:5

God is love. Romans 8:35 says, "Who shall separate us from the love of Christ? Shall tribulation, or distress, or persecution, or famine, or nakedness, or danger, or sword?"

As beautiful as human love is, it cannot compare to the love God has for us, His children. I speak from experience when I say that when everyone you know turns their backs, God never will. As long as you have God, then you have everything and everyone you need. With God, you are complete. In Him, your hope will be reassured.

God's kind of love is unconditional. It is not one that demands something in return. God's never withdraws His love when it is not reciprocated. Believe me when I tell you today that God is all you need. As long as God's got your back (if you permit Him to), then you are good to go. When human love fails, God's love is always available, whether or not we feel we deserve it.

Confession: *Dear God, I'm thankful because I know nothing can separate me from Your love. You will never stop loving me. I will always be enough for You regardless of what other people say or do. You are all I need, Lord. Your love is all-encompassing. Amen.*

JANUARY 10

WHEN WE TURNED OUR BACKS

Come to me, all you who are weary and burdened,
and I will give you rest.
Matthew 11:28, NIV

If God decided to give us exactly as we deserved, some of us would have perished a long time ago.

Remember those times when you and I lost our way? This awesome God never gave up on us. He guided us with His grace until we found our way back home. When we eventually found our way, He didn't chastise us as our earthly parents would have. Instead, He nurtured us till we could stand on our own feet again. This is my story and that of countless others who have, at some point, backslid.

This God we serve is one who has His arms wide open, ready to receive us whenever we decide to return to Him. If you are out there today with a repentant heart but feel engulfed in guilt, God has two words for you: "Come home." The devil condemns and castigates, but God just welcomes you back into the family. Walk into His outstretched arms today, and embrace the loving Father, who is delighted to have you back.

***Confession:** Dear Lord, You are my rescue story. You never give up on me. When I lose my way, You always find me. I shed all the weight of condemnation. This day, I choose to walk into the freedom only You can give. Amen.*

JANUARY 11

WHO GOD IS NOT

When you ask, you do not receive, because you ask with wrong motives, that you may spend what you get on your pleasures.
James 4:3, NIV

I heard a story about a group of people who decided to agree in the place of prayer. They had a specific prayer point: that God should kill their employer because he was not favoring them. My first thought was "Who do these people think God is?" My second thought was about how sad it was that some Christians would assume God would consider such prayers. God will never listen to a prayer that carries an ungodly motive, period! God is never and will never be an unjust God.

God is also not a magician. Some lazy people are in the habit of praying for overnight success without wanting to work. These people may need to understand that such prayers will most likely not be answered. Yes, God changes people's stories overnight, but those are usually ones that have sown something worthwhile into the ground. God then blesses and multiplies such seeds and makes room for abundant harvests. God is so many things and can assume so many names to His covenant children. But before we go to Him with any request, let's check to be sure it carries the right motive.

Confession: *Dear Lord, You know my shortcomings. If there is any way that I have been selfish or prayed amiss, please forgive me. Have mercy upon me, dear God. Amen.*

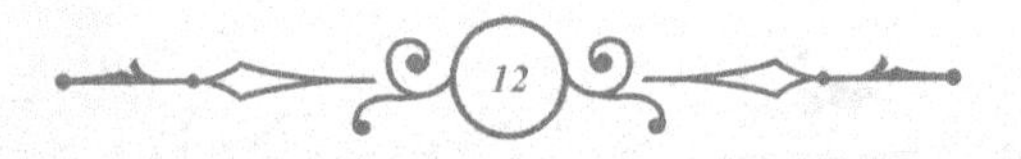

JANUARY 12

A LOVING FATHER DISCIPLINES

...For the Lord disciplines the one he loves,
and chastises every son whom he receives.
Hebrews 12:6

Like every loving father, God also disciplines his children. Sometimes He disciplines us to correct, train, break, and remold us. God disciplines us as a preparation for the journey ahead.

Some parents say the best way to teach a grown child adamant about playing with fire is to let that child feel the heat from the fire. This will automatically set the child straight. Well, with God, sometimes we may also have to learn the hard way. This is especially true if we refuse to follow God's instructions. If we keep doing that which He disapproves of, we may keep experiencing difficulties. Learning the hard way is one measure God uses to discipline His own. There are several others as well.

God is a disciplinarian; we cannot take that away from Him or ignore it. But in all He does or does not do, one thing remains constant: His love for us. God will never stop loving us even as He disciplines us. Our place is to embrace and not rebel against God's discipline. Discipline makes us better in the end. Success can hardly be attained without some level of discipline.

Confession: *Dear Lord, You correct those whom You love. Help me, Holy Spirit, so I will not learn the hard way. I humbly accept Your discipline today. Keep molding me until I become all You have destined me to be. Amen.*

JANUARY 13

A LOVING FATHER SAYS NO

For I know the plans I have for you, declares the LORD, plans for welfare and not for evil, to give you a future and a hope.
Jeremiah 29:11

From my experience, when God says no to a particular request of mine, it's because He has something better for me. Parents in the habit of pampering their children often feel they must give them everything they want. They also feel it is their sole responsibility to make their kids feel like the most important people in the world. These parents will always endeavor to see that their children receive all they request, regardless of the cost. However, many other parents understand the danger of kids getting their way all the time. These kinds of parents have no problem saying no to their kids when it is called for. Their no is always a firm one. No matter how much their kids plead, throw tantrums, or get upset, their no remains no. A firm but loving parent understands that a child may not appreciate hearing no, but they also know that same child will most likely understand it better in the future. Everything the parents do, they do purely out of love. The same goes for our God.

Just because we desire something doesn't mean we need it. And just because we feel we need it doesn't mean it is good for us in the long run. Our God (who knows and sees all) says no for many reasons, but hatred has never been one. God is love. A no from God sometimes is His way of showing us how much He loves us.

Confession: *Dear Jesus, You always have my best interest at heart. All You do and refuse to do is only for my good. I'm thankful for this. Help me, Lord, to never get ahead of myself. Guide me so I may never be derailed from Your plans for my life. Amen.*

ATTITUDE OF GRATITUDE

JANUARY 14

INGRATITUDE

And you will say in that day: "Give thanks to the LORD, call upon his name, make known his deeds among the peoples, proclaim that his name is exalted." **Isaiah 12:4**

Someone may ask, "Why do I need to be especially grateful? Everything that happens in my life is only normal. I sleep, wake, eat, and go about my daily business like a normal person. There is nothing extraordinary about my life that requires me to give any special thanks."

When asked to testify about God's goodness, hardly anyone responds. According to them, one should only testify when certain "real incidents" or "near-miss incidents" occur. These people may say things like "It wasn't like I was involved in a fatal accident that claimed everyone's life but mine." They may even say, "It wasn't like I was diagnosed with a terminal illness that God healed me from. Therefore, I do not have any special testimony to give."

Until we have those big testimonies, many of us will not believe God has done anything special. If we allow the Lord to open our spiritual eyes for just a few moments, we will marvel at what God does for us every minute. The most extraordinary miracles are not those that are necessarily visible. Please never let your life get to a point where your testimony is only based on you escaping tragedy. Be grateful for everything, even the so-called little mercies. Your life is a testimony right now.

Confession: *Dear Lord, thank You for making me a testimony. You bless me every day with so much. Thank You for the blessings I see as well as the ones I don't. When given the opportunity to testify, I will be the first in line. Amen.*

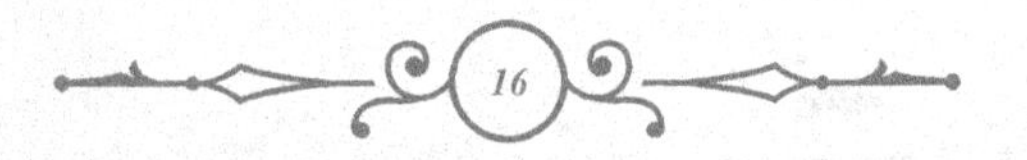

JANUARY 15

EVIDENCE OF GOD'S GOODNESS

Let them give glory to the LORD, and declare his praise in the coastlands.
Isaiah 42:12

We should not need any persuasion to be grateful to God. Nonetheless, for the sake of those who may need some, I will give a few. A trip to the mortuary, hospital, or prison should serve as a good prompt. Beggars and homeless folks are everyday people like you and me.

There are so many day-to-day situations that prove how good God has been to us. The most important proof is Christ's death on the cross. Christ died so that we can live abundantly on Earth and also enjoy eternity in heaven. Unfortunately, the "blessed" and "highly favored" ones are those who often feel they have little to be thankful for. This is because these people get comfortable quickly. Hopefully this is not our case too.

Every new day is a gift from God, and we have a billion reasons to be thankful. We cannot even see many of God's blessings with our physical eyes. Let's make gratitude a part of our lifestyle if we are not in that habit yet. No matter what we are going through at the moment, our case is not the worst. God has been good to us. In examining our lives thoroughly, we will find evidence of His goodness.

Confession: *Dear Jesus, thank You for the grace to see another day. My being alive is only by Your mercies. You are marvelous. For all You do, I appreciate you. Even if I had ten thousand tongues, I know I still could not thank You enough. You are amazing!*

JANUARY 16

SHOWING APPRECIATION

Those who are wise will take all this to heart; they will see in our history the faithful love of the LORD.
Psalm 107:43, NLT

Imagine going the extra mile to do something nice for someone, but the person then forgets to say thank you because he or she feels you have done nothing special. Perhaps the person just says a casual thank you. How would you feel? You would feel hurt, wouldn't you? Well, this can also be likened to God's position with us.

Whatever measure we choose to show our appreciation to God can never be equal to what God does for us. Still, it is important we give our thanks in the best way we can. Psalm 116:12 (NLT) says, "What can I offer the LORD for all He has done for me?" and Psalm 103:2 (KJV) reminds us, "Bless the LORD, O my soul, and forget not all His benefits."

It's one thing to show appreciation, but how we show it also matters. Whenever we choose to show our gratitude, let's do it like we mean it. When we give our thanks to God, let's do so because we want to and not because we have to. Thanksgiving should go beyond a mere routine we observe. It should be what we delight in doing. Our God has done so much for us, and He has been beyond good to us. How then do we show our gratitude? We do so when we make thanking God our lifestyle.

Confession: *Lord, I'm sorry. Please forgive me for the ways I have acted unappreciative of Your blessings. You have kept me and all that concerns me. You have blessed me with even more than I have asked for in times past. Today I lay all my worries aside and praise You. You have been good to me. Thank you, Jesus.*

JANUARY 17

THANKSLIVING

And when he had removed him, he raised up David to be their king, of whom he testified and said, "I have found in David the son of Jesse a man after my heart, who will do all my will." **Acts 13:22**

There will always be a difference between those who live thankfully and those who don't. Thankless people are naturally pessimistic, gloomy, and negative. They are the ones that complain about everything. Nothing is ever good enough for them. What an unhappy life! A good thing you and I are thankful people.

Today we are being challenged to go a notch higher from just being thankful to "living" thankful. "Thanksgiving" becomes "thanksliving" when we offer praises to God ceaselessly. Thanksgiving becomes thanksliving when we live every day in humility and gratitude. Thanksgiving becomes thanksliving when we perceive life and all we've been blessed with as a gift and not a right. We live thankfully when compliments and appreciation consistently flow from our lips.

Thanksliving is a way of life that pleases God. In the Scriptures, those who made Thanksliving a lifestyle were easily drawn to God. God even called one of them, David, a man after His own heart. When we make living thankfully a lifestyle, we become excellent candidates for God's devoted attention. There is a special place in God's heart for grateful people.

Confession: *Dear Lord, thank you for being my portion in the land of the living. Today I choose thanksliving. I will worship You every day. Every moment of my life will be filled with praise. As I go about my day-to-day activities, I will take every opportunity I get to say something thankful to You. Amen.*

JANUARY 18

THAT WHICH COST ME NOTHING

But the King said to Araunah, "No, but I will buy it from you for a price. I will not offer burnt offerings to the Lord my God that cost me nothing." So David bought the threshing floor and the oxen for fifty shekels of silver.
2 Samuel 24:24

A busy rich man may find it easy to write a million-dollar check. Should this man offer God his money as opposed to his quality time, he has offered God that which cost him nothing. To the rich man, his time is of more value than his millions. So in choosing to give that which is of little worth, he has offered nothing. In Mark 12:41–45, a poor widow chose to contribute her last cents to the offering box. Jesus noticed this and was very pleased. He regarded her offering as more valuable to God than the contributions of the rich men (Mark 12:43).

Nothing we give to God is too much. How do we even give back to the One who created and owns everything? If we truly understood what it means to give to the Lord, we would hardly struggle to do it. Out of the abundance we have been blessed with, God has only asked us to return so little. What a gift!

When we give, we should aim to do so with joy in our hearts. The person who benefits the most from giving to the Lord is the giver and not God Himself. No transaction done in faith with God goes unrewarded (Galatians 6:9). Henceforth, let's endeavor not just to give but to only give that which costs us something.

Confession: *Father, You are my everything. I decree this day that my offerings will cost me something. Even if it is my last, I will drop it at the altar. I give You all of me today. Use me for Your glory. Amen.*

JANUARY 19

WHERE ARE YOU COMING FROM?

Then King David went in and sat before the Lord and said, "Who am I, O Lord God, and what is my house that you have brought me thus far?"
2 Samuel 7:18

Many of us get so caught up in our everyday routine that we forget to look back at where we are coming from. Some of us do not even recognize how far God has brought us. In our search for more, we often forget our yesterday. The act of remembrance is vital for all believers. No, this is not the same as living in the past. Rather, it is continually going down memory lane. It entails bringing back to mind where we have been, where we are now, and where we are going. This way, we appreciate life more. It's essential we remember our former lives and all that we were years ago—or maybe even days ago.

The thankful habit reminds us to never take anything for granted. According to today's text, David knew the importance of reminding himself of where he had come from. No wonder he danced naked, cried, and rolled on the floor while praising God. He never once forgot where God picked him from. David acknowledged God every opportunity he got. At every phase of his life, he was appreciative. This habit also helped him keep his life in check. Let's have a thankful attitude today. Being thankful triggers more blessings from God. Besides that, it helps us recognize how much we have to be grateful for.

Confession: *Lord, You are my refuge and fortress. I remember where You picked me from. I remember those days when I had lost all hope. But You, O Lord, came onto the scene and turned my life around. You have given me a brand new song. You have turned all my travails to triumphs. For this, I bless You. Amen.*

JANUARY 20

ATTITUDE OF GRATITUDE

Out of them shall come songs of thanksgiving, and the voices of those who celebrate. I will multiply them, and they shall not be few; I will make them honored, and they shall not be small. ***Jeremiah 30:19***

Life is all about choices. If there is anything God has given us, it's the free will to make these choices. In life, you will always be given an option to celebrate the thorns that have roses. You will also be given the freedom to complain about the roses that have thorns. I urge you today to please choose gratitude.

Life has its ups and downs. Sometimes the situations we find ourselves in make us very happy. Other times, they make us sad. Still, no situation comes labeled. We are the labelers. The good news is, God has given us a free will to label our situations any way we want to. Nothing happens on this beautiful Earth that God hasn't allowed. Yet in everything, He still expects us to be thankful wherever we find ourselves, even in unfavorable circumstances.

Everyone is naturally happy when things are going fine, but how about those times when problems arise? What about those times when it feels like our entire world is crumbling? We could complain, grumble, and murmur. We could also rebel and go look for help outside of God's presence. Or we could trust God to bring us out of that situation. Remember, it is very easy to lament when things are not going our way. It is also challenging to be thankful through tough times. Yet gratitude is what God expects of us. No matter how terrible a situation may seem, there will always be something in it to be grateful for. I implore us to look into our lives today and start celebrating those thorns that have roses.

Confession: Dear Lord Jesus, I label my situation great. Even if it may not appear so right now, I choose to work in faith. I choose gratitude today. Regardless of all that may be going on in my life, I praise You. I know I am exactly where You need me to be right now. Thank you, God. You are good.

JANUARY 21

AS AN OFFERING TO THE LORD—YOUR HEART

I appeal to you therefore, brothers, by the mercies of God, to present your bodies as a living sacrifice, holy and acceptable to God, which is your spiritual worship. **Romans 12:1**

Our hearts are the best gifts we can give God. In fact, our hearts are the first gift God requires from us as Christians. Permit me at this junction to ask if you have truly given your heart to God. Please note that I am not asking if you regularly attend weekly church services. This is not even about whether you give alms to the poor or if you prophesy. I'm asking if you have genuinely surrendered it all to Him.

The ultimate sacrifice one can give is one's life. Christ did this on the cross for you and me to show how much He loves us. But if we hold on to that which we should release to Him (our hearts), His death on the cross may be a waste as far as we are concerned.

Are you one who has not totally let go of your life? Are you one who has backslid and soiled your relationship with Jesus? Should you be unsure of what your relationship with Jesus Christ is like, all you have to do is dedicate or rededicate your life right now. Please do not wait, as tomorrow may be too late. Go ahead this minute; surrender your life to Him. Do so in your own words, and believe that as of this moment, you are a confirmed child of God. Congratulations!

Confession: *Lord Jesus, thank You for the gift of salvation. I humbly come to Your throne of grace and ask for mercy. Please forgive all my trespasses. Please come into my heart today. I yield my life to You. Take it all. Amen.*

JANUARY 22

AS AN OFFERING TO THE LORD—YOUR PRAISE

And at midnight Paul and Silas prayed, and sang praises unto God: and the prisoners heard them. And suddenly there was a great earthquake, so that the foundation of the prisons were shaken: and immediately all the doors were opened, and every one's bands were loosed. **Acts 16:25–26, KJV**

You might be surprised what a few minutes or hours of regular worship can do. In the place of praise, there is healing, breakthrough, joy, and miracles. Paul and Silas understood this. According to today's scripture, Paul and Silas prayed and praised. As a result, the prison doors opened, and they were set free from their captivity. The power of praise can bring about liberty from bondage. These and more are the many benefits of praise. But are these benefits the only reason we should give our praise offering to God? Definitely not!

We should praise God because we love Him. We should praise God because when we look at our lives, we can see Him workings. We should also praise God in remembrance of all He has done for us. Oh how sweet it is to be loved by God! How beautiful it is to be called one of His own. This God is good!

The more we grow in God, the more we will long for an atmosphere of fellowship with Him. The more we fellowship with Him, the more we will lose ourselves in Him. There is something extraordinary about the power of praise. The connection it magnates from heaven is topmost. Spend quality time in the place of praise today. Praise nourishes the soul.

Confession: *Dear Lord, I praise You. When I think back to all You have done and are still doing, I can only bless You. There is enormous power in praise. Today I will sing to You. Every day I will dance and praise You. You are good, and Your mercies endure forever. Amen.*

JANUARY 23

AS AN OFFERING TO THE LORD—YOUR TALENTS

In the same way, let your light shine before others, so that they may see your good works and give glory to your Father who is in heaven.
Matthew 5:16

Our talents and gifts are the attributes that set us apart from everyone else. They are those things we find ourselves doing effortlessly. They are the potential that God had deposited in us from birth. These gifts are not mistakes or coincidental. God put them in us for this major purpose—to offer them to our world and His Kingdom. God blesses us with gifts, and how we best make use of these gifts is our offering to Him. The question today is, have you and I been blessing the world with our gifts? Can we honestly say God is happy with our attitude toward all we have been blessed with? Are we making good use of these gifts or wasting them?

God has brought us into the world for moments like this. The world needs our talents. The special package God put in us before we were born is what the world is desperately in search of today. It's high time we opened our parcel. As Christians, we have an obligation to bless our churches, communities, and nations with our gifts. Our talents may seem insignificant in our own eyes, but if we would step out in faith and bless the world with them, we would be surprised at how much of a difference we can make.

Confession: *Dear God, thank You for the gift of creativity You have given me. I will serve You with my gifts, and I will bless the world with all I have been blessed with. Help me not to waste my talent. Help me make a difference in my world. Amen.*

JANUARY 24

GIVING BACK TO THE LORD

And Solomon awoke, and behold, it was a dream. Then he stood before the ark of the covenant of the Lord, and offered up burnt offerings and peace offerings, and made a feast for all his servants.
1 Kings 3:15

Giving back to the Lord comes in many forms. As Christians, many of us are accustomed to our usual thanks offerings, tithes, and vows. But the Bible has revealed that giving does not have to center around a particular doctrine. For example, Hannah gave her child as an offering to the Lord (1 Samuel 1:27–28). Solomon offered a thousand burnt offerings at the altar (2 Chronicles 1:6). Jesus Christ, our Savior, offered His very life (Matthew 27:50). All these examples show us that we can give just about anything worthy of thanks as an offering to God.

An offering is something between God and His child. It is an act that displays one's gratitude for all God has done in time past. Many disciples in the Bible gave their lives solely for the gospel. So if we give our entire being to God, it will not be considered too extreme. Giving does not have to be conformed to a particular rule or principle. So long as it comes from the heart, God will accept it.

When we give, we do so as a testament of all God has done and all He will do. Besides our regular offering, we can also give to God through other acts. These include our time, services, testimonies, worship, and more. In whatever form we choose to give is at our discretion. The act of giving is what truly matters.

Confession: *Dear Lord, I offer You my praise today. Solomon's offerings provoked You into giving him a blank check of any blessing he desired. Holy Spirit, teach me to make my offering to God in like manner. Henceforth, I will not merely give an offering to the Lord but give that which will catch God's attention. Amen.*

THE WORRY-FREE LIFE

JANUARY 25

THE WORRY-FREE MIND

Peace I leave with you; my peace I give to you. Not as the world gives do I give to you. Let not your hearts be troubled, neither let them be afraid. **John 14:27**

Worry has many definitions. It includes feeling uneasy, anxious, or unhappy about something. When worry becomes extreme, it can lead to sleepless nights and panic.

Worrying all the way is what we humans do. We worry about the past, present, and unseen future. Parents worry whether their children will be safe and turn out great. kids fret over feeling left out or not measuring up to their peer's standards. Students worry whether they will do well on their examinations. Health-care professionals worry about their patients' lives. Patients worry about the result of their test and treatment. The worry list is endless.

Mankind is in a state of constant worry, but what do the Scriptures have to say about the act of worrying? Is it possible or realistic not to worry at all? These and more will be explored as we consider the new theme, "The Worry-Free Life."

Confession: *Dear Lord, I thank You for Your peace. Today I come against any force that may be threatening my peace of mind, and I receive the grace to live worry free. Amen.*

JANUARY 26

THE GRACE TO LIVE WORRY-FREE

Fear not, for I am with you; be not dismayed, for I am your God; I will strengthen you, I will help you, I will uphold you with my righteous right hand. **Isaiah 41:10**

A human being is made up of the flesh, soul and spirit. This is why no matter how spiritual a person is, there are just certain things he or she cannot run away from. One of those things is worry. But why do we worry? We do so because we are human. We worry because unlike inanimate objects, we have feelings. We are bothered because we care. We fret because we do not have control over everything in life. We worry because this is one way we can connect to or understand a situation. We also worry because it is in our nature to do so.

God created us, and He knows all about our inadequacies. Therefore, He does not expect us to act like or pretend to be supernatural beings when we are not. In fact, the Scriptures make us understand that pretense is something God detests. Jesus repeatedly preached against pretense while He was on Earth (Matthew 6:16, Mathew 23:27). This lets us know that God wants us to come to Him as we are and with all our "fleshy" shortcomings. This includes the act of worrying.

Unexplainable peace of mind and inner joy are some added benefits that come with living a worry-free life. Living free of worry can never be attained by our human might. It is a way of life that can only be achieved through the grace of God. This special grace is available today just by asking.

Confession: *Father, I'm grateful for the grace to be myself in Your presence. Today I come boldly to the throne and lay all my weaknesses at Your feet. I receive the grace to live worry-free and focus on You, my Author and Finisher. Amen.*

JANUARY 27

THE PROS AND CONS OF WORRY

Casting all your anxieties on him,
because he cares for you.
1 Peter 5:7

The act of worrying comes naturally with the human package. Since this is the case, it is expedient that every person knows the disadvantages and advantages that come with this act.

Starting with some health disadvantages, excessive worry leads to stress, which may lead to high blood pressure, depression, panic disorder, fatigue, and more. Untamed worrying may lead to sleepless nights and to appetite loss, poor job performance, and deteriorating relationships. Those that worry excessively grow old and wrinkly before their time. These are just a few disadvantages out of many. There aren't many advantages of worrying. Still, here is one: When we worry about an issue, it helps us feel like we are dealing with that issue and helps us feel like we care.

Worry steals our time and energy. If unwatched, anxiety will rob us of our peace. Worry achieves nothing and is unproductive. Most of the things we worry about don't even happen and can't be prevented by worrying anyway. What will happen will happen no matter how much we worry about it. Worrying is futile, and its disadvantages will always outweigh its advantages. But there is one who can help us deal with our worry issues. His name is Jesus. He has simply asked that we cast all our worries upon Him because He cares deeply for us.

Confession: *Dear Lord, the act of worrying bears hardly any good fruit. All it does is steal my joy. Henceforth, I cast all my cares on You because I know You care for me. I decree this day that worry no longer has a hold on my life. Amen.*

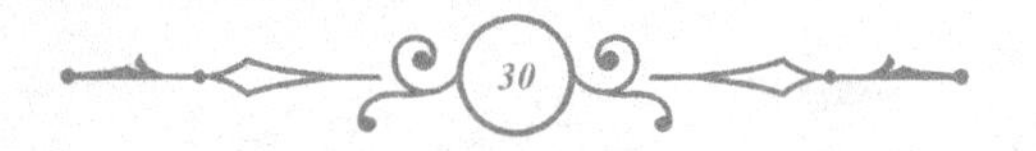

JANUARY 28

PONDERING VS. WORRYING

But Mary kept all these things,
and pondered them in her heart.
Luke 2:19, KJV

Mary went through a lot, no doubt. Despite all of this, the Bible's never once reported that she worried. Instead, she exuded a calm attitude and trusted and praised God (Luke 1:46-47). On one occasion shortly after Jesus was born, the Bible recorded that "she pondered things in her heart." This must have been how she dealt with arising situations.

Mary's story lets us know that it is possible to live a worry-free life. When we face strange circumstances, it's only natural for us to think about them. But the moment we begin to worry excessively, the flesh kicks in. We then unconsciously distance ourselves from God.

We are humans, so worry will come naturally to us. Mary teaches us that it is possible to stay calm during challenging times. In essence, we can reflect on issues but not lose our peace about them. When we worry ourselves sick over problems, we take God out of the picture. There is nothing so terrible that God cannot fix, for with him all things are possible. God can help us get through whatever situation we find ourselves in. Our place is to believe He will.

Confession: *Dear Lord, I know there will be times when life's issues may leave me confused. I also know that it is during moments like this that You want me to trust in You more and not my flesh. Today I receive the grace to remain calm and trusting despite my circumstances. Amen.*

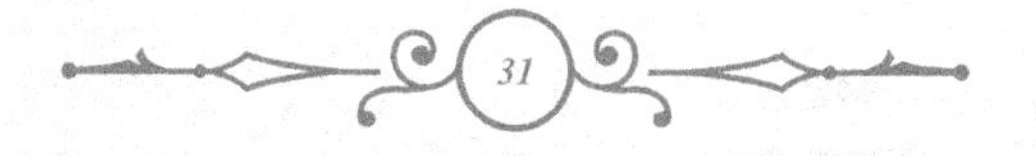

JANUARY 29

THE WORRY TOOL

Let not your hearts be troubled.
Believe in God; believe also in me.
John 14:1

I used to worry a lot, and the worry tool is something the devil has used in times past to keep me distracted and in bondage. I remember those times when I would always have something to worry about. In week 1, my worry could be all about my health. In week 2, I would have centered my worrying around family and friends. In weeks 3 and 4, I might worry myself about all the wrongs going on in the world. By week 6, I probably would be back to worrying about my health again and would then continue the cycle. Crazy, isn't it? Do you also fret like this?

The devil knows the human makeup, and he is always ready to exploit our worrying weaknesses. How does the devil do this? First, he feeds our minds with issues he knows we care about. Then he twists those issues with fears and horror until we begin to worry about them. Once trapped in the worry bubble, he loads us with more worry thoughts. All these he does in an attempt to put us in bondage and our minds in captivity.

Worry is what the enemy uses to distract us from our God-given assignment. Now that we know how the devil works, it's time to stop letting him win the battles over our minds. When we say no to worry, we also say no to the devil.

Confession: *Dear Jesus, in times past, the enemy has used the worry tool to keep me in bondage. Today, I break free from his captivity. I receive my deliverance from all the traps of the devil. My mind will no longer be troubled. From here on, I choose to think like the winner I am. Amen.*

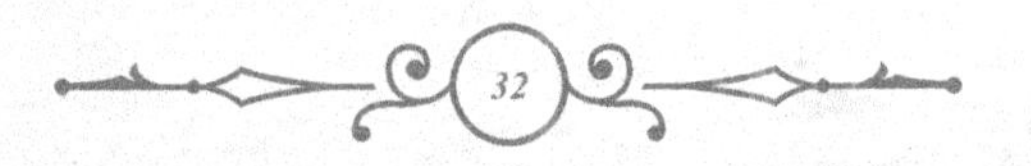

JANUARY 30

WORRYING ABOUT THE PAST

No, dear brothers and sisters, I have not achieved it, but I focus on this one thing: Forgetting the past and looking forward to what lies ahead. **Philippians 3:13, NLT**

Everyone has a past. Some may have a yesterday they are proud of, but this is not the case for many people. There are different ways people react to their pasts. Some hold on to it, some run away from it, some live in denial of it ever happening, some let it terrify them, and some allow it to control their present. Which category do you fall into?

I made up my mind at a young age that my past will always remain in the past. Should I mess up in the future, I will do everything within my power to fix it. If I cannot, I will take responsibility for my flaws, forgive myself, and then find a way to make up for it. No one has a spotless past. Paul, who wrote today's scripture text, had one of the most eventful histories recorded in the Bible. In fact, his past is one many would term as "dark." But what did Paul do with his dark past? He put it behind him. He let go of it.

Time spent worrying about the past is futile. Nothing can be done about all that has already happened. The future, however, has endless possibilities that can be exploited. This is what Paul is challenging us to look into. No matter how horrible your past looks, it's time to leave it where it belongs.

Confession: *Lord, thank you for Your promise of a better tomorrow. I leave all my past deeds and mistakes in the past. Old things have passed away, and my future is bright. This is what I choose to look forward to. Amen.*

JANUARY 31

WORRYING ABOUT THE PRESENT

Do not be anxious about anything, but in everything by prayer and supplication with thanksgiving let your requests be made known to God.
Philippians 4:6

God's original plan was that humans should live completely worry free. He made this evident when He put the first man and woman in the Garden of Eden after creating them (Genesis 2). The garden had everything Adam and Eve needed. All they were to do was eat, take care of Eden, communicate with God, and live every day with joy. They were to worry about nothing and enjoy everything. This was God's plan, not just for Adam and Eve alone but for generations to come. Things got complicated in Eden because the first couple refused to keep their end of the bargain. Despite the complication, God's plan for humans to live worry free has still not changed.

God has taken care of everything, and we do not have to worry about anything. This may sound illogical to some people, but it is the truth. There is a certain simplicity that comes with walking with God (Isaiah 46:4). We can experience this too if we stop sieving God's words through our human reasoning. It's imperative we take God's Word at face value.

While we may still have to earn a living, God has taken care of our needs. He has made available all the provisions necessary for our daily livelihood. All we need is the revelation of the Holy Spirit to access all of God's blessings that are available for us.

Confession: *Dear Lord, I'm grateful for the gift of another day. Your wish is that I live in plenty. You have taken care of everything, so today I choose not to worry about anything. I lift all my concerns to You. Amen*

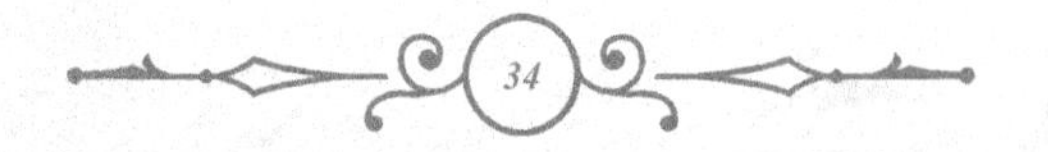

FEBRUARY 1

WORRYING ABOUT THE PRESENT PART II

Look at the birds of the air: they neither sow nor reap nor gather into barns, and yet your heavenly Father feeds them. Are you not of more value than they? And which of you by being anxious can add a single hour to his span of life? And why are you anxious about clothing? Consider the lilies of the field, how they grow: they neither toil nor spin, yet I tell you, even Solomon in all his glory was not arrayed like one of these.
Matthew 6:26-29

A close friend worked hard to get a job for months but was unsuccessful. After he got a job, he testified to God's goodness. During his testimony, he confessed that how he survived those jobless months still baffles him. He also added that how he was able to live without a paycheck was something he could not explain. All he knew was that somehow God had met his daily needs.

Today's scripture reference encourages us to do one basic thing: take every day as it comes. It also describes how God takes care of the birds of the air and the lilies of the field. If God can be so concerned for animals and flowers, how much more those He made in His own image?

God will never leave His own to hang out to dry. So long as we keep doing our best daily and trusting God for everything, He will surely take care of us. Believe in God's supernatural provision, and the God of wonders will prove Himself in your life.

Confession: *Lord, at the center of my life, it is You that I see. Thank You for Your care thus far. You have always come through for me in the past, and I know You will not fail me now. Help me to always depend on You in all that I do. Amen.*

FEBRUARY 2

WORRY-FREE VS. LAZY CHRISTIANS

Therefore, I tell you, do not be anxious about your life, what you will eat or what you will drink, nor about your body, what you will put on. Is not life more than food, and the body more than clothing?
Matthew 6:25

There is a big distinction between being worry free and being lazy. Lazy Christians are ones who live nonchalant lives. They are unwilling to put in the work but expect all the rewards. It is imperative to note that the Bible never asks us to sit idle while expecting miraculous returns. In fact, 2 Thessalonians 3:10b says, "The one who is unwilling to work shall not eat." God does not condone laziness in any form.

God discourages a lazy life, and living worry free is what He expects from His children. Worry-free Christians know that they have to always put their best foot forward. They are constantly willing to do the work required, no matter how hard. Worry-free Christians know better than to depend on their own abilities. They never put their trust solely in their paycheck. Instead, they put their trust in God, who makes the paycheck available. After doing their best, worry-free Christians leave the rest to God. Should worry-free Christians have concerns about anything, they pray. They do this while trusting with all their hearts that God will take care of them.

Can you call yourself a worry-free Christian?

Confession: *Lord, thank You for Your strength that enables me to keep pushing on each day. If there are moments I have been lazy when I should have forged ahead instead, please forgive me. Through my daily toil, help me realize that Your blessing is ultimate. Amen.*

FEBRUARY 3

WORRYING ABOUT THE FUTURE

So don't worry about tomorrow, for tomorrow will bring its own worries. Today's trouble is enough for today.
Matthew 6:34, NLT

How many times have we woken up to a day that turned out to be the opposite of what we planned? I would say countless times. We can predict, anticipate, or guess what the future holds, but no one knows for sure what will happen the very next minute. Even those who have the gift of prophecy cannot say for certain all that is to come next. So how can we deal with these upcoming events we have no control over? We can reach out to God's Word, which has the answers to all of life's questions.

The Bible encourages us to take every day as it comes because tomorrow has a way of taking care of itself. It also encourages us to live for each day and never to be anxious about the days that will follow. We can only see the present moment. This is all God wants us to be concerned about while we trust Him for the moments to come. Life doesn't always go the way we plan it. And so long as it's just our own future plan and not God's, those plans are subject to change as unexpected events overtake them.

The Lord has supplied us with all that we need to handle the present day. He will also provide what we need to handle tomorrow's demand. It is futile to worry about a tomorrow we have no control over.

Confession: *God, every day I am alive I count as a blessing from You. Your Word instructs me not to worry about tomorrow, but sometimes I fail at this. I ask for your help today, Holy Spirit. Teach me to never depend on my plans but rather Your plans for me. Amen.*

FEBRUARY 4

WORRYING ABOUT THE FUTURE PART II

For I know the plans I have for you," says the LORD. "They are plans for good and not for disaster, to give you a future and a hope.
Jeremiah 29:11, NLT

A close friend once had a heart-to-heart talk with me. He told me he was not scared of my past or present but was worried about my future because of some of my tendencies. Well, this person had every right to be. Why? For one, I have workaholic tendencies. I also come off as blunt and too independent. A few people have interpreted these habits as pride-like in the past. I also have other ugly sides. In all honesty, I am sometimes scared of myself too. I was going to tell this person this, but all I remember was opening my mouth, and then this came out: "Indeed, I have my weaknesses, but I also have God, who has helped me and is still helping me deal with them. I choose not to worry about my future because God has everything taken care of." Although these words came out of my mouth, I knew they came directly from the Holy Spirit.

There is no human on Earth that does not have a weakness. We all do. But as long as the "God factor" is present, then we believers can be at peace knowing God will get us where He needs us to be. We are not perfect yet, but in our everyday walk with Christ, we take another step toward perfection. Our human weaknesses should not be a reason to worry about what our future will be.

Whatever God needs to fix in us, He will fix. Our place is to make ourselves available in the fixing process. We are not who we once were. By the special grace of God, we will get to where God needs us to be in due time.

Confession: *Dear Lord, I remember where You picked me up from. I have come a long way. Thank You for making me better than I was yesterday. I know You hold my future in Your hands. For this reason, I choose not to be afraid of tomorrow. I look forward to my future with great joy, knowing that You will take care of things. Amen.*

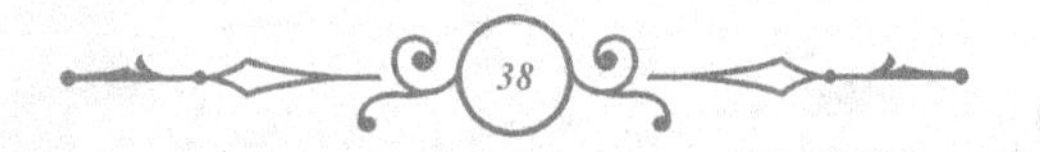

FEBRUARY 5

WORRYING ABOUT OTHER'S FUTURE

This is a trustworthy saying, and everyone should accept it:
"Christ Jesus came into the world to save sinners"—
and I am the worst of them all. **1 Timothy 1:15, NLT**

Saul, who today's scripture reference is about, was a murderer. He was an absolute threat to the kingdom of God and a religious terrorist. He would persecute God's people with everything he had. With the way he was living, those around him would have been right to be concerned for him. It would have seemed logical to predict that his end would be nothing short of God's wrath.

However, when God was ready for Saul, He turned him around. God changed him not just to be a better person but to become His own soldier. His name was even changed from Saul to Paul. This shows us that no one is beyond redemption.

God has plans for everyone. Of course, it's in our nature to worry about the future of defiant folks with ungodly lifestyles. Yet, God is letting us know today that we should not. We can reach out to them. We can also seek the face of the Lord on their behalf. The bible says, "If Paul plants and Apollo waters, without God all will be in vain" (1 Corinthians 3:6). Worrying sick about our loved ones is something we should do less of. I want to encourage us to pray more for them and speak into their destinies. In due time, God will find them and make them instruments for His use.

Confession: *Father, in times past, I have excessively worried about those I care about. I repent of this. Today I lift my spouse, kids, parents, friends, colleagues, and other loved ones to You. I know You will get them to where You need them to be. In the meantime, I ask that You give me Your peace and grace to worry less and trust You more. Amen.*

FEBRUARY 6

ONLY GOD CAN FIX IT

But Jesus looked at them intently and said,
"With man this is impossible but with God all things are possible."
Matthew 19:26

One medical slogan reads, "We care, but God heals." The same goes for all human effort. We can try, but only God can fix. God has been the one fixing things throughout history, and He is still doing the same today. God is the glue that holds our lives together.

Do we remember those "it could only have been God moments"? What about those times when God came through for us when we did not even deserve it? If we remember, why have we now let a new situation make us weary to the point where God is no longer enough? Is it because of these endless life concerns? Is it because of past occurrences that did not go the way we prayed and hoped they would? Is it because of some present unfavorable conditions? Or maybe it's because of fear and anxiety for tomorrow.

God sees the end from the beginning. No matter how hard we try to control, fix, or change things, it will not work unless God says it would. The more we grow in the Lord, the more we will understand the importance of leaving things in His hands. Our vocabulary will then contain sentences like "Fix it, Jesus," "I leave it to You, Lord," and "Take absolute control, my Savior."

Confession: *Dear God, thank you for being God. Every time I have acted as the god over my life, I have failed. Today I acknowledge that I have no power of my own. I hand everything to You. Fix it, Jesus. I lift all my worries, fears, and concerns to You. Please help me. Amen.*

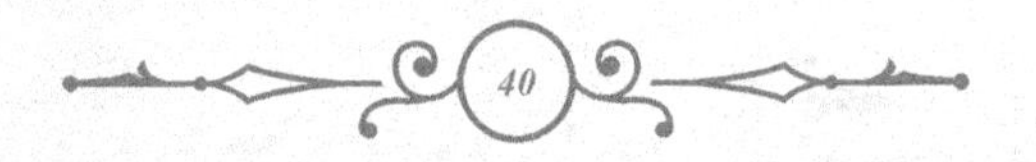

FEBRUARY 7

THE "GOD'S PROBLEM" BOX

Then Jesus said, "Come to me, all you who are weary and burdened, and I will give you rest."
Matthew 11:28, NLT

Some time ago, a woman spoke about how she handles her everyday worry issues. She said she has a box labeled "God's problem." Every time a matter arises that causes her to worry, she writes her concern in the form of a letter to God. She also dates the letter and puts it in the "God's problem" box. After this, she leaves the box in her closet and goes about her business. According to her, she does everything possible to take her mind completely off the matter. Thus, she hands all her problems to God.

Someone asked her what had brought about this method. She replied, "I'm a fixer. I've never been able to let things go. I always want to play God. Every time I do, things go awry, so I started doing this. It may look like an ordinary box to many, but it reminds me to put my faith in God and not in myself. The bonus comes when I see my prayers answered. Once a particular prayer has been answered, I won't put the note back in the box." Another person asked, "What if God doesn't answer?" She smiled and replied, "Then He's got something better in store for me."

We may not all buy into the idea of getting a box labeled "God's problem," but we can take a cue from some of this woman's remarks. Whatever the situation may be, hands off and let God fix it. He will fix it—maybe not according to our own timing but His own.

Confession: *My Father, thank you for the insight of Your Word. I did not create myself; You did. In ways I have played God over my life, have mercy. Please take control of my life, for You are the true God. Direct my life. Amen.*

FEBRUARY 8

SETTLING THINGS IN THE PLACE OF PRAYER

Trust in the LORD with all your heart, and do not lean on your own understanding. In all your ways acknowledge him and he will make straight your paths. **Proverbs 3:5-6**

Can we always correctly predict the outcome of all we set out to do? The answer most likely is no. Even the best of plans are usually allotted a 99% success rate. This means that there is a 1% chance it still won't work out. That one percent belongs to God. Only God ensures 100%. As God's children, this is the upper hand we have.

Our scripture today admonishes us to acknowledge Him in all our ways. Acknowledgment, in this context, means to recognize God's existence. When we recognize God's existence in our dealings, we understand our place in Him and His in us. Once we know our place in God, we realize that He is concerned about all that concerns us. We then gradually begin replacing our worries with firmer confidence in God. When others panic, we just go on our knees and settle issues there. Without a doubt, things are 100% certain with God.

Confession: *Dear Lord, You are my all in all. Whenever I call, You listen. You care about every aspect of my life and make this obvious. Because of You, I am a winner. I am assured that You got my back 100%. Success is mine in all I do. Amen.*

FEBRUARY 9

THE BEST GIFT FOR YOUR CHILD

Do not be anxious about anything, but in everything by prayer and supplication with thanksgiving let your requests be made known to God.
Philippians 4:6

Like every mother, mine may not be perfect, but when it comes to praying for her children, she is like a machine that doesn't have an off button.

While growing up, I observed that my mother would pray in the morning, at night, and every chance she got. Before my siblings and I left for school, she would pray for us. When we got back, she would do the same. While we were eating, she would come and pray for us. When we were sleeping, she would do it again. Her prayers for us were never-ending. My mother devoted a lot of time to praying into all her children's present and future. To date, I still feel the effects of her prayers in all I do.

We can send our kids to the best of schools and leave them a big inheritance. However, one of the best gifts any parent can give their offspring is the gift of ceaseless prayers. When we pray for our kids, we invite God into all their undertakings. We also shield them from the evils we cannot protect them from. In our persistent prayers, we hear from God concerning the plans He has for them, and we can use this to direct them. Praying for our kids gives us the grace to worry less about them and to trust God more for their lives. Today, whether or not we have children, let's take time to pray for all the kids we may know. Let's mention all their names to God. Let's pray that God will guide and bless them and make them useful vessels all the days of their lives. Amen.

Confession: *Lord Jesus, thank you for making our children the heritage of the Lord. Today I pray for all the kids I know. May Your goodness and favor follow them, and may they always remain under Your care. Amen.*

FEBRUARY 10

EYES ON JESUS

But when he saw the strong wind and the waves, he was terrified and began to sink. "Save me, Lord!" he shouted.
Matthew 14:30, NLT

Jesus' disciples were on a boat when Jesus appeared to them, walking on the water. Their initial reaction was fear as they thought Jesus was a ghost. Peter, one of the disciples, believed in his heart that it was Jesus and not a ghost, so he asked if he could join Jesus to walk on the water. Jesus agreed. Peter started walking on the water toward Jesus but began to sink after he took a few successful steps. Why would Peter, who started out well, fail in the middle of a journey? Simple! He took his eyes off Jesus.

The Bible records that Peter was fine walking on the water until he noticed the "strong wind." The Bible also mentioned that this wind was present before Peter started his journey. But Peter wasn't concerned about the weather or any other factor as long as his focus was on Jesus. As soon as he took his eyes off Jesus, his human consciousness kicked in. He started worrying about all that was going wrong around him. Before long, his worry turned into panic. After that, doubt set in. At that moment, the divine connection, which was supposed to help him do that which only faith in God can do, broke. Peter was then left with his human strength. Well, we all can guess how far his human strength got him—nowhere!
This story is food for thought for all.

Confession: *Father, on several occasions, I have doubted Your power. Today, I repent of this. Your instruction is that I keep my eyes on You regardless of the surrounding turbulence. But there are so many distractions in today's world that often make me lose my concentration. I need Your help. Please show me how to stay focused on You. Amen.*

FEBRUARY 11

EYES ON JESUS PART II

But when he saw the wind, he was afraid and,
beginning to sink, cried out, "Lord, save me!"
Matthew 14:30

A believer in God can only have his or her focus in either of these two directions: vertical or horizontal. The vertical focus means one's concentration is leaning toward heaven. The horizontal focus means one's attention is more toward all that is going on around them.

Just like the story of Jesus' disciples journeying on a boat (Matthew 14:22–33), life itself is a journey. Peter would have successfully walked on water in the middle of the strong wind had he not taken his eyes off Jesus. Throughout life's journey, there will be seasons of strong winds. So long as we have our sights set on heaven, we will be able to navigate whatever storms life throws at us on our journey. If our focus is primarily on everything going on around us, we are bound to be weighed down with life's concerns.

Once we choose to view our challenges through heaven's eyes, Jesus will take us through them, and the journey will be struggle-free. Which direction will we keep our focus on today, horizontal or vertical?

Confession: *Lord, when my soul experiences turbulence, it stumbles. When this happens, I find myself afraid and anxious. I pray for your strength today. Please grant me the grace to walk on your set path for my life. Help me so I may never sink. Help me to always see my life through heaven's eyes. Amen.*

FEBRUARY 12

EYES ON JESUS PART III (IT'S NEVER TOO LATE)

But when he saw the wind, he was afraid, and beginning to sink he cried out, "Lord, save me." Jesus immediately reached out his hand and took hold of him, saying to him, "O you of little faith, why did you doubt?"
Matthew 14:30–31

Peter gave into his fears and as a result, started to sink. However, Peter was also wise enough to know that only one name could take him out of his "sinking place." As soon as he recognized his mistake and its consequences, he called on his only help in time of need—Jesus. Peter did not call on his fellow disciples. He did not begin moaning about how bad he had it or how he would probably die. He simply called on Jesus.

No matter how much we have messed up, it's never too late to call on Jesus. No matter how chaotic the situation is, the Lord is always ready to intervene as soon as we cry out to Him for help.

The scripture records that Jesus immediately reached out to Peter. The emphasis is on "immediately" as this establishes how swiftly Jesus responds when we call. The scripture also records that Peter called out. We cannot just assume that Jesus will pull us out of our "sinking place." We have to open our mouths and call on Him for help. Jesus is never far away. He is right beside us with His arms outstretched, ready to lift us out of whatever may be drowning us.

Confession: *Dear Lord, I admit that there are times when I have wavered and doubted You. Please forgive me. Today I cry out to You. Whatever in my life may be drowning me, please lift me out of it. Help me, Jesus. Amen.*

FEBRUARY 13

EYES ON JESUS PART IV (THE OPPOSITE OF WORRY)

Jesus immediately reached out his hand and took hold of him, saying to him, "O you of little faith, why did you doubt?"
Matthew 14:31

First, Jesus pulled Peter out of his "sinking place." As soon as this was done, Jesus told Peter why everything went wrong when it did: Peter doubted! For a person to doubt, a series of events will likely occur. First, a situation will arise. Then the person may begin to consider all that could go wrong with that situation. This creates room for worry. Worry may lead to panic and panic to doubt.

Peter desired to walk on water. To do extraordinary things like this, faith is required. To perform exploits, it's necessary to trust God. When Peter believed that the power of Jesus could get him to his destination, he had complete backing to accomplish his mission. However, in the middle of the journey, Peter lost his faith. At that moment, Jesus' power was no longer consequential. This was because Peter was no longer playing his part.

For God to use us, we have roles to play. To perform miracles, we must trust and believe in Him. When we play our parts, God will perform mind-blowing wonders through us.

Confession: *Lord, thank you for bringing me out of my "sinking place." I long to trust You more, but I still need help to achieve this. Please teach me how to rely on You at every junction of my life. Amen.*

FEBRUARY 14

EYES OFF ME

Let each of you look not only to his own interests,
but also to the interests of others.
Philippians 2:4

I knew someone whose life was only about her. All her concerns centered around what she would eat and wear. Some of her other concerns were also about what people thought of her. She confessed that those days, her worry level would be so elevated she could go into depression. Then she started her walk with God. She said she did not notice any significant change at first, but after some time, she noticed she stopped being as frustrated, tormented, and worry-crazed. So she started doing some soul searching about what had happened. It hit her! Her focus had changed from being self-centered to caring for others.

One way to practice the act of worrying less is by taking our focus off ourselves and putting it on others. When we cultivate the habit of reaching out, we gradually feel our worry fade away. Those that may need reaching out to are the needy, the less privileged, and others that need our assistance.

When we open our eyes to other people's suffering, we realize that there is so much we can do to help. We also realize that our own problems may be nothing compared to the issues many are facing. What some of us need is a change of focus. When we focus on other things, our worry level will drop significantly.

Confession: *Today I will reach out to those around me and will be a blessing to others. I will ensure that I perform at least one act of kindness for another person. From here on, I refuse to be self-centered. Amen.*

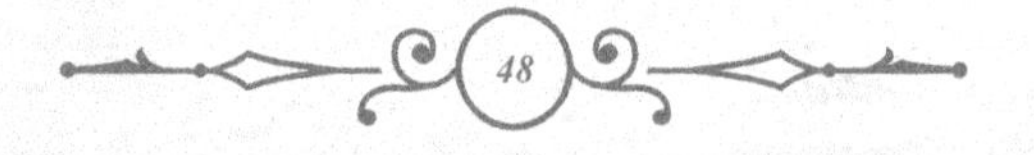

FEBRUARY 15

SEEKING FIRST GOD'S KINGDOM

But seek first the kingdom of God and his righteousness, and all these things will be added to you.
Matthew 6:33

As young believers, we may start out by seeking God only for material things. Our prayers may only be about our immediate needs and wants. This is okay. However, as we grow in God and make Him our top priority, He will meet our needs even without our asking Him to.

Today's scripture is an agreement God gives those willing to enter into a partnership with Him. The first part of the contract says we are to seek first God's kingdom and His righteousness. The second part is God's promise for whoever will obey. God is willing to meet all our earthly necessities. The emphasis is on "all" because this goes beyond daily meals, shelter, clothing, or a means to get by. It includes "all these things." In essence, we as children of God get everything—wealth, peace, good health, joy, a great home, and many more.

To seek God's kingdom, first we are required to have a personal relationship with Jesus. After this, we can then seek God's kingdom in other ways. These include working in God's sanctuary and winning souls for Christ. We are also to reach out to those in need. When we joyfully do these things, we can trust that God will fulfill His own part of the partnership.

Confession: *Lord, thank you for the gift of salvation. Your instruction is that I seek You first; then Your added promises will come. I know there are many ways You desire that I seek You. Please reveal these ways to me. I want to know You more. Help me find You. Amen.*

FEBRUARY 16

THE ULTIMATE PREPARATION

And while they were going to buy, the bridegroom came, and those who were ready went in with him to the marriage feast, and the door was shut.
Matthew 25:10

The Scriptures strongly caution us against "worrying" about the future. Nevertheless, they encourage us to "prepare" for tomorrow. One story that teaches about planning ahead is that of the ten virgins. According to Jesus, who told this parable, five of these ten virgins were wise, and five of them were foolish. The wise virgins were termed so because they took extra oil for their lamps when they went to meet the groom. In essence, they prepared for the future. But the other five did not. There was an unexpected delay by the groom, during which time the five foolish virgins ran out of oil. As a result, they had to run out in search of more fuel. Before they returned, the groom came, and the door was shut against the five unprepared virgins.

Preparing for our future on Earth is necessary, but what should be our topmost priority is preparing for where we will spend eternity. Heaven is every believer's ultimate goal. Jesus, the groom, is coming soon to take His beloved to heaven. But will He find us ready or unprepared? Will we have run out of oil to power our lamps?

Our lifestyles and relationship with God will determine whether we will follow the groom when He returns. Again, the question is, will our lamps still be burning when Jesus comes for us?

Confession: *Jesus, help me. I do not want to be unprepared in those final moments. When You come for me, I pray that my lamp will still be burning. Please strengthen me daily. As I navigate through life, help me always remember that this earth is not my final destination.*
By Your special grace, I will make it to heaven. Amen.

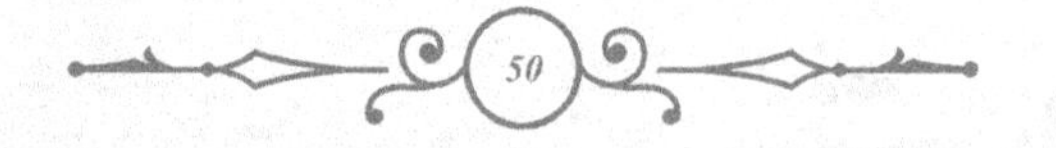

A LIFE DEVOID OF REGRET

FEBRUARY 17

WHAT IF TODAY WAS YOUR LAST?

...whereas you do not know what will happen tomorrow. For what is your life? It is even a vapor that appears for a little time and then vanishes away.
James 4:14, NKJV

No one would like to hear that they only have twenty-four hours left to live. What if your doctor, for example, told you today is your last day and nothing can be done to prevent it? What would be your immediate response? Who and what would come to your mind? What would you make sure you address? What are the things you would quickly try to make up for? What would be the pressing matters?

Some will immediately accept Christ into their lives or rededicate their hearts. Some will quickly mend friendships with those they haven't spoken to in years. Some will immediately visit parents they have ignored. Many will begin to make amends and put their house in order. The list goes on. For you, the first ten people, things, and thoughts that flash through your mind are of utmost importance. I hope heaven is one of those things. This exercise is mainly to help us recognize the critical factors in our lives.

Some things may look crucial only for us to realize in the long run that they hold little to no value. A life devoid of regret is what everyone wants when they reflect on their lives in their final moments. How to do this? God will reveal to us more as we delve into this new series: "A Life Devoid of Regret."

Confession: *Lord Jesus, thank You for the gift of life. Thank You because I will always live my life to please You. Teach me to walk in Your ways every day without regrets. Amen.*

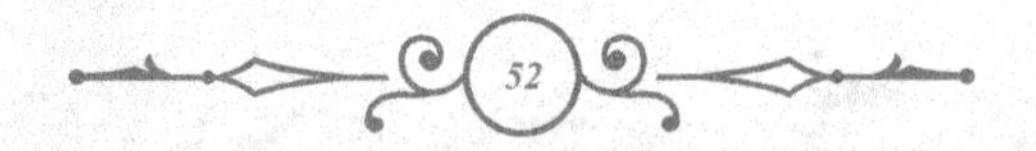

FEBRUARY 18

WHAT IF TODAY WAS YOUR LAST? PART II

Do not boast about tomorrow, for you do not
know what a day may bring.
Proverbs 27:1

When people are given a death sentence, the thought of leaving everything behind is not the only thing what makes them sad. The idea of exiting life may be terrifying, but what makes some truly sad is regret about how they lived.

No one knows what the next hour holds, and no one has been given the promise of eternity on this earth. The best hope we have is living a long life. So it is safe to say that at some point, we will all leave this earth. In our final moments, what will our thoughts be? Let's say God gives us the grace to live to 100. Eventually, when it is time to depart from this earth, will we do so with great satisfaction with how we lived? Considering the way we are living now, what will our final moment's contemplation be? Unfortunately, a good number of people will still not get this until their final moments on the earth. I hope that will not be our case. I also hope we will choose to live our lives with the understanding that one day it will all be over. I pray we will begin aspiring to live every day as though it may be our last.

Confession: *Lord Jesus, thank You for the blessing of another day. Today I choose to do my best and live every day like it's my last. Help me to understand that every moment here on Earth is a gift from You. Amen.*

FEBRUARY 19

IT'S NEVER TOO LATE TO BEGIN AFRESH

Immediately the rooster crowed the second time. Then Peter remembered the word Jesus had spoken to him: "Before the rooster crows twice you will disown me three times." And he broke down and wept.
Mark 14:72, NIV

The stories of Judas Iscariot and Peter are great examples of what starting afresh is all about. Judas is the disciple popularly known as the black sheep who betrayed Jesus. His betrayal eventually led to the death of Jesus on the cross. Like Judas, Peter also wronged Jesus, but his wrong was in the form of denial. In fact, not only did Peter disown Jesus once but three times.

The court of public opinion is quick to dismiss what Peter did as not as profound as what Judas did. However, I believe Peter's denial probably hurt Jesus more than Judas's betrayal. For one, Peter was closer to Jesus than Judas was. Also, Jesus had already predicted Peter's denial, and Peter swore to Jesus that he would never do that. Well, he eventually disavowed Jesus.

Judas and Peter messed up, period! But what made all the difference between these two was their responses to their actions. While Peter went back to the throne of grace to obtain mercy from God, Judas let regret consume him. Judas concluded within himself that he didn't deserve a second chance, so he let guilt drive him to suicide. Peter, on the other hand, received God's mercy and was mightily used by Him. Both stories tell us that no matter what we have done in times past, God's mercy is always available to start afresh. Like Peter, will we receive this mercy, or like Judas, will we conclude that we are ineligible for it? Please accept the gift of a new beginning today.

Confession: *Lord Jesus, I appreciate all You have done for me. In ways I have denied and betrayed You, please forgive me. Help me, O Lord, to never let negative thoughts overshadow Your love for me. Thank You for the gift of a new beginning. Amen.*

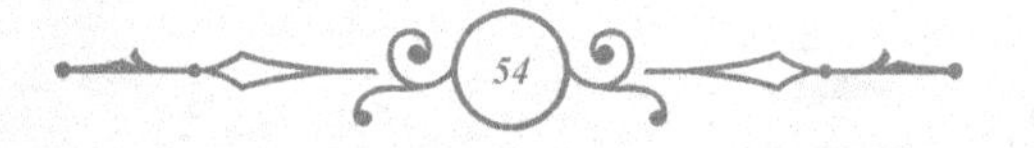

FEBRUARY 20

OUR REASONS ON EARTH

You are the light of the world. A city set on a hill cannot be hidden.
Matthew 5:14

Life can be likened to a jigsaw puzzle. It takes beyond mere filling to make it meaningful. For the puzzle to be completely assembled, it has to be in compliance with its blueprint. That is, each space must be filled with the correct puzzle piece. If the earth is the puzzle board, then every person is one of the puzzle pieces needed to complete the puzzle. In essence, for life to be balanced, everyone would have to bring his or her own contribution. Alas, not everyone does this.

One big regret many people take to their graves is that they never lived a purpose-driven life. It's like their existence never mattered because they did not make a contribution to the world. So many people leave life the same way they entered it. Many just breeze in and breeze out, adding nothing to their world before departing from it. When they finally exit life, nothing can be said of their existence or how they impacted their world. I hope this won't be our story too. I wonder what will be said about you and me when we depart from the earth. Would it be said that we made our world a better place than we met it? Would it be said of us that we fulfilled that which we came into the world to fulfill? Would we have left a mark on the earth for the coming generations to remember us by? This is food for thought for us today.

Confession: *Lord Jesus, thank You for making me a light to my world. I desire to leave life better than I met it. Show me ways to live an impactful life that will leave a mark for generations to come. Amen.*

FEBRUARY 21

THE PURPOSE-DRIVEN LIFE

In the same way, let your light shine before others, so that they may see your good works and give glory to your Father who is in heaven.
Matthew 5:16

Not everyone will be an inventor. Nonetheless, everyone has something unique they can offer the world. The question then is, what do you and I do for our world? How can we make life better for others? What have we been created for? Why are we here on this earth? God will not come down from heaven to help us figure all this out. It's our responsibility to do so through the help of the Holy Spirit.

Many of us get caught up in the same daily cycle. This may include earning a living, raising a family, and providing for our loved ones. Life's obligations have a way of consuming us to a point where we forget that we also have other responsibilities. One of these responsibilities is to dig into ourselves and bring out what God has deposited in us.

In each of us are books yet unwritten. In each of us are beautiful things yet unfounded. The world immensely needs something you and I have. Although our gifts may not be as fancy as those of others, they will still make a difference if we bless our world with them. If you haven't already, begin digging deep within yourself. Note those things you are exceptionally gifted with. Begin to explore them in whatever way you can, whether little or big. The best gift any person can give themselves is living purposefully. The fulfillment that comes with this act is almost indescribable. Most people who live purposeful lives go to their grave with peace. They do so knowing they gave their best to their world while they could.

Confession: *Lord Jesus, thank You for the understanding of Your words. Teach me how to tap into my gifts. Help me to fully understand my purpose here on Earth. Order my steps, dear Lord. Amen.*

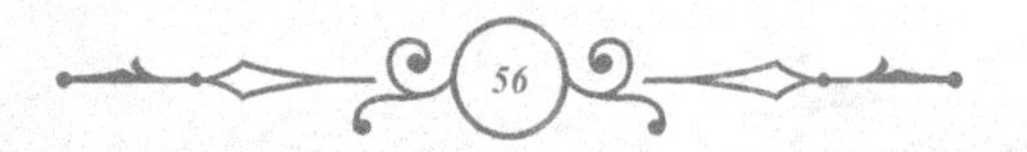

FEBRUARY 22

THE LITTLE ONES

One who is faithful in a very little is also faithful in much, and one who is dishonest in a very little is also dishonest in much.
Luke 16:10

Many people grow old while waiting for their big break. While many get those "big breaks" in life, others will not. Life does not always offer a rosy path. What life offers everyone instead are the daily little breaks. What does this mean? The "daily little breaks" mean everyday little jobs as opposed to the dream jobs. It also means the dirty task one may need to do in the interim, if only just for the sake of survival. It's what the Bible describes as "he that is faithful in very little."

How we handle the "little" is crucial because it will likely determine whether God will give us the "much." If God cannot trust us to be humble while He puts the little in our hands, how do we expect Him to give us the big breaks? Besides, God did not promise every child of His the life of a celebrity or billionaire. What He promised everyone is joy, peace, and that everything will work for our good. Whatever it is we do, let's determine to do it well. Whether it is big or little, dignifying or degrading, clean or dirty, let's give it our all. When we do this, God will trust us with bigger things. No, not all of us will get the billions we so desire, but God will bless us with better things than we had in the past.

Confession: *Dear Lord, thank You for Your mercies. You love me, and I know it. Teach me, Holy Spirit, to be faithful with the little You have committed into my hands. Help me, Jesus, to never be ungrateful for all You have done for me. Amen.*

FEBRUARY 23

•••

THE EXEMPLARY LIFE OF JOSEPH

But his brothers hated Joseph because their father loved him more than the rest of them. They couldn't say a kind word to him.
Genesis 37:4, NLT

The life of Joseph makes a fantastic example of what true faithfulness is all about. Joseph wasn't just a faithful one-timer; he was a faithful all-timer. First, he was a faithful son. While he lived with siblings who disliked him, he was a faithful brother. When he was sold as a slave, he remained a faithful servant to his master's household. Interestingly, when he was accused of an assault he did not commit and was sent to jail, Joseph was still faithful as a faithful prisoner. While serving time in prison, he was a loyal friend to those around him. When God eventually took him from prison to the palace, Joseph was a faithful prime minister of the nation of Egypt.

Joseph was tested and trusted, but throughout his ordeal, he was always found worthy. He continually proved to God that he was palace material. Because of this, God took him to the palace.

God will hardly give you all your desires just because you make the request. More often than not, you will be put to the test by being given a little to start with. Perhaps you are one who is just starting out or still at your small beginning; please do not be discouraged. Instead, encourage yourself in the Lord. Remember, it's the small blessings that later become big.

Confession: *Dear Jesus, thank You for another day. In whatever situation I find myself in, help me to remain faithful. Give me the grace to be a committed all-timer. Even through tough times, help me so I will never waver. Amen.*

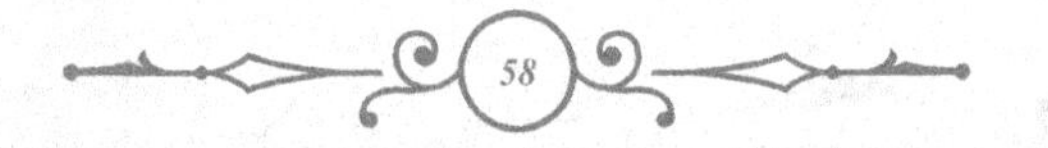

FEBRUARY 24

THE GIFT OF A BETTER EVER AFTER

He will wipe every tear from their eyes, and there will be no more death or sorrow or crying or pain. All these things are gone forever.
Revelation 21:4, NLT

I was born into a flawed family...I was raised in a terrible environment...My community of influence is backward...I did not attend college...I have an embarrassing past.... These are a few of the many reasons people give when I ask why their lives turned out the way they did. In truth, the hardships many people have had to endure are deep and real. When people tell their stories, it cuts deep to know many are victims of traumatizing pasts. Past experiences may be agonizing. But do they have the sole potential of defining a person's future? No, I do not think so.

Traumatic events are powerful. They may even alter an individual's life. But do they denote death sentences? Not necessarily. This has been made evident by those who have passed through trauma and are still standing. Why and how were they able to? I believe these ones were determined never to allow past experiences to write their entire life stories. These ones most likely got help where necessary. They dealt with their internal warfare and kept working on themselves. The result was the beautiful future they foresaw for themselves.

Every day is a gift from God. It is a gift that opens the door for a fresh start. Regardless of yesterday's bitter experience, there is hope for a joyous tomorrow. A better-ever-after is within everyone's reach. We may not be able to control all that has happened to us, but we definitely have a say in what our future will be.

Confession: *Dear Lord, thank You for the gift of this day. Thank You for the gift of tomorrow. Today, I choose to look forward and leave all regrets, trauma, and mistakes in the past. I receive Your grace for a new beginning. I know my future is brighter and better than my past. Amen.*

FEBRUARY 25

PROCRASTINATION KILLS

A little sleep, a little slumber, a little folding of the hands to rest and poverty will come upon you like a robber, and want like an armed man.
Proverbs 24:33–34

Some elderly people were asked if they had any significant life regrets. Some of them said they did. When asked what their regrets were, several of them had this to say: I wish I did more when I had the time and energy to. Procrastination can be described as pushing things off or delaying things habitually. This attitude is familiar to many of us.

We think we have all the time in the world, but we really don't. One day we will wake up and realize we have aged. Most people will then wonder where all the time went and what they did with their lives. I have observed that the best way to live life is to do things the moment they should be done. As a result, I am continually reminding myself by saying, "That which you know you should do, do now."

Postponing things to the next hour or day, especially when unnecessary, steals the time we need for future accomplishments. In each of us are ideas of the kind of life we long to have. We can have that life if we manage our time diligently. Procrastination kills time, opportunities, and growth. Procrastination, if not curbed, will slowly kill a person's dreams.

Confession: *Dear Lord, teach me to never waste the precious moments You have blessed me with. Help me to fully utilize my time here on Earth. Henceforth, I will do that which I am supposed to do at the right time. Amen.*

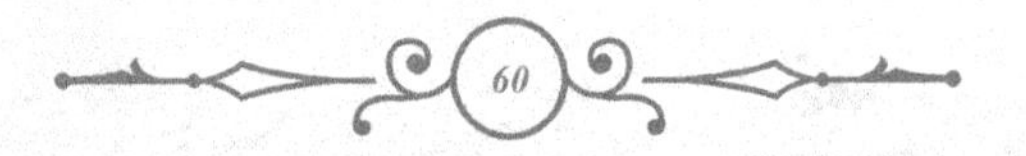

FEBRUARY 26

THE BLAME GAME

...but God said, "You shall not eat of the fruit of the tree that is in the midst of the garden, neither shall you touch it, lest you die."
Genesis 3:3

The serpent tricked Eve in the garden of Eden, and she fell for it. She ate the fruit from the forbidden tree and gave some to her husband, Adam, who was with her. God then appeared to both of them, asking what had happened. He also asked why they had disobeyed Him because He had explicitly asked them not to eat from the tree. God simply asked Adam, "Have you eaten of the tree of which I commanded you not to eat?" While Adam could have just said, "Yes, Lord, and I'm sorry I did." His reply instead was "The woman whom you gave to be with me, she gave me fruit of the tree, and I ate." When Eve was asked, her response was "The serpent deceived me, and I ate."

In truth, the serpent tricked Eve, and she persuaded Adam. Still, both Adam and Eve had a choice not to eat of the tree, but they did anyway. God, who is all-seeing, already knew what the first couple had done before asking them. He only wanted to hear their responses. Unfortunately, their excuses only made things worse. God went on to punish them for that which they had done.

Blaming and excuses are the hallmarks of an unsuccessful life. Sadly, this is the same way many are still living their lives—playing the blame game. Everyone is responsible for his or her own actions. It is a shame the first generation did not understand this early enough. They had to learn the hard way. It did not work for people in the past, and it will most likely not work for those who exhibit this attitude in the present. The blame game is a bad habit that will not take anyone very far in life.

Confession: *Dear Lord, today I come to You with a humble heart. I'm sorry about all my past excuses. My life is my responsibility. Teach me, Holy Spirit, not to disobey you. Help me to always walk in Your light. Amen.*

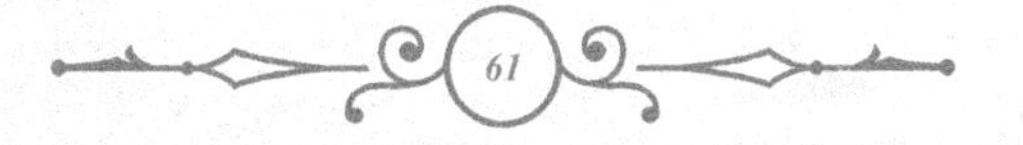

FEBRUARY 27

ACCEPTING RESPONSIBILITY

For we are each responsible for our own conduct.
Galatians 6:5, NLT

I once knew a woman for whom nothing was ever her fault. If she fell, it was because someone put something in her way. If she forgot to do something, it was because someone failed to remind her. If anything wrong ever happened, someone other than her was responsible for it. Life for those around her was practically unbearable. There are so many who live in the same manner, although maybe not as extreme. Many people are unconsciously in the habit of blaming someone or something for their own errors. These people never see anything wrong with anything they do. They rarely admit to any mistake. Folks like these say things like "If you did not, then I wouldn't have." They always find excuses and justifications for their actions.

If we search deep within and know that this pertains to us, we are being challenged to do better today. We are not yet perfect, and we will make mistakes occasionally. When we do, let's take responsibility for them, apologize if need be, and get on with life. In practicing this lifestyle, we make life bearable for others around us. We also get to live peacefully in return. We will not get it right 100% of the time. Whenever we are at fault, maturity in Christ dictates that we take full responsibility for our conduct.

Confession: *Dear Lord, thank You for helping me see that which I may have been blinded to. Teach me, Lord, to take full responsibility for my actions when I am wrong. Help me to be humble enough to say I am sorry when I am at fault. Amen.*

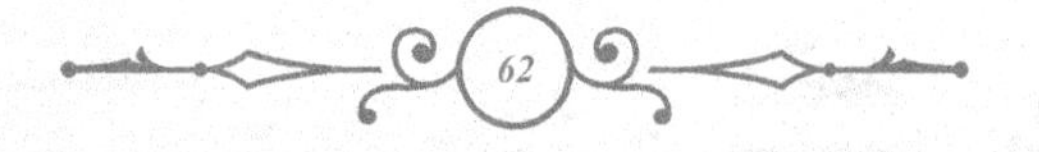

FEBRUARY 28

THE STAGNANT POND

The LORD our God said to us in Horeb, "You have stayed long enough at this mountain."
Deuteronomy 1:6

There will always be a difference between a flowing lake and a stagnant pond. While the former is clean and full of life, the latter is disgusting and full of germs. A stagnant pond has a history of becoming home to algae, mosquitoes, and severe contaminants. It is called stagnant because it does not flow in or out. It remains in the same state day in and day out. Stagnant water stinks! One of the worst places anyone can ever find themselves is in a stagnant pond.

Just as water can become stagnant, a person can stagnate. An individual can tell when he or she is feeling stagnant. One of the most telling signs is boredom. Other symptoms may include feeling choked, stuck, frustrated, uneasy, or generally unhappy. If you notice these signs, it may be time for a shakeup.

Stagnant people gradually become unproductive, and some lose their creative potential over time. The good news is that no one has to live like this. How can one then become more of a flowing lake instead of a stagnant pond? We will discuss this next.

Confession: *Thank You, Jesus, for the gift of another day. You said I will be rivers of living water. Today I choose to no longer remain stagnant. I choose to become all that You have given me the capacity to be. Amen.*

MARCH 1

THE IMPORTANCE OF GROWTH

Every tree that does not bear good fruit is cut down and thrown into the fire.
Matthew 7:19

Growth is part of the human cycle. Anything that stops growing will begin to stagnate and die with time. Stagnancy mostly results from doing the same thing repeatedly. To break the stagnancy cycle, an individual must purposely seek to introduce new elements into his or her routine. Spontaneity is vital. We all should endeavor to spice up our lives.

Growth requires hunger—a hunger for new ideas and learning experiences. Everyone should attempt to be better than they were yesterday, and we all should strive to progress in all areas of life. When change comes, we should not be too quick to run away from it. Instead, we should embrace change and seek ways to use it to propel ourselves to greatness. Also, we all should not forget to always nourish our bodies and minds with wholesome nutrients, as this promotes growth.

To live a life devoid of regret, growth is necessary. A growing person is a happy and healthy person. People who are growing today are ensuring their happiness for tomorrow. These people will most likely live a life devoid of regret.

Confession: *Dear Lord, thank You for yesterday. Thank You for the grace to grow every day. If there is any aspect of my life that has been dormant, help me to recognize this aspect today. Amen.*

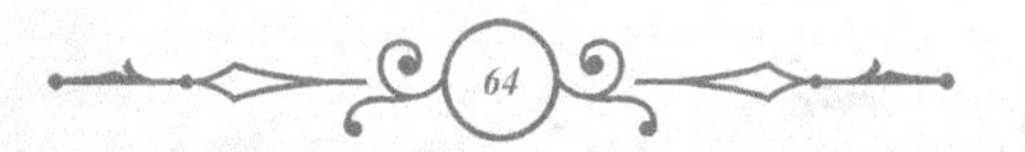

MARCH 2

COMPLACENCY

I know your deeds, that you are neither cold nor hot.
I wish you were either one or the other!
Revelations 3:15, NIV

While some feel dissatisfied with their lives, there are those who feel too satisfied with theirs. These people are also called the rather complacent ones. Many complacent folks are known to exhibit the "I have achieved it all" or "I am all that" attitude. However, not all complacent people display this pride-like outlook. Some are just laid back and become too comfortable after achieving a few milestones in their lives. One of the greatest enemies to anyone's potential is his or her accomplishments. Potential, in this case, means inbuilt ability. No matter the level of success a person may have attained, there is still something within that has not yet been tapped into. Regardless of one's achievement, there is still always something to be exploited. It's left to every one of us to keep digging in. The more we dig into ourselves, the more we realize many surprising things.

There is a popular saying that the graveyard is one of the wealthiest places on Earth. This is because a lot of potential dies with people who refuse to use it while still alive. A life devoid of regret is one lived to the fullest, not one lived too relaxed or carefree. We live to the fullest by fully harnessing all our potential. Let's begin doing this today.

Confession: *Lord Jesus, thank You. Today I search myself for any complacency.*
Help me use all my potential for my world and for Your glory.
I choose to press on until I achieve all that You have created me to do. Amen.

MARCH 3

LIVING FOR OTHERS ALONE

To acquire wisdom is to love yourself;
people who cherish understanding will prosper.
Proverbs 19:8, NLT

I met an elderly woman who held some resentment toward her children. She was quick to tell anyone available to listen about how her children were treating her poorly. On meeting some of her children, they said, "We are not surprised because she tells everyone that." They further said, "Although we do not give our mother all she wants, we try to meet her needs. But no matter what we do, it's never enough."

Eventually, the root of the problem surfaced. This elderly woman felt cheated because she had spent her life living for her children alone. She practically did everything for them, and she expected reciprocation. But as soon as her children grew and had their own families, they made their nuclear family their priority over her.

A story was also told of a woman who gave everything for her spouse when they first started out as a couple. For decades, she gave him all that she had. They finally caught their break and became very successful. She then began resenting her spouse. This resentment mostly had to do with her losing her own dreams while helping her spouse find his. She felt lost.

Have you ever experienced or witnessed something related to this? Do you know anyone who has? Stories like these are all too common in our world today. Why would someone who was once selfless become someone who resents? We can ponder this as we go about our day today.

***Confession:** Lord, Your word is life. Help me to better understand our hearts as humans. Please search my heart today, and if I hold any resentment toward others, help me recognize and deal with it. Amen.*

MARCH 4

LIVE FOR YOU TOO

And a second is like it:
You shall love your neighbor as yourself.
Matthew 22:39

The Bible's instruction is simple: Love others as you would love yourself. Philippians 2:3 also added that out of humility, we should value others more highly than ourselves. However, the Bible never encourages us to disregard or not treat our own selves right. Many people drown themselves in other's lives. They give themselves entirely while assisting others. After giving their all, they end up feeling empty and purposeless.

Today's discussion does not in any way suggest that we should not be part of people's lives. We should do that. But the danger comes when we resort to being "all" of other people's lives instead of being "a part" of it. Living a balanced life is important

One regret many elderly people take to their graves is that they never lived for themselves. If you have not already, please get into the habit of taking care of yourself. It's not selfish to occasionally do nice things for yourself. Life is about finding stability. Too much selflessness can lead to self-sabotage. Love your family. Love your neighbor. Also, love yourself.

Confession: *Dear Jesus, I am grateful for Your word. Teach me how to find stability. Help me never to be unkind to other people. In the same way, help me never to be unkind toward myself. Amen.*

MARCH 5

THE NEED FOR APPROVAL

Woe to you when everyone speaks well of you,
for that is how their ancestors treated the false prophets.
Luke 6:26, NIV

As humans, we all long for approval. The only difference is the rate, form, and level at which we crave this. When we are approved by others, we feel somewhat validated. We also feel confident, relevant, and accepted. Drinking from the well of approval no doubt quenches a certain thirst on the inside, but the problem with this is that this approval well never truly satisfies. The more a person drinks from it, the thirstier that person becomes.

Some people, when old and gray, say they regret living their lives just for other's reactions. Their regular thoughts throughout their lifetime ran somewhat like this: What will others say? How will people see me? Is this socially acceptable? Will others like this? It's surprising the lengths to which we humans will go to be admired. In fact, many have made life-altering decisions that have negatively impacted their lives. All this was done for social acceptance.

Unfortunately, the downside of approval is that it is not constant. It comes and goes. Those that approve of us today may disapprove of us tomorrow. Do we then live our lives based on how others feel? The answer to this question is no. Being validated is great. However, the incessant need for approval carries a lot of baggage and headache. Like everything in life, finding a balance is key.

Confession: *Father, You know my heart and all I have done in search of validation. Please have mercy on me this day. Help me to see my life through heaven's eyes and not the eyes of mere men. Amen.*

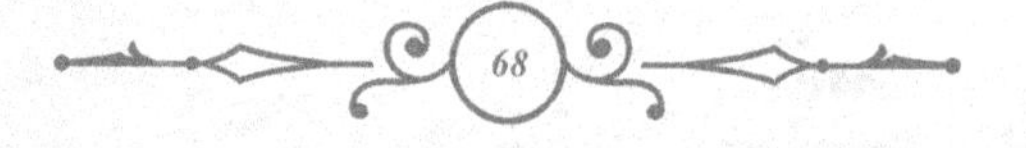

MARCH 6

SELF-APPROVAL

Do not be conformed to this world, but be transformed by the renewal of your mind, that by testing you may discern what is the will of God, what is good and acceptable and perfect. **Romans 12:2**

Just as people have a choice to approve of you, they also have an option to disapprove. It's within people's rights to do as they please. Everyone is entitled to feel the way they want or say what they like. And should those who praise you today decide that you do not deserve their praise tomorrow, this has to be okay with you.

The best form of approval is that which comes from within one's self. Not only is self-approval constant but it is also positive, healthy, and lasting. Getting validated by others is fantastic, but on days when the approval is not forthcoming, remind yourself of your self-worth. On days when people forget to compliment your looks, compliment yourself. And should it seem like people are ignoring you, do not take it to heart. Maybe the reason they are not acknowledging you is that they are dealing with their own issues.

We may think we need other's approval, but we don't. What we truly need is self-approval and approval from God. You cannot force others to approve of you. Thus, it's important you live your life on your own terms. When people decide they do not love you anymore, endeavor to utilize the self-love you have already stored within your personal bank.

Confession: *Dear Jesus, You have deposited so much in me. Teach me how to love and approve of myself. Help me understand that true validation has to begin from within me first. Amen.*

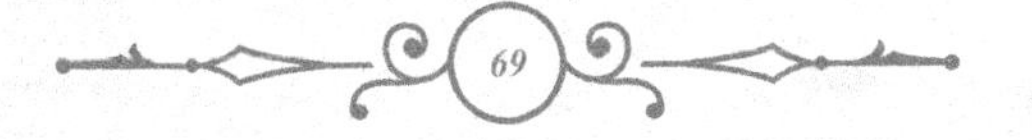

MARCH 7

THE SATISFYING DRINK

Jesus replied, "Anyone who drinks this water will soon become thirsty again. But those who drink the water I give will never be thirsty again. It becomes a fresh, bubbling spring within them, giving them eternal life."
John 4:13–14, NLT

Choosing to strictly live off other's approval can be likened to traveling down a road. At first, the path may look promising. However, the farther one travels, the more one may realize that the route has no destination in sight. What it has, on the other hand, is emptiness and misery. Sadly, depression in recent times has been linked to social pressure.

There is a void in every human that can only be filled by God, but the devil manipulates people into thinking this void can also be filled with a good social status and being liked. Does the devil stop there? No, he doesn't. He continuously feeds our minds with thoughts of not being good enough or being a reject. He does until he gets us to a place where we will do anything just to be admired by society.

There is One whose love we do not have to beg for. His name is Jesus. When folks whose attention we crave fail us, Jesus is always available to give us all the attention we need. If approval is what we are thirsty for, Jesus has the satisfying drink that will quench our thirst. Whenever we feel down, let's call to that One who has unending joy within His reach. He will always be there for us.

Confession: *Dear Jesus, thank You for your unconditional love. You loved me even before I was formed. Today I choose to only drink from the well that satisfies. This well is You, my Lord, and Savior. Amen.*

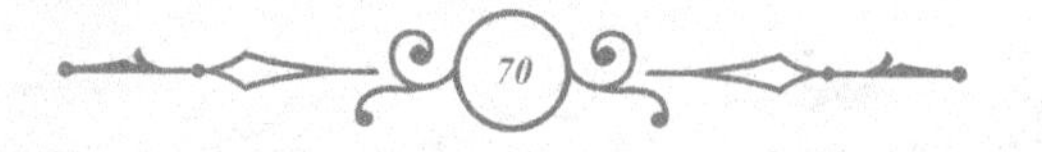

MARCH 8

•••

THOSE WHOSE APPROVAL REALLY COUNTS

For they loved the glory that comes from man more than the glory that comes from God.
John 12:43

Grace started to feel invisible. It was as if people did not see her anymore, and she felt ignored. This bothered her so much that she started doing crazy things to get people's attention. This went on for a while. One day she was home playing with her kids when she heard a voice. The Holy Spirit said to her, "Why do you keep searching for love when you have been surrounded with more than enough?" She stopped for a moment to ponder what she had just heard. Then she truly looked into her life, and for the first time, she realized how blessed she was. She had her spouse and children, who adored her. She had a few friends, who had her back come what may. She had her parents, who regularly sang her praises and loved her tremendously. She had her siblings, who were always there for her. She also had a few other people whom she knew genuinely cared for her. Those whose approval really mattered already approved of her. Why was she then so hungry for love and admiration from people who were mere acquaintances?

Grace was hungry for love from others because she is human like the rest of us. Everyone wants to be loved. Unfortunately, not everyone will love us. No matter how hard we try, there are those that will just not like us. This is why we need to have that inner circle that we know we can always draw strength from at our weakest. Those whose approval of us should count are those that know and genuinely care for us, not mere strangers. To live a misery-free life, these are the only people whose opinions should matter: ours, God's, and our inner circle.

Confession: *Dear Jesus, now I know that Your approval is all I need. You have already validated me, and I am thankful for this. I embrace Your love. Please open my eyes that I may see all I have been blessed with. Help me to stop seeking validation in the wrong places. Amen.*

FOR AS A MAN THINKETH

MARCH 9

FOR AS A MAN THINKETH

For as he thinketh in his heart, so is he.
Proverbs 23:7a, KJV

Getting into the right frame of mind was something I struggled with for a long time. One could say it has a lot to do with my temperament, and I would not disagree much with that. For one, I used to be a major worrier. When I wasn't worrying, I would try to fix or control things. And when that didn't work, I would try to calculate how and when everything must take place. I did this until I became frustrated or went into a minor depression. After wearing myself out, the Holy Spirit then picked me up and set me straight. Thankfully, with my consistent walk with God, my mind has become renewed.

The mind of a person is God's gift to him or her for several reasons. Some of these reasons are communicating with heaven and performing exploits on Earth. However, the weak spot of this gift is that it can be manipulated and used to bring about the ruin of an individual. The devil has been aware of this from the beginning of time, so he utilizes this weakness for his evil purposes. This is also why there is always an ongoing battle within every human—the struggle between good and evil.

The mind of man is complex yet simple. How can something be simple and still be complex? We will discuss this in detail in our new series, "For as a Man Thinketh."

Confession: *Dear Jesus, thank You for loving me in spite of my shortcomings. Every day You make Your love for me obvious. I yield my mind to You today. Please mold me into all that You have created me to be. Amen.*

MARCH 10

PUTTING THE MIND IN PERSPECTIVE

But what comes out of the mouth proceeds from the heart,
and this defiles a person.
Matthew 15:18

Some time ago, a prominent establishment was attacked. The main aim of the perpetrators was to paralyze the company, bringing all its work to a complete halt. One would think the strategy of these perps would be to eliminate the head of the company. One may even think they would destroy the company's building and all those in it. However, what they did instead was head straight to the control room. As soon as they got the necessary gadgets and crash sequence, they shut the company down. What they did, did little to affect the infrastructure and staff of the company, but they went into the heart of the company, destroying it from the inside out.

The mind can be likened to a control room. It can also be equated to the engine of an automobile, pillar of a structure, or nucleus of an atom. Our minds have more profound impacts than we may ever know. What takes place in the mind eventually defines the person.

We cannot do more than our minds allow. Our minds form our thoughts, and our thoughts dictate our actions, which impact our destiny. All that will be needed to control a person is to control that person's mind.

Confession: *Dear Lord, thank You for the gift of a functioning mind. Now I know that all that takes place in my mind will define me. Help me, Holy Spirit, to always keep my mind positive. Amen.*

MARCH 11

THE PLACEBO EFFECT

The heart is deceitful above all things, and desperately sick; who can understand it?
Jeremiah 17:9

The placebo is a fake medication. It is sometimes shaped to look exactly like the original pill. But its components are entirely different from the real thing. The placebo has little to no pharmacological content. Some are merely sugar, saline water, or vitamin tablets. Sometimes this fake drug is administered to patients to deceive as well as satisfy them. In recent times, the use of the placebo has been discouraged in caring for patients. Still, when used, it has often proven to be effective.

The placebo works hand in hand with the average patient's expectations. Those that perceive the assumed treatment to be the real thing are often cured. The placebo has been used to treat depression, headaches, and many other disorders. The placebo effect does an excellent job of demonstrating the relationship between the mind and the body. It also explains how one can trick the mind into believing just about anything.

If the mind can have such a significant impact on our health, we can only imagine its effect on other aspects of our lives. The placebo example goes a long way in showing how powerful our minds are and why they should be treated as such.

Confession: *Father, Your Word says that out of my mind flows the issues of life. You have made me a master over my thought life. Henceforth, I choose to act in this knowledge. May springs of living water continually flow out my mind. Amen.*

MARCH 12

WHAT THE MIND FEEDS ON

Above all else, guard your heart,
for everything you do flows from it.
Proverbs 4:23, NIV

If we ingest anything toxic into our bodies, it will most likely cause harm. Having figured this out, many people have learned to avoid damaging substances. Unfortunately, a good number of us haven't learned how to do the same for our minds.

To guard something means to protect, oversee, or preside over a thing. It could also mean to monitor. This is precisely what today's scripture reference is asking us to do. According to the text, we are to guard our hearts. Also, we are to do it above everything else, in essence, making it our number one priority. The reason for this is that the mind is very delicate and easily penetrated. It is like a sponge that absorbs anything it is exposed to.

The outer part of the body needs nutrients for everyday activities. The internal part of the body needs its nutrients too. Whether we humans like it or not, our minds will feed! It is a 24/7, non-stop clock. The choice of what it feeds on depends on what we provide it with. Even if we do not furnish our minds with anything, somehow they still find something to feed on. This is why what we expose our minds to is crucial. What we permit into our minds will end up shaping our lives. The question is, exactly what do you and I let into our minds regularly?

Confession: *Dear Jesus, I'm thankful for the word that has come my way this day. I declare that I am renewed in the spirit of my mind. From now on, I will no longer feed my mind with defiling thoughts. Help me achieve this. Amen.*

MARCH 13

WHAT DOES YOUR MIND FEED ON?

Keep vigilant watch over your heart; that's where life starts.
Proverbs 4:23, MSG

Previously, we established that the mind feeds on whatever is available. These things could be positive or negative. But why the need to guard the heart? We will use examples of two different people living in the same community.

The first is an inventor. His invention is aimed at helping others and making life easier; he is also a happy person. The second is one who is barely getting by. He is known to be one who complains about everything. According to him, life has been unfair. Somehow, everyone apart from him is responsible for all the wrongs in his life. To describe him in one word, he is mediocre. The major difference between these two people may be their surrounding circumstances, for instance, their family background, financial position, and more. More importantly, it may also be an issue of what goes on in their minds. Our reference text today says life starts from our hearts. Everything we do flows from the mind. Whatever we will become in life originates from our thinking.

The need for a proper frame of mind can never be overstated. It is essential for anyone who desires a meaningful and successful life. The question again is, what is your frame of mind? When you compare all that goes on in your mind with what happens in your life, can you draw a link?

Confession: *Dear God, thank You for Your word of wisdom today. Your instruction is that I guide my heart diligently as life begins from my heart. All I will become in life largely depends on my thinking process. I decree this day that my thoughts will produce life and abundance. Amen.*

MARCH 14

FRUITS THAT POISON THE MIND

For out of the heart come evil thoughts, murder, adultery, sexual immorality, theft, false witness, slander.
Matthew 15:19

When I find myself unhappy, sometimes I am led by the Holy Spirit to conduct a mental check. On one occasion, I found that my foul attitude was a result of feeling irrelevant. I just felt out of place with people. On another occasion, I found the reason to be envy. I got into the habit of comparing myself with those around me. Somehow I convinced myself that others were ahead, and I was just trailing behind them in life. On several occasions, I found the reason for my bitterness to be no reason at all. I had allowed the devil to play some funny tricks with my mind, which ended up making me frustrated.

Some people live in constant fear of the unknown. Some have been deeply hurt by others and are still bearing the emotional bruises. Many are still carrying guilt and shame from their past mistakes. Others may have developed habits that have constantly threatened their peace of mind. This may include anger, jealousy, backbiting, addiction, and many more. These are fruits that poison the mind.

Conduct your own self-search today. As you do so, determine what poisonous fruit has been threatening your peace of mind.

Confession: *Dear Lord, thank You for blessing me with a sound mind. I decree that henceforth, my thoughts will be divinely inspired. Help me overcome fruits that poison my mind. My thoughts will no longer drag me backward but propel me forward. Amen.*

MARCH 15

RENEWAL OF THE MIND

...and to be renewed in the spirit of your minds.
Ephesians 4:23

If we continue to believe as we have always believed, we will continue to act the same way. If we continue to act this way, we will keep getting the same results. Should we want a different result in our lives, most times all we need is a renewal of the mind. A change of mind usually precedes a change of attitude because where the mind goes, the man follows.

As humans, some of the biggest problems we face are because of wrong thinking. Our minds will either work for us or work against us, depending on their disposition. The mind is a battlefield. It is where we lose or win. It is also where we become victims or victors.

Getting the right mindset takes a lot of work and determination. A productive mindset requires intentional effort. It may even require altering our belief system and how we see life as well as warranting a change from our former way of thinking. Most of us could use a good renewal of the mind. Its advantages cannot be overemphasized. Renewal of the mind helps us become better versions of ourselves, and we can achieve this as we continue our walk with God. The necessary coaching needed for an improved thinking process and a better life is just a few steps away.

Confession: *Dear God, I am no longer conformed to this world but transformed. My mind is renewed, and my knowledge is refreshed. My mind blossoms in Jesus' light and truth. I no longer reason with my understanding but the mind of Christ. Amen.*

MARCH 16

THE THOUGHT–ACTION PROCESS

Finally, brethren, whatever things are true, whatever things are noble, whatever things are just, whatever things are pure, whatever things are lovely, whatever things are of good report, if there is any virtue and if there is anything praiseworthy—meditate on these things. ***Philippians 4:8, NKJV***

When a seed is sown, several factors must be in place for it to grow into a plant successfully. These factors may include fertile soil, sunlight, water, fertilizer, and others. Once these resources are available, chances are high that the seed will yield a good harvest. The thought-action process works in the same way and is sequential. First, a seed is planted; this seed usually comes in the form of a thought. The thought may come from anywhere. It could be a movie one is watching, something one is listening to, or anything one comes in contact with. Interestingly, a person may be doing nothing, and a random thought could just drop into his or her mind.

Once this thought-seed is implanted, the next thing that is done is what makes all the difference. For the seed to survive, only one nutrient is required. This nutrient is called "meditation." To meditate means to think deeply about something over time. Today's reference text has given us specific things to meditate on. Therefore, thoughts that don't align with the listed reflections should be immediately discarded.

Why would the Word of God ask us to meditate on certain things and not others? What exactly are we to do with other thoughts that find their way into our minds? We will focus on these questions next.

Confession: *Today I decree that my thoughts will no longer hold me in bondage. I refuse to think thoughts that are limiting and discouraging. Lord, help me always remember this decree when negative thoughts pour into my mind. Amen.*

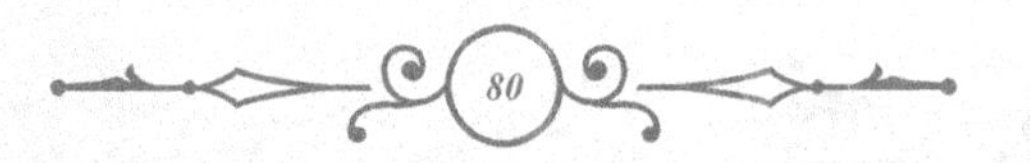

MARCH 17

THE THOUGHT–ACTION PROCESS PART II

Therefore, preparing your minds for action, and being sober-minded, set your hope fully on the grace that will be brought to you at the revelation of Jesus Christ.
1 Peter 1:13

How many times have we been taken aback by someone else's horrible action? For me, I would say countless times. People have a way of surprising us, especially those we least expect such actions from.

I believe people do not just wake up one day to be serial killers. I also believe people do not become overnight inventors. Yes, there are instances when people act on the spur of the moment without thinking twice. But more often than not, people usually follow the thought–action process. A particular train of thought at first presumed to be harmless can gain strength. The thought may then flourish until it becomes a stronghold that prompts actions. People that do bad things are not necessarily bad people. Sometimes these people are just victims of evil thoughts that took root in their minds. Over time, these thoughts gained power and caused torment until they became executed.

When a thought comes to our minds, we can ask ourselves these questions: Is it pure? Is it honest? Is it of good report? Is it true? Is it lovely? Is it worthy of praise? (Philippians 4:8). If the answer is no, there is only one thing to do—immediately discard the thought. We have no business thinking about it. Unfruitful thoughts should never be allowed to grow roots. They should be cut off at the planting stage and never allowed to germinate. If they are not cut off, their execution may be inevitable.

Confession: *Father, You have availed me the good thoughts I should meditate on. Henceforth, the thoughts I will linger on will be ones that are just, noble, and pure. Amen.*

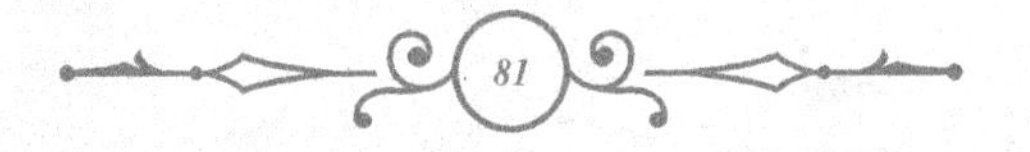

MARCH 18

EARLY IN THE MORNING

The thief comes only to steal and kill and destroy.
My purpose is to give a rich and satisfying life.
John 10:10, NLT

I visited a woman some time ago and noticed something unusual. This woman was God-fearing, compassionate, and lovely but would just throw a fit from time to time. This usually took place as soon as she opened her eyes in the morning. Surprisingly, this same lady might go to bed happy but then wake in a different mood. At dawn, she would nag everyone around her. She would remind them of everything they had done and were still doing wrong. She would complain about everything. This could go on for hours or until everyone left the house for their daily activities. This attitude of hers was a mystery. Over time, I found myself pondering over the "whats" and "whys" behind her actions.

Early in the morning is one of the most vulnerable moments in a person's life. It is the time when the mind is very fresh and notices anything within sight. Once we open our eyes in the morning, our minds are on high alert and will let anything in.

It took me a while to realize that I do not have to meditate on every thought that pops into my mind as soon as I wake. I can choose what I want to think about. Although it may take a lot of training and self-discipline, this is very much achievable. Whatever we let our minds meditate on sets our course and mood for the day. If there is ever any time we need to guard our minds, it is early in the morning.

Confession: *Lord Jesus, thank You for the gift of another day. The devil's mission is that I live in frustration. Teach me how to guard my heart with all diligence. I choose to live daily with the joy and peace You have furnished me with. Amen.*

MARCH 19

OTHER TIMES WHEN THE MIND IS MOST VULNERABLE

Be sober, be vigilant: because your adversary the devil walks about like a roaring lion, seeking whom he may devour.
1 Peter 5:8, NKJV

Previously, we discussed that the mind is permeable in the morning. Besides this time, there are other moments when the mind is porous as well. One significant moment is when a person is angry. People often say and do things they don't mean when they are upset. This is simply because the mind has been displaced from its correct state at that moment of anger. Another major moment when the mind is vulnerable is when one is depressed. Depression is an ongoing struggle for so many. People with this disorder often experience overwhelming mind conflict and lack of motivation. The anger or depressive states are just a few of the many times when the mind is most vulnerable.

We may not be able to control being angry or gloomy. Frankly, we may not be able to control the negative thoughts that pour into our minds at such intense moments. What we can control, however, are those specific thoughts we meditate on.

Lifelong decisions made during the mind's vulnerable moments are hardly the right ones. Therefore, it's crucial that we do not make any drastic decisions until we are calm and in the correct frame of mind. Unguarded moments are the times the devil uses to trick us. Being vigilant is not just a choice; it is a must for a successful life.

Confession: *Father, You own the hearts of kings, and You own my heart. I set aside every distraction this day, and I set my heart on You. Help me guard my heart against anger and depression. Amen.*

MARCH 20

A GOOD THERAPY FOR DEPRESSION

Give thanks in all circumstances; for this is the will of God in Christ Jesus for you.
1 Thessalonians 5:18a

Depression is real. Those who have never struggled with this disease may not realize how real the disorder is.

Life can be overwhelming, and situations beyond our control may occur. A lot of times, life's issues and challenges may drag us down; this is only natural. Still, today's reference scripture encourages us to give thanks in all things. Thanksgiving is a powerful spiritual tool that permeates upliftment and inner joy.

When we are at our lowest, we can overcome this state by making a list of all we can be thankful for. This list may include life, health, family, shelter, a job, provision, friends, safety, and so on. Making this list will help us realize how good God has been to us. This list also helps us take our eyes off our problems and set them on God, who alone can fix them. God, in turn, will then reward us with gladness of heart. Drugs are good and therapeutic sessions are fantastic, but one of the best therapies for depression is "being thankful in all things." I and many others can attest to this. Try it today. It works!

Confession: *Lord, thank You for Your word that reminds me to give thanks at all times. In the ways I have lifted my worries above You, please have mercy. I call forth my inner joy today. Amen.*

MARCH 21

COACHING THE MIND

Then you will experience God's peace, which exceeds anything we can understand. His peace will guard your hearts and minds as you live in Christ Jesus.
Philippians 4:7, NLT

Out of nothing, the mind can create things as it possesses the power of life. Unfortunately, if not properly channeled, the mind can become a tool of destruction. In training our thinking, a few things must be established.

First, we must make an acknowledgment. This acknowledgment is an acceptance of the fact that the mind is a battlefield. Thoughts will always come in. Some of these thoughts belong to us (internal), while some are due to our surroundings (external). Other thoughts that come pouring into our minds are from the devil, whose sole aim is to destroy. Because our hearts are thought magnets, thoughts cannot be stopped from pouring in. So what do we do with these thoughts? We hold on to the positive ones and discard negative ones. We can also properly channel our minds by meditating on the truth of God's Word. We alone have the deciding vote on what to do with our thinking process. Wherever our thoughts lead is up to us.

We are more than conquerors. Jesus has availed us His peace that passes all understanding. We can coach our minds into thinking the way we want them to. A superior quality of life can be attained when we develop the habit of being alert to what our minds absorb.

Confession: *Dear Lord, today I declare that out of my soul shall flow rivers of living water. I channel my mind to positivity and shut out every negativity. Amen.*

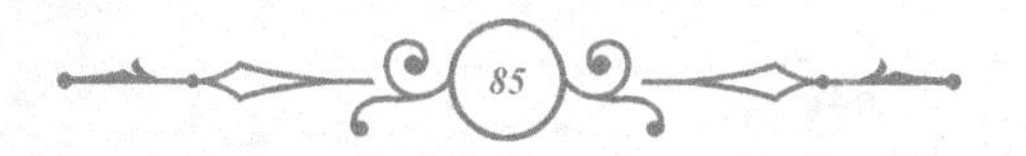

MARCH 22

LEAVING THE PAST WAY OF THINKING BEHIND

And no one pours new wine into old wineskins.
Otherwise, the new wine will burst the skins, and both the
wine and the wineskin will be ruined. No, they pour new
wine into new wineskins. ***Mark 2:22, NIV***

According to today's text, new wine put in an old wineskin will ruin both the new wine and the old wineskin. New wine will be at its best if stored in a new wineskin. In essence, new must follow new. Any iota of old leads to contamination and destruction. The same goes for our minds. The mind must be renewed. For it to be truly refreshed, anything of the old life must be wiped clean. All the baggage from the past must be left where it belongs—the past.

Certain underrated weapons have the power to derail one's thought process. One of these weapons is guilt. Guilt has just one job: to keep people in bondage. Unhealthy guilt makes people self-punish themselves. They do this as a means to atone for their past wrongdoings. Fear is another weapon aimed solely at messing with one's mind. Fear is False Evidence Appearing Real. Fear is in our imagination and tricks us into believing our worst nightmare will come true. This belief is incorrect.

To leave the past in the past, we must expunge certain old thought poisoners. These include guilt, fear, shame, disappointment, defeat, and self-loathing, among others. We must also embrace a fresh way of thinking, one that only promotes positivity. This is very achievable. All we have to do is say no to the old way of thinking and yes to a renewed thinking process.

Confession: *Lord Jesus, thank you for the gift of a new beginning. Today I leave my past way of thinking behind. I leave all thoughts of fear, guilt, and condemnation in the past. Help me as I forge ahead and work toward a better thinking process. Amen.*

MARCH 23

ASSOCIATION MATTERS!

Walk with the wise and become wise:
associate with fools and get in trouble.
Proverbs 13:20, NLT

There is a danger in exposing our minds to anything and everything. An exceptional student that hangs out with those that only do okay may also begin doing average in school. A unique student that hangs out more with outstanding ones will likely do great in class. The question here is, with whom do we spend most of our time? Whether we like it or not, our company affects us. They can either influence us positively or negatively.

Personally, certain things just set me on track. These include hanging out with good friends and attending quality social gatherings. Reading good books and watching positive shows also improve my thinking process. But when I watch a good deal of bad news or befriend negative people, I feel demoralized.

Association matters! Who and what we let in will shape us and our thinking. What we expose our minds to carries ripple effects on our thoughts. Our thoughts will either act as a catalyst that propels us or as a stumbling block that hampers us.

Confession: *Dear Lord, Your peace passes all understanding. May this peace guide me and my heart this day. I dissociate myself from anything dragging my thought process backward. I will only follow Your leading. Amen.*

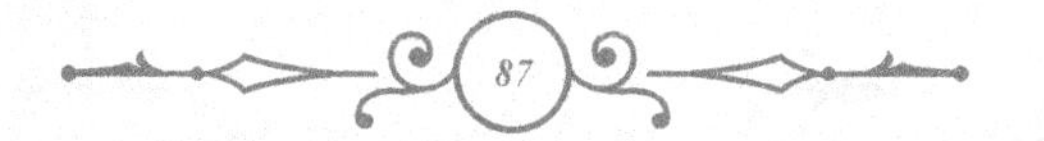

MARCH 24

SELECTIVE THINKING

For God has not given us a spirit of fear and timidity, but of power, love and self-discipline.
2 Timothy 1:7. NLT

To win the battle of the mind, we have to habitually think about what we are thinking about. This simply means to always examine the nature of our reasoning. As Christians, are those thoughts what we should meditate on? Will they make our lives or the lives of those around us better? Are those thoughts in alignment with our set goals for the future?

Another way to win the battle of the mind is to replace vile thoughts with good ones. We may not be able to control random thoughts that drop in our minds. However, nothing stops us from creating our own thinking. For instance, when thoughts of sickness come, we can replace them with thoughts of good health and a long life. When ambushed with thoughts of our terrifying pasts, we can replace them with ones of a victorious future. The more we do this, the more we will believe God's Word concerning us.

God's Word works! Let's begin seeing ourselves in the promises Christ has in store for us. In doing so, we can access all our blessings.

Confession: *Lord, as I begin to intentionally examine my thought patterns, please help me. I want to be like You, Jesus. I pray that my thoughts henceforth will be ones of victory and not defeat. Amen.*

MARCH 25

WORDS MATTER!

Kind words are like honey—sweet to the soul
and healthy for the body.
Proverbs 16:24, NLT

Stupid! Ugly! Useless! Dummy! Unattractive! Nasty! Inadequate! Weird! These are a few of the words some have heard people call them all their lives. Some have even been called worse. Words have a way of influencing our thought process, and it does not take long before words uttered begin to sound believable to those on the receiving end. Eventually, these people may start to filter their own thoughts through the sieve of these words.

Unfortunately, you may not be able to convince others to change what they say to you or how they perceive you. So what can you do then? You can begin by refuting those appalling words in their entirety. Are those who call you ugly right? No, they are not. You are not ugly. Who sets the standard for ugliness or beauty, anyway? Is it not we humans? So as a fellow human, I say you and I have an equal right to set our own personal standards. You are the image of God and made in His likeness. His creations are flawless, and you are no exception. Wake up every morning, look in the mirror, and tell yourself how awesome you are. Say it repeatedly until your inner being believes it. Then start treating yourself as someone exceptional.

The more you do this, the likelier others will begin to see you in all your splendor as well. Like everything else, the words we choose to be defined by begin within. Our minds are life's well. Whatever we decide to draw from it is what we will receive.

Confession: *Dear God, I am thankful for today's words. I confess today that I am excellent. All your creations are perfect, and I am no exception. Since you made me, only You can define me. Because You call me good, I believe it with all my heart. Amen.*

MARCH 26

KEEPING THE MIND BUSY

...making the best use of the time, because the days are evil.
Ephesians 5:16

The word boredom may sound innocent, yet it is often responsible for the horrible things people do. There is a popular saying that an idle mind is the devil's workshop, and an idle person is certainly one with a permeable mind. A person may choose to be idle but not the person's mind. Although the mind can be redirected, it can never be turned off, as it will always function. To keep busy means to keep the mind occupied with something productive. This just means giving the mind a positive thing to focus on.

It's one thing to be busy as anyone can be busy doing nothing. It's another thing to be busy being productive and fulfilled. Productivity keeps the mind focused and gives the mind something to work on. If we do not intentionally provide it with something to do, the mind will find something on its own. This is how people find themselves involved in all sorts of foolishness.

When I am busy doing something that fulfills me, I am focused. I am less interested in unimportant things. I am also friendlier, happier, and optimistic. Have you noticed this about yourself too? If yes, then you may agree that a well-focused mind brings joy. If you are not satisfied with your present life, give being productive a try. When you engage in fulfilling activities, you will live a satisfying life.

Confession: *Dear Lord, thank You for calling me Your own. I am not a mediocre, so I refuse to live that way. Today I tap into the creative mind You have blessed me with. Not only will I keep my mind busy but I will also stay productive and achieve all You have destined me to. Amen.*

MARCH 27

VERIFYING THE TRUTH BEHIND OUR THOUGHTS

...but test everything that is said. Hold on to what is good.
1 Thessalonians 5:21, NLT

Not all thoughts are accurate. Just because we assume or think something to be true doesn't mean it is. Often the mind is outright wrong about what is going on. An example is two people laughing behind me. My mind may tell me that those people are laughing at me because of my appearance. However, they could be laughing at something different and may not even notice my presence. Another instance could be when my friend withdraws and begins to keep some distance. My mind may think my friend does not want to associate with me any longer. But in reality, my friend could be going through some tough times. She may only be staying away because she is trying to figure things out on her own.

Today's discussion does not suggest that we should discredit all our thoughts. Far from it! As a matter of fact, going by the examples, those two people may be laughing at me. Also, my friend may be intentionally keeping her distance. However, this is not so in all cases. Things sometimes appear different than they really are. It's imperative that we verify the facts first before reacting to thoughts that pop up in our heads.

Sometimes others around us have no idea as to what we think they feel about us. These people may regard us highly in their minds, but our minds may tell us otherwise. Misconceptions should be avoided as this will save us from a lot of future heartaches. This will also help improve our relationships with others.

Confession: *Today I receive my deliverance from all limiting thinking patterns. From here on, I will only think the right thoughts. I will begin verifying the truth behind my thoughts before giving them life. Amen.*

MARCH 28

THE WORD WORKS!

...casting down arguments and every high thing that exalts itself against the knowledge of God, bringing every thought into captivity to the obedience of Christ.
2 Corinthians 10:5, NKJV

Nothing in this life is constant. At one time we were babies, and then we grew to become adults. The more we grew, the more we experienced transitions in our lives. The point is, things in life are subject to change. One thing, however, has remained constant from the very beginning: the Word of God. People we are in relationships with will change. Circumstances surrounding us fluctuate. But throughout life's shifts, God and His Word will never change.

Whom and what we center our lives around is significant. When we make a person (no matter how close he or she is) the center of our existence, what happens when that person fails us? When we make our jobs our lives, what happens when the job is gone? Our God is the only constant figure. He is the only unchanging One through all life changes. When He is our anchor, not only does He lead us aright but He regularly sets us on the right path.

One way to get closer to God is through His Word. The more we meditate, chew on, and confess these words, the more we key ourselves into all the promises in store for us. If the mind is a battlefield, then the Word of God is the weapon we need to wage and win the battle. A verse or a chapter of the Bible daily is sometimes all we need to turn things in our lives around. His Word has the power to set our minds on the correct pathway and guarantees hope. God's Word is life!

Confession: *Dear Lord, I acknowledge that Your word is truth. The more I surround myself with Your truth, the more at peace I become. Please reveal Yourself more to me. I long to know You more. As I study the Scriptures daily, speak to my mind, Jesus. Amen.*

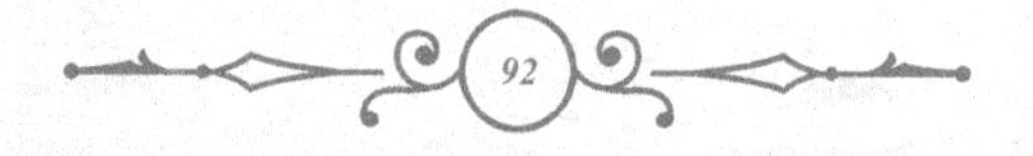

MARCH 29

THE CRAFTY SERPENT

Now the serpent was more crafty than any other beast of the field that the LORD God had made. He said to the woman, "Did God actually say, 'You shall not eat of any tree in the garden'?"
Genesis 3:1

When the devil tempted Eve in the Garden of Eden, he was very strategic. His plan was very simple—manipulate her into believing what was false was real. His agenda was successful. Unfortunately, he still uses this same trick to deceive many today.

I was once a victim of this scheme. In my late teens, I remember being so scared of myself. My fear grew from thoughts of me hurting people. In my head, I literally started seeing myself stabbing people, but in real life, I could not hurt a fly. This torment continued for a while. But one day, I realized the thoughts were actually not mine. They were planted by the devil. That day the chains of bondage broke, and I was set free from those evil thoughts. The devil has still not stopped attempting to mess with my mind, but then again, I do not expect him to stop. A few days before writing what you are reading, a thought of me being terminally ill was planted. By the grace of God, I now know better than to let the devil mess with my mind.

Life and death begin in the mind. Sadly, there is one other who knows about this all too well—the devil. The devil hates everything the human stands for. His only goal is to make an individual miserable here on Earth and afterward spend eternity in hell. How does he do this? He goes after the person's powerhouse (the mind) to mess with it. The devil knows that to destroy a person, he need not come after him or her physically. As soon as he can gain control of the person's mind and manipulate it, he has the person already. It's high time all children of God understood this and began their own warfare against the enemy.

Confession: *Lord, I rebuke every captive thought and bring them into Your obedience. Today I come against the devil and his hold upon my mind. I am free of negative, fearful, and limiting thoughts. I will keep my mind fixed on You. Amen.*

MARCH 30

PRAYER IS STILL THE ANSWER

For with the mouth one believes and is justified,
and with the mouth one confesses and is saved.
Romans 10:10

The power of prayer has been significantly downplayed in recent times. This has actually been a strategic ploy from the pit of hell to keep God's children in a passive state.

How do we react when we receive notice about a potential attack on our homes? Many of us will probably improve our security so that the perps won't gain access to our property. The same should go for our spiritual lives. The war the enemy is waging against God's children is serious. He is after our minds, so we must be guarded and ready to defend ourselves. Enough of this lukewarm attitude toward the battle of the mind! This is our lives we are talking about. We Christians must respond to the enemy's attacks as if our lives are on the line because in truth, our lives really are on the line.

It's time for the children of God to arise from their slumber! It's time for us to take our rightful places as true heirs with Christ. We are more than conquerors through Him (Jesus) who loves us. Jesus died for us so that we might have lives that are not lives of misery but of peace of mind and joy. How do we stop the devil in his tracks? We pray without ceasing! We cast and bind! We command the devil out of our minds and thoughts! We confess God's promises to us daily! When negative thoughts come to our minds, we open our mouths and rebuke them! We pray and speak in tongues at every point! When the devil comes with his tricks to torment our minds, we remind the devil of who we are in Christ! He has no place and no rights whatsoever in our lives. Stop giving the devil permission to enter into your affairs. Pray without ceasing!

Confession: *Lord Jesus, whenever I call, You always hear me. From this day on, I will no longer wallow in bondage. I take hold of my inheritance in You. I take dominion over my mind and think anointed thoughts. I think victorious thoughts. I am a winner. Amen*

IN THE PURSUIT OF HAPPINESS

MARCH 31

IN THE PURSUIT OF HAPPINESS

May the God of hope fill you with all joy and peace in believing, so that by the power of the Holy Spirit you may abound in hope.
Romans 15:13

We all search for happiness. How and where we search for it is what differs. Happiness means different things to different people. To some, happiness implies amassing wealth. Some define it as having peace of mind and solace. Many describe it as the joy that comes with living a fulfilled life.

Unfortunately, when in search of happiness, some have sacrificed life's essentials for alternative pursuits. For instance, some who define happiness in terms of a successful career have lost their family in their pursuit. But does it always have to be this way? Must certain things be sacrificed before an individual can be truly happy? Of course not.

As we delve into this new series, "The Pursuit of Happiness," there are a few things you need to understand. First, happiness begins with you as a person. Happiness is rarely about what you have, where you are, or what you do. Also, happiness is your right that God gave to you (Psalm 144:15). Finally, true happiness does not just show up; it has to be pursued purposely. How to maintain our happiness, the sacrifices we may need to pay for this cause, and more are what we will be focusing on in the following pages.

Confession: *Father, in time past, I may have stepped out of Your will to find happiness. I pray that You have mercy upon me for those missteps. I want to be happy, and I long to wake every morning with gladness of heart. I desire to sleep at night with my joy and peace intact. Teach me how to be happy with who I am and all You have blessed me with. Amen.*

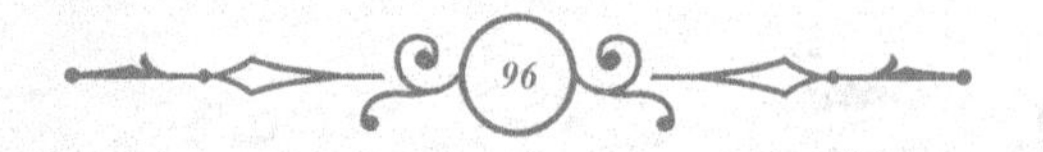

APRIL 1

•••

HAPPINESS IS A CHOICE

There is nothing better for a person than that he should eat and drink and find enjoyment in his toil. This also, I saw, is from the hand of God.
Ecclesiastes 2:24

Abraham Lincoln once said, "Most people are about as happy as they make up their minds to be." I tested this statement and found it to be true. Before carrying out this test, I used to be a rather moody person. One minute I would be all excited about life. The next, I would be downcast and joyless. Somewhere deep within me, I knew there was a better way to live than my default high–low mood. So one day I decided to be happy and to pursue happiness alone. I made up my mind that I would not let anyone or anything (including me) steal my joy anymore. Through the help of the Holy Spirit, I aggressively shut my eyes to all negativity. I kept monitoring my thoughts, actions, and emotions. If anything threatened my peace of mind, I addressed it right then and there. Through tough and disappointing moments, I chose to maintain my inner joy. And it worked! In truth, it wasn't an easy task, but I kept at it. The peace that has come with this practice has been beyond amazing.

Happiness is a choice that begins with every individual person. We are going to be happy when we decide to be happy and not when situations start going our way or when everyone likes us. We will be joyful only when we choose to. Today, choose a happy life. It is within your reach.

Confession: *Dear Lord, You have already blessed me with all the happiness I need. Today I choose happiness. I declare that nothing will steal my joy. From here on out, I will intentionally protect my peace of mind. Show me how to go about this, Jesus. Please teach me how to stay happy. Amen.*

APRIL 2

LOST JOY

Rejoice in the Lord always. Again I will say, rejoice!
Philippians 4:4, NKJV

Most of the time when we start feeling depressed and miserable, the devil is behind it. Today we will discuss how and why.

Once we lose our peace, our minds become exposed. This creates room for the devil to play all kinds of tricks with our thoughts. How? The devil starts by exaggerating our issues, making them look more dreadful than they are. He further compounds things by reminding us of all the things that have gone wrong in times past. He may also intimate us about all that could go wrong in the future. He flashes all manner of lies and deceit until we begin to believe them. Before long, fear creeps in. Panic follows. We may even lose our joy in the process. Then the devil wins.

Yes, it is challenging not to give in to our feelings, especially when going through tough times. But today we are being encouraged to be careful that we do not expose ourselves to the evil one to allow him to do his damage. The devil can hardly permeate a cheerful heart. This is why the Scriptures urge us to guard our hearts with diligence, as out of the heart flows the issues of life (Proverbs 4:23). Please keep your mind joyful, and keep it thankful. Keep it full of trust for God. Should you have problems threatening your happiness, take these to God in prayer. He'll fix them.

Confession: *Heavenly Father, thank you for making me a victor. I have been given the authority to trample upon the enemy. This power I take hold of today, and I say no to the devil. I refuse his lies, deceit, and games. My happiness is mine. The devil will no longer win over my life. I am a happy child of God. Amen.*

APRIL 3

GOD HAS NOT FORGOTTEN YOU

"For I know the plans I have for you," says the LORD. "They are plans for good and not for disaster, to give you a future and a hope."
Jeremiah 29:11, NLT

Years ago, my family went through a rough patch, and it felt like God had forgotten us. In fact, it got so bad that people started insinuating that we must have offended God in some way. It just seemed like God was mad at us and had turned His back on us. I was a little girl who loved God, but I took this challenging time personally because I always thought I was God's favorite. I knew He wanted me to be happy, so why did He have to forget my family and let us go through such suffering for so many years? I cried every other day during that time. Things just kept going from bad to worse. At one point, I stopped being hopeful because I did not want to be disappointed. I just started expecting bad news, and it kept coming. I also began training myself to adapt to that kind of life. For all I knew back then, maybe God's love for me was a fairy tale. This was my thinking as a little girl who thought her God had forsaken her.

Decades later, looking back at how far God has brought my family and me, all I can do is thank Him. At that time, it really seemed like God had forgotten me. But all He was doing then was training me for the future. He put me through tough moments to bring me out tougher, wiser, more mature, and broken. Now I see the big picture better. I wake up every morning, blessing Him for every phase of my life, both the good and the bad.

Today, should you feel abandoned, forgotten, or rejected, please keep trusting and believing. He did not forget me then, and He will not forget you now.

Confession: *Jesus, thank you for both the good and not-so-good times. Everything You do is for a reason. In it all, I know You have my best interest at heart. You will never forsake me; I know this. I trust You, and I know You will bring me out of my challenges better than I am now. Amen.*

APRIL 4

GOD HAS NOT FORGOTTEN YOU PART II

...for it is God who works in you, both to will and to work for his good pleasure.
Philippians 2:13

It is easy to be happy and thankful when things are going well. It may be challenging to "count it all joy" when things are not going so well. Still, Proverbs 3:5 admonishes you to "trust in the LORD with all your heart and do not lean on your own understanding." If you are currently going through some ordeal, today's words are for you. This is God's promise: You will laugh again. You will be happy again. You will look back and be able to bless God for how far He has brought you.

Whatever you may be going through now, please know that God has not and will never forsake you. His love is unconditional. God is letting you pass through the fire but not because He hates you. His intention is to refine you and make you better than you used to be.

Trust God through every situation in your life. Trust Him not because you have no other choice but because you know He is molding you into the person you should be. It's only normal for the potter to be tough on his clay. The tougher your challenges, the bigger the victory coming your way. Hang in there—God loves you.

Confession: *Heavenly Father, I'm grateful for Your unconditional love. Your love is constant, and it is not dependent on what I do or don't do. What I am going through, I count it all joy. I know You are molding me into all You need me to be. Amen.*

APRIL 5

A LIFE DEVOID OF REGRET

For God has not given us a spirit of fear and timidity,
but of power, love, and self-discipline.
2 Timothy 1:7, NLT

So many people are in the habit of asking questions like "What if I don't make it?" or "What if it doesn't work out?" My responses to these people have always been "What if you make it, and what if it works out?" Below are excerpts from my writing titled "What's the Worst That Could Happen?"

- As opposed to hesitating, ASK. The worst that could happen is you get a no. No means to try again with a different approach.
- As opposed to holding back, GO FOR IT. The worst that could happen is that you fail. The best stories often begin with failures.
- As opposed to procrastinating, DO IT NOW. The worst that could happen is that you arrive at your destination early.

A one-minute hesitation could land a person in a lifetime of regret. That missed opportunity may never present itself ever again. So if we haven't been grabbing opportunities as they present themselves, we could start now. An unhappy life is one filled with thoughts of "what if" and "what could have been." An unhappy life is filled with regrets. These can be avoided by doing all God leads us to do at every moment.

Confession: *Dear Lord, thank You for the gift of life. I also appreciate You for the gifts of courage, tenacity, and a sound mind. Your will is that I live a fulfilled life and not one filled with regrets. I pray for the strength to forge on and achieve all I have been created to. Amen.*

APRIL 6

EMBRACING YOUR UNIQUENESS

But you are a chosen race, a royal priesthood, a holy nation, a people for his own possession, that you may proclaim the excellencies of him who called you out of darkness into his marvelous light.
1 Peter 2:9

God enjoys variety and loves diversity. In every one of His creations, He made this obvious. Within all of God's creation, He placed in them a certain uniqueness. This uniqueness is individualized so that every person is different. In each of us are specific qualities that are peculiar to us. Only in embracing this uniqueness will we be able to understand our purpose on Earth. Unfortunately, not everyone embraces this uniqueness. Instead, many people imitate others and try to "be among" instead of "standing out."

Finding one's uniqueness can take a lot of digging deep into oneself. It takes a lot of self-introspection and we can begin doing this today. How? First, we have to study ourselves well enough to know what makes us different. When we find those qualities, we can then utilize them adequately. Yes, these qualities may not fit into the world's "acceptable attributes," but in harnessing and refining them, we can create a place for our kind of "unique."

Fitting into the crowd is comfortable. By the world's standard, being different is considered weird and appalling at first. But we are not of the world. We are of Jesus' lineage. Today, God is asking us to show forth the light He placed in us. When we do this, the promise of a fruitful, joyful, and happy life will be made evident in our lives.

Confession: *I am royalty. I am special. I have been created in the image and likeness of the Most High. Therefore, I am God's masterpiece. I decree this day that I will never again hide my head in shame. I am unique. I am the light of the world. I will show forth my light. I will search within and bless my world with all I have been gifted with. I will no longer let the world and its standard define me. Amen.*

APRIL 7

TRUE HAPPINESS

Yes, joyful are those who live like this! Joyful indeed are those whose God is the LORD.
Psalm 144:15, NLT

One does not need a dictionary to define happiness. Happiness comes naturally when you are at peace with yourself, your world, and your God. Happiness comes when you are advancing in the direction of your dreams, and true fulfillment comes from achieving one's goals. Happiness is the feeling you get when you know you are doing the right thing. You are joyous when you become a blessing to your generation. You are happiest when you feel you are growing and when you know you are better than you were yesterday. You are a happy person when you decide to start enjoying your life. You enjoy tranquility when you take time out of your busy day to smell the flowers. You are cheerful when you cultivate the habit of smiling. Happiness is a state everyone feels. When you are happy, you know it.

Happiness is one of the gifts God has blessed humans with. But like every other free gift from heaven, it cannot be bought or sold. The good news is that happiness is within everyone's reach. Choose it today. It promises a lifetime of excitement.

Confession: *Lord, thank you for making me a blessing to my world. Thank you for the grace to live stress-free. When I am down, please lift me up. Open my eyes to all the beauty You have surrounded me with. Help me to be able to be happy at every moment. Amen.*

APRIL 8

EVERY MORNING SELF-TALK

This is the day that the LORD has made;
let us rejoice and be glad in it.
Psalm 118:24

Have you ever noticed how tons of thoughts come pouring into your mind as soon as you wake? Many of us probably have. Sometimes these thoughts are good. Other times these thoughts are filled with negativity.

Our thoughts inspire our actions. In essence, whatever we permit and let linger in our minds may likely dictate how we will act. How, then, do we control our thoughts? We can do so by speaking back to ourselves. When we wake up in the morning and thoughts of failure come pouring into our minds, we can talk back to ourselves. We can say things like "I am a success, I am the apple of God's eye, and God's grace is sufficient for me." When thoughts of those who upset us flood our minds, we can say. "I choose to be at peace, so I release all hurt and pain to God." When we wake, our words to ourselves should be centered on how great our day will be and how favor will follow us.

This method of daily self-talk works! It helps us to voice joy into our situations. It also keeps the devil and his tricks far from our lives. When we speak words, we speak life, so talk into your life every morning. Tell yourself all that you would love to accomplish. Agree with heaven concerning all that is connected to you. Then go ahead to do all you have set out to do. This is one sure secret to a happy and productive life.

Confession: *I agree with heaven concerning my life today. I speak joy and happiness. I speak light into all that may be dark. I speak life into all that may be withering. From now on, when I wake every morning, I will only declare positivity into my situations. Please help me, God. Amen.*

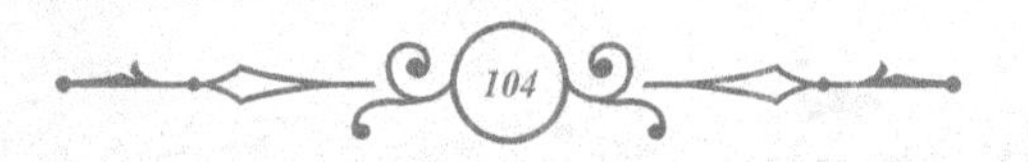

APRIL 9

LIVE FOR TODAY

So I concluded there is nothing better than to be happy and enjoy ourselves as long as we can.
Ecclesiastes 3:12, NLT

Lauren believes when she gets married, she will be happy forever. James believes when he has kids and starts a family, he will be content. Tony believes when he gets his dream job, his joy will be fulfilled. And Thomas believes that as soon as he retires, he will be happy. All these people have beautiful hopes and desires. They also share something in common—destination fixation.

Yes, it is great to have high hopes for our lives. The question, however, is, what about the present moment? What about this day? The idea that our happiness is somehow tied to a particular event or person is very misleading. Of course, the future should be looked forward to with great excitement, but the present also matters. We can choose to be happy with who we are and what we have now. Our happiness should not only be tied to when our dreams finally come true. Instead, it should be lived every day even as we plan for a better tomorrow.

If we are not happy today, chances are we will not be happy tomorrow. The "destination" may bring us joy, but if we do not make a conscious effort to choose happiness daily, the joy that comes with "destination accomplishment" may be short lived. Today is as special as what the future promises, so enjoy each day. Make every moment count. Involve yourself in things that bring you happiness and peace of mind. Live for today!

Confession: *Father, You have created me to be happy. I am to be joyous every day. So today I choose to be cheerful. Today is as special as tomorrow. I will no longer postpone my gladness of heart to a future date. Amen.*

APRIL 10

INGREDIENTS OF HAPPINESS: A CALM MIND

But he was in the stern, asleep on the cushion. And they woke him and said to him, Teacher, do you not care that we are perishing. And he awoke and rebuked the wind and said to the sea, "Peace! Be still!" And the wind ceased, and there was a great calm. **Mark 4:38–39**

One day while Jesus and His disciples were on the sea, a storm arose. At the time of turmoil, Jesus was asleep. Everyone aboard started to panic because they thought they were going to die. As soon as Jesus woke up, He simply said, "Peace be still," and the turmoil ceased. One school of thought believes that one of the reasons Jesus could calm the storm was because He was calm. Jesus was at peace both on the inside and outside. Unfortunately, His disciples were not. One who doesn't possess a peaceful mind may never be able to perform great exploits. One who has a troubled spirit will never be able to enjoy life to the fullest.

Guilt, jealousy, envy, self-condemnation, and all forms of sin are causes of a disturbed mind. Intense stress, worry, anxiety, and agitation are also causes of a restless spirit. A troubled mind limits the powerful workings of God for a happy life.

Any individual who desires to perform extraordinary exploits must possess a calm spirit. A calm mind can be gotten by meditating on positive words, praying, and trusting God for all things. A quiet spirit can be obtained by cutting out distressing thoughts and people. Sleeping adequately, exercising regularly, and connecting with nature also refresh our thought process.

Confession: *Lord, You are my peace. Only in You will I find long-lasting comfort. I trade my ashes for Your beauty and my despair for Your peace. I long to perform exploits in life. Please use me. Take away my turbulent heart, and fill me with Your serenity. Teach me how to maintain the rest You have blessed me with. Amen.*

APRIL 11

INGREDIENTS OF HAPPINESS: A THANKFUL HEART

Give thanks to the LORD, for he is good;
his love endures forever.
1 Chronicles 16:34, NIV

A glass filled halfway can be seen as either half full or half empty. It just depends on the perception of the person looking at the half-filled cup. Two people can be looking at the same situation, and where one may see all that is wrong, the other may see all that is right.

To possess a thankful heart simply means to have an appreciative attitude. Grateful people make it a point to always count their blessings, whether big or small. Thankful people naturally are friendly and humble. They achieve more and cope well with stress. They feel great about their own accomplishments and are not envious of others. Thankful people are less prone to depression, and they see every day as a gift and not a right.

One method you can use to determine how much you have been blessed with is the writing method. This entails putting down all the good in your life versus all the not-so-good things on a sheet of paper. Upon doing this, you will realize how much you have to be thankful for. You may also begin to see your cup as filled and not empty. I am personally encouraged by the Holy Spirit to do this when I feel downcast and discouraged. Shortly after I write all that God has blessed me with, I start feeling cheerful again. After writing the good things, most times I don't even have enough space left to write the not-so-good things. There is joy in thanksgiving. Try it today.

Confession: *Father, today I celebrate Your goodness in my life. You have blessed me with so much—much more than I deserve. As I make a list of all Your grace upon my life, please open my heart again. Help me realize how much You love me and have blessed me. Also, help me understand the need for living thankfully every day. Amen.*

APRIL 12

•••

INGREDIENTS OF HAPPINESS: ONE'S APPEARANCE

You were bought at a price. Therefore honor God with your bodies. ***1 Corinthians 6:20. NIV***

One's appearance goes a long way in influencing one's self-carriage. A good number of times, the way we dress is the way we will be addressed. And the way we are treated will likely affect our self-esteem.

Some people are smart, hardworking, and God-fearing and possess all it takes to succeed in life. Yet these people may not succeed because they have refused to pay attention to their outward appearance. Well-laundered clothes, a neat hairstyle, fresh breath, and a pleasant smell are all key and must be paid adequate attention to. For the person to function efficiently on the inside, the person must be well taken care of on the outside too. Appearance has the power to either enhance or cripple a person's potency.

There is a level of confidence that comes with looking and smelling good. A person's outward appearance is often directly proportional to his or her productivity. This makes it paramount for us to keep doing our best when it comes to taking care of ourselves. We stand a higher chance of being happy when we take time to look good.

Confession: *Dear God, it's an honor to be created in Your image. Thank you for counting me worthy of being called Yours. If there is any way I have devalued Your creation (me), please have mercy. I have been bought with a price; therefore, I am precious. From now on, I will place a greater value on myself. I will represent You decently and appropriately everywhere I go and in everything I do. Amen.*

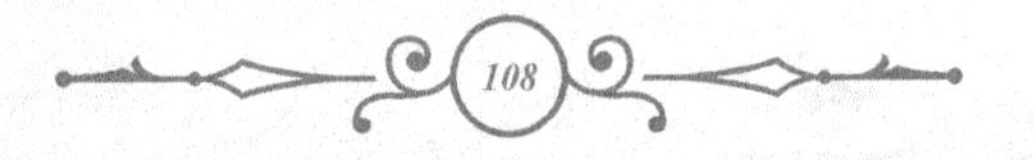

APRIL 13

INGREDIENTS OF HAPPINESS: THE WORD OF GOD

Contentment, simplicity, cheerfulness, meekness, good humor, and peace of mind are all ingredients of a happy life. But there is one ingredient that surpasses all other ingredients put together. Some call it the primary element. Others call it the distinctive flavor. I call it the main component of a happy life. This ingredient is the Word of God.

We can go searching for happiness wherever we deem fit. However, the scriptures will always be the best place to find it. Some Bible texts that addresses happiness include:

- **Psalm 118:24** – This is the day the LORD has made; I will rejoice and be glad in it.
- **Isaiah 12:3** – With joy, you will draw waters from the wells of salvation.
- **Psalm 37:4** – Delight yourself in the LORD, and he will give you the desires of your heart.
- **Psalm 144:15b** – Happy are the people whose God is the LORD!
- **Philippians 4:4** – Rejoice in the Lord always; again I will say, rejoice.
- **Psalm 128:2** – You shall eat the fruit of the labor of your hands; you shall be blessed, and it shall be well with you.

Human strength is limited, but God's strength is not. There is joy and fulfillment in God's Word. Speak these words into your life and situation today.

***Confession:** Lord, Your Word gives me joy for the future. When I am down, Your Word brings me hope. Today I connect to every promise in the Bible. I will delight myself in You, knowing that You will give me my heart's desire. Thank you for Your Word of life.*

APRIL 14

CHOOSING OPTIMISM OVER PESSIMISM

And we know that all things work together for good to them that love God, to them who are called according to his purpose.
Romans 8:28, KJV

Life can assume a lot of interpretations. It just depends on how we choose to see it. While some see life from an optimistic angle, others do so from a pessimistic view. When an optimistic man looks into his life, all he sees are things he can be thankful for. He sees that which he has been blessed with. He often says to himself, "My life may not be perfect, but until better things come, I will enjoy all I have." The pessimistic man, on the other hand, may take one glance at his life and only see the difficulties. His regular thoughts are mostly about the things he doesn't have. He often complains about all the wrongs in his life and how complicated everything seems to be for him.

In truth, optimism is not easy to practice. It is especially hard to exercise in this so-called "tough life." But how would one be able to find happiness without some hope for a brighter tomorrow? Sometimes things aren't nearly as horrible as we think they are. All we have to do is look at those who are not as privileged as we are. Then we will know how much we've been blessed with.

We may not have perfect lives, but we have beautiful lives. Regardless of our current predicaments, we still have hope. Today we are encouraged to focus more on the good in life. Where we are right now is exactly where God needs us to be. All things will eventually work for our good.

Confession: *Heavenly Father, You have overcome the world for me. Your Word has always encouraged that I stay joyful regardless of my circumstance. After taking an inventory of my life, I know I have been blessed with so much. Thank you for these blessings. My life is beautiful, so I choose to be optimistic about life. Amen.*

APRIL 15

ALL YOU HAVE IS NOW

Sluggards do not plow in season; so at harvest time they look but find nothing.
Proverbs 20:4, NIV

Fear of the unknown comes with not knowing what will happen next. Life is a risk. Deciding to leave our beds in the morning to go out is a huge risk because the truth is, anything can happen out there. In fact, choosing to close our eyes to sleep in the first place carries its own risks. While we are asleep and unconscious of our environment, anything can happen. Whether or not we choose to believe it, life is all about risks. So if there is something we shy away from because of our fear of the unknown, today is a good day to reconsider.

Please note that it is okay not to know the outcome of what you want to do. If you are being led by God, just do it. Whatever it is, do it! If you don't, chances are that a few years from now, you may look back and ask yourself, what could have been.

Let's stop the habit of overanalyzing things before venturing into that which God is urging us to do. Perfect is the enemy of good. There is no perfect place, time, or resource anywhere. All you have is now, so do it this moment. Take the risk! Explore your faith! Begin today!

Confession: *Jesus, my perfect example, I adore You. While You were on Earth, You made every moment of Your existence count. You trusted in the purpose for which You came to the world, and You gave the world Your all. You kept pressing on until You fulfilled Your objective. I pray You grant me the strength to keep pushing through today. Please give me the grace to forge ahead despite my fears. Amen.*

APRIL 16

ALL YOU HAVE IS NOW PART II

Then I saw and considered it;
I looked and received instruction.
Proverbs 24:32. ESV

Yesterday we discussed stepping out in faith. Today we will be discussing some attributes that come with this action.

First, it is important to stress that stepping out in faith and being overly impulsive are two different things. Stepping out in faith requires deep conviction within oneself. This is far from acting on the spur of the moment or doing things without thinking. Also, when we venture into something new, the first results may not be as anticipated. In fact, we may meet several hurdles along our way. We may even fail a few times. But failure does not signify the end of the road. It only allows us to learn and grow. It also gives us opportunities to be better than we used to be.

Many accomplished people confess they did not get it right on their first attempt. But with persistence, they eventually got the desired result. The real world doesn't reward perfect people. It rewards people who get things done. So again, take risks! Go with God's leading. Let go of the fear of failure. Do that which you know you should do. God will walk you through the rest of the journey.

Confession: *Dear Lord, all things work together for those who love You and are called according to Your purpose. Even when I do not get the result I hope for, I know You have a reason for it. Failure will not stop me. As long as I know You are with me, I will keep pressing on until I achieve that which You have called me to. Amen.*

APRIL 17

MONEY IS GOOD MOTIVATION

For you say, I am rich, I have prospered, and I need nothing, not realizing that you are wretched, pitiable, poor, blind, and naked.
Revelation 3:17

At a youth seminar some time ago, this question was thrown to the crowd: "Can you do just about anything for money?" One young man's response was "If the pay is worth it, why not?" This young man can be likened to the average man who starts out life climbing the corporate ladder, often blinded by money.

In truth, money is important and pushes things in the right direction. Money assists in making dreams come true. Whether we admit it or not, we all need money. However, the question is, at what expense? Unfortunately, because of money, many people have done despicable things. When you do foul things to make money, you may get the money but may also end up losing a part of your soul. This is why some of the so-called "rich" people cannot enjoy little things like a good night's sleep. Money has not been able to fill the emptiness and frustration in the lives of so many people out there. What money brings, at best, is temporary happiness that wears off after a while.

Personally, I made up my mind a long time ago that I would rather live in a little house and be happy than live in a mansion and be miserable. But by the grace of God, I know I can have my mansion and still be happy should I pursue righteousness over riches. What will you or won't you do for money?

Confession: *Dear Lord, thank You for all You have blessed me with. For moments I have gone out of Your will in search of money, I pray that You forgive me. Your will is that I prosper, but I do not want to do so outside Your will. I want to be happy. Please teach me how to remain content while I work and trust You for a better life. Amen.*

APRIL 18

FOLLOW YOUR PASSION

"Now when David had served God's purpose in his own generation, he fell asleep; he was buried with his ancestors and his body decayed."
Acts 13:36, NIV

We have all been brought into this world for a purpose. There is this part in us that rejoices when we discover that which we have been created for. This part of us further jubilates when we begin exploring our newfound purpose to the fullest. To follow one's passion means to pursue that which one loves to do, and it's not a coincidence that what we love to do is usually what we have been created for. God will never send a person on a journey He hasn't first equipped that person for. God is hardly in the habit of sending people on forced missions. God has already placed all that we need on the inside of us.

What do you enjoy doing? What brings joy to your heart just at the slightest thought? When you look at the world, what problems do you see? What ideas do you know can best solve these problems? What would you gladly do without being paid? What are the things you do effortlessly? Where does your curiosity strongly lie?

In all these questions lies the answers to what you have been created for. Please find your passion today if you haven't done so already. Pursue that which you love with all you've got. In doing so, you will find happiness and fulfillment like never before.

Confession: *I declare this day that I will fulfill purpose. I will fulfill that which I have been created for. I will tap into the creative mind I have been blessed with and begin to explore its potential to the fullest. I will not just be a spectator in life. I will impact my world positively. Amen.*

APRIL 19

THE MYSTERY BEHIND GIVING

One gives freely, yet grows all the richer; another withholds what he should give, and only suffers wants.
Proverbs 11:24

Being on the receiving end is wonderful. What is even more lovely than this is being on the giving side. Why is this so? Well, today's scripture reference explains it all.

When giving takes place, something supernatural occurs. Of course, what is seen in the natural is that the giver releases and the receiver takes. However, unknown to us, what happens is the very opposite. This is the simple explanation behind the popular saying that givers never lack. A true giver with a generous heart will hardly be deficient in the good things of life. This becomes more evident when one takes a closer look at the philanthropists, caregivers, and benefactors around us. These people just always seem to have more to give, even after giving so much.

Those who habitually ask will always keep asking, and those who keep giving will always have a surplus—this is a principle in life. This is also what today's scripture is revealing to us. Yes, owning things gives us some form of security, and the thought of letting them go could be scary. But living a "giving" life is one of the best ways to live happily. Just like today's reference text has pointed out, those who hold back only suffer wants in the long run, but those who give freely will always receive more.

Confession: *Dear Jesus, on the cross of Calvary, you blessed the world with the ultimate gift—your life. Through this one act, you saved humanity. Today I ask that you open my eyes to your thoughts concerning giving. I do not want to merely give. I want to be a true giver. Please teach me how to do this. Amen.*

APRIL 20

THE MYSTERY BEHIND GIVING PART II

The point is this: whoever sows sparingly will also reap sparingly and whoever sows bountifully will also reap bountifully.
2 Corinthians 9:6

One particular day, I was feeling depressed. Everything just felt wrong. Nothing anyone could say or do made me feel any better. Then I got on my knees, with tears in my eyes, and asked God to help me out of this terrible state. His response to me was the last thing I thought I would hear. He simply said to me, "Go and do something nice for another." I got up and did just that. To this present day, I still do not think I have experienced any rapid miracle like I did that day. Suddenly I wasn't depressed, confused, or sad anymore but the very opposite.

Giving works miracles, and it hardly takes anything away from us, even if it might look so at first. Giving destroys the demon of possessiveness, and it helps us rely more on God for His provision. Giving humbles us. It helps us relate better to other's predicaments. The act of giving multiplies our possessions and helps us feel better about ourselves.

In a real sense, giving brings more advantages to the one who offers than the one who receives. Giving is a true source of joy and happiness. Whether it is your money, food, time, clothes, or kind words, offer it to others today. Be a blessing to another, and watch how you are blessed in return. Giving is a worthwhile and fulfilling investment. Givers are happy souls.

Confession: *Heavenly Father, thank you for Your provision. It's a privilege to bless others, but I can only give because I have been blessed with so much. Help me to never hold back. Whether I have little or plenty, give me the grace to give it away as You lay it on my heart to do so. Amen.*

APRIL 21

WHEN WE SMILE

A glad heart makes a happy face; a broken heart crushes the spirit.
Proverbs 15:13, NLT

Happiness is an attitude of the mind. However, certain external factors also contribute to our state of happiness. One of these factors is the habit of smiling.

When we smile, we feel better, and everyone around us feels better too. Another advantage of making this a habit is that it makes us more approachable. This act makes us appear calm, confident, and in control. Smiling even makes us look younger. It decreases our stress level and eases our tension. When we smile, we add years to our lives; we also add lives to our years. I have noticed that smiling brings about a corresponding reaction from others. In essence, when we smile at someone, they will most likely smile back at us. This explains why people say smiling is contagious.

The act of smiling is an action that radiates joy. Not only does this act radiate joy from the inside out but it also radiates joy from the outside in. The act of smiling tricks the mind into worrying less and being happy more. The good news is, this habit costs nothing and blesses us with so much. It is one of God's unique gifts to mankind. Wear a smile today, and wear a smile always.

Confession: *Dear Lord, thank you for being concerned about every aspect of my life, even my state of mind. Today I declare that I am a happy person. I will not allow my circumstances to dictate my mood. I will always smile. Even when I don't feel like doing so, I will. Please remind me to always wear a warm smile everywhere I go. Amen.*

APRIL 22

A GOOD DOSE OF LAUGHTER IS GOOD TOO

Being cheerful keeps you healthy. It is slow death to be gloomy all the time.
Proverbs 17:22, GNT

It's one thing to smile and another to laugh. A smile usually comes from within, whether it is evoked or not, while laughter is generally invoked by something funny. Laughter is good for the soul, and good humor often goes a long way in rejuvenating a sour mood into an excited state. This is why today's scripture reference is recommending a regular dose of laughter.

We would do well to include a humor time out in our daily endeavors. We could do this by reading comics, watching funny movies, listening to comedians, and more. So long as whatever we do is not repugnant to heaven, then God is in support of it.

A happy life is one in which laughter is not too far away. A genuinely happy person is one who knows how to create room for both seriousness and humor. No wonder medical experts recommend at least five minutes of daily laughter time-out. Over time, this time out has proven to perform great wonders. Humor is the good cheer that we can all use from time to time. Laughter is a powerful medicine for a healthy mind and body.

Confession: *Lord Jesus, when I laugh, I feel better. This tells me that laughter is a blessing from You. A joyful heart is good medicine. There is abundant joy and healing in laughing. From here on out, I choose to surround myself with cheerful things. I will intentionally create time for humor in my life. Amen.*

APRIL 23

TAKE TIME OUT

For we brought nothing into the world,
and we can take nothing out of it.
1 Timothy 6:7, NIV

Many of us take life too seriously. We work every hour and hardly pause for a rest. Some of us have a planned daily to-do list that has little or no space for leisure. We are either working, attending church activities, or caring for the home. Of course, all these things are essential as they are our responsibilities. But relaxation is also paramount. We can only give 100 percent to things if we are adequately fit ourselves.

It is crucial we regularly give ourselves a little time out. This could be just a fifteen-minute walk by ourselves or going to a quiet place to meditate during a work break. It could also include taking mini-vacations or going somewhere different for a while. The whole idea here is to do something that takes away from everyday tension. It's all about finding a serene environment where we can be ourselves and relax, even if it's for a couple of minutes or a few days.

Taking time out helps you look back at where you are coming from, where you are, and where you are going. It enables you to reflect and study the course of your progression in life. It helps you determine if you are satisfied and happy with where you are at present. It also refreshes, strengthens, and prepares you for what lies ahead. Start taking some time out whenever you can today.

Confession: *Dear God, Your Word says I should come to You, and You will give me rest. This tells me You always want me to take time out and refuel. In my pursuit of a better life, sometimes I overwork myself. Today I repent of this. Teach me how to take good care of the body You have given me. Help me learn how to unplug and recharge. Amen.*

APRIL 24

HAPPINESS IS RELATIVE

...also that everyone should eat and drink and take pleasure in all his toil—this is God's gift to man.
Ecclesiastes 3:13

Some time ago, I was chatting with my former high school classmate. The conversation extended to other classmates, and I started asking about their well-being. Everyone seemed to be doing great except one, whom I was told was a sales attendant at a small grocery store. This came as a surprise to my shallow mind. Why? Because this person was at the top of the "most likely to succeed" list for our set. Back in school, he was the best academically. So why would someone so exceptional become a grocery store employee? I pondered on this for a while; then it hit me! Maybe this is what this classmate of mine really wants to do. Maybe being in sales made him happy.

Happiness means different things to different people. The way we define happiness is not the same way other people do. To some, happiness is being a stay-at-home mom. To others, happiness may be being the CEO of a company. To some, offering services and being a helping hand may be where they derive satisfaction from.

Whatever it is people decide to do, it's not our place to judge them. We are not to look down on others because they do not fit into our standards of "success." Happiness is relative. What others define as happiness may not be what we define as happiness. We are all different and have all been called to live different lives. The question today is, what makes you happy?

Confession: *Dear Lord. For those times when I have judged others because of their life choices, please forgive me. You created people for different purposes. Help me find my purpose. Help me also to be happy for people, whether or not I like their choices. Amen.*

APRIL 25

BE THE BEST AT WHATEVER YOU DO

Show yourself in all respects to be a model of good works, and in your teaching, show integrity, dignity and sound speech that cannot be condemned, so that an opponent may be put to shame, having nothing evil to say about us.
Titus 2:7–8, ESV

To be the best means to be exemplary. If we must do well at whatever we do, then we must strive to be people who pursue excellence. Excellence is a habit that anyone who wants to make headway in life must cultivate. This excellence culture is also prevalent with successful and highly accomplished people. Hardly would these people lend their signature or name to anything of inferior quality. So should we desire to make headway and associate with those at the top, we also must speak their language, the language of excellence.

It is imperative that people associate us with quality standards. Never should mediocrity or inferiority be traced to us. When we pursue excellence, people will be more willing to associate with us. Should we have something to offer, they will be happy to patronize us.

Being an outstanding person carries several advantages. First, it makes one diligent. Also, it improves one's self-confidence. Above all, it makes one feel good about himself or herself. So whether it is at your home, school, place of work, or whatever sphere of life you may currently be in, please always give it your best. Be exceptional in your dress, conversations, and relationships. Choose to stand out both in your big and small endeavors. This is a useful tool for a successful life. Be excellent—not perfect but excellent.

Confession: *Excellent God, I adore You. You created me in your likeness. As you are, so am I. I pray for the grace to represent you well everywhere I go. Help me never to be slothful in my dealings. Help me to always give my best to all my endeavors. Amen.*

APRIL 26

IN THE MEANTIME

When times are good, be happy; but when times are bad, consider this: God has made the one as well as the other. Therefore, no one can discover anything about their future.
Ecclesiastes 7:14, NIV

Contented people are those who are at peace with their state of affairs. These people are not lazy or complacent. Rather, they are the ones who choose to stay happy at whatever phase they may be in as they look forward to a better future.

Most of us have things we look forward to. Sometimes we feel that once we achieve those set goals, we will finally be happy. However, the question is, what about now? What about this moment? Does our happiness necessarily need to be postponed to a future time? In the meantime, do we not deserve some level of happiness at the very least?

The only permanent destination in life is death. While we are still alive, the promise of the present moment is what we can say for sure is really ours. Tomorrow is uncertain. Most times we plan for a better tomorrow, but within the twinkle of an eye, an unforeseen event can change those plans completely. It is important we treat each day like it may be our last. Let's stop postponing our happiness and joy to the future. Let's do things that will make us happy now. Let's enjoy the gift of the present moment. In the meantime, let's choose to be cheerful even as we trust God for a better tomorrow.

Confession: *Father, each moment I breathe is a gift from You. Thank you for the blessings of this day. Yesterday is in the past, and tomorrow holds no promises. Help me begin living in the here and now. Teach me how to have a good relationship with the present even as I look forward to a great future. Amen.*

THE BALANCED CHRISTIAN

APRIL 27

THE BALANCED CHRISTIAN

Live as people who are free, not using your freedom as a cover-up for evil, but living as servants of God.
1 Peter 2:16

Many individuals use spirituality to dissociate and escape from earthly happenings. These people are constantly on what some call the "spiritual high."

To enjoy deep spiritual fellowship to the ultimate, we have to first embrace our human side. This was very much evident in Jesus' life while He was on Earth. Jesus spent a lot of time with His Father and in the place of worship. He was also seen associating with people and doing human stuff too. He would dine with "sinners," tell jokes, attend parties, rest, make friends, and lots more. Being 100% God, Jesus did not have to do these things. Still, He did them to acknowledge his 100% humanity. Notably, while Christ enjoyed His earthly experience, He never got caught up in it. Worldliness and carnality could never be traced back to Him.

Living a godly life entails living a balanced life. But how do we find that balance? What type of Christians do we need to be? Also, what does it mean to be a devout follower of Christ? These questions and more are what we will explore under the new theme, "The Balanced Christian."

Confession: *Jesus, my perfect example, I praise You. A balanced life is all You require of me. I do not want to be over righteousness and neither do I want to be worldly. I want to be like You, Lord. Please show me Your ways. Amen.*

APRIL 28

THE TWELVE & SIX O'CLOCK CHRISTIAN

Be not overly righteous, and do not make yourself too wise.
Why should you destroy yourself?
Ecclesiastes 7:16

It's twelve midnight or noon when both hands of the clock meet at twelve, facing upward. Many Christians are also twelve o'clock in nature. These people are seen to have their gaze strictly fixed on heaven. They appear to look so perfect; it would almost seem like they have no human weaknesses. However, some of them can be very judgmental. They would shove the gospel down another's throat if given the opportunity. Some of these "twelve o' clock Christians" even look down on those they perceive are not nearly as perfect as they are. According to them, every other person is headed on the path of destruction and will end up in hell.

With the timepiece at six o'clock, one hand of the clock will be on the twelve and the other on the six. The same goes for a Christian who has one foot in heaven and the other in the world. Rarely would there be any difference between the six o'clock Christian and an unbeliever. They are also known as lukewarm Christians.

Today's scripture reference lets us know that it is possible to be overly righteous. This is not the life we have been called to live. Other scripture passages also discourage living an unrighteous life (Titus 2:12). So if we are never to be overly righteous or unrighteous, there is only one way of life that heaven approves of. This is the "Balanced Christian" lifestyle. And should we still have questions about what it means to live balanced, the study of Jesus' lifestyle while on Earth will give us accurate answers. After studying Jesus' life, we can take things up a notch by emulating His way of life.

Confession: *Dear Lord, thank You for the freedom You have availed me. I want to be in line with You. I want to be the exact type of Christian You need me to be. Teach me please. Amen.*

APRIL 29

APPEARANCES

So let us come boldly to the throne of our gracious God. There we will receive his mercy, and we will find grace to help us when we need it most.
Hebrews 4:16, NLT

Appearance is a facade people use to cover up all the hurts, fears, regrets, and wrongs in their lives. Many people have so perfected the art of deceiving people that they almost believe their own deceit. Unfortunately, this does not work with God. He sees the heart, and appearances cannot deceive Him. He knows what is going on within. Really, there is no point praying 24 hours a day or fasting every other day if one's heart is not right with God. What is the point of preaching the gospel everywhere if one does not practice all its instructions?

Christ can never be fooled by our actions. He is more concerned about our motives and not the actions themselves. At every point in our lives, we must make it our goal to keep our hearts in sync with Jesus. Jesus' requirement is not that we come to Him perfect. He wants to see us spiritually naked but unashamed. Let's appear before God's throne dirty, stinking, tattered, and broken. Let's openly reveal our inner man to our Maker. Let's boldly approach Jesus today, looking exactly as we are on the inside. In doing so, we will receive His mercy and grace.

Confession: *Dear Lord, I bring it all to Your altar today—my pain, shame, guilt, sorrows, anguish, and problems. You know and see everything. Henceforth, I will no longer pretend. At every moment, I will bare my soul to You, knowing that the Great Fixer will fix my issues. Amen.*

APRIL 30

THE PERFECT HEART

"I the LORD search the heart and test the mind, to give every man according to his ways, according to the fruit of his deeds."
Jeremiah 17:10

A perfect heart isn't one that is flawless but one that is teachable, searchable, and child-like. While perfection can be faked, a perfect heart is lived. Jesus, while on the earth, had a perfect heart and was quickly drawn to those with the same trait, like Peter and His other disciples. Of course, these imperfect ones had many shortcomings. Still, Jesus was able to work with their yielding hearts. And through that, those who drew close to Jesus drew closer to God.

The Pharisees, on the other hand, couldn't be caught doing any wrong. They would always seem to appear upright, but since a perfect look doesn't equal a perfect heart, Jesus wasn't pleased. In fact, more often than not, He rebuked them for their hypocrisy.

Our heavenly Father hates sin, but He is more concerned with the state of our hearts. He doesn't want us to be actors like the Pharisees. Instead, He wants us to be broken—broken enough for Him to work through. A perfect heart is one after God's own heart. A perfect heart trusts God and not "self." A perfect heart seeks to always do right by his or her Maker. Do you have a perfect heart?

Confession: *Dear Lord, give me a yielding heart. The hearts of kings are like streams of water in Your hands, and You direct them wherever You desire. I want to be right with You. Help me. Amen.*

MAY 1

THE CHOICE NOT TO COMPROMISE

But even if he doesn't, we want to make it clear to you, Your Majesty, that we will never serve your gods or worship the gold statue you have set up.
Daniel 3:18, NLT

The three Hebrew men, Shadrach, Meshach, and Abednego, refused to bow to the king's statue (Daniel 3). For disobeying the decree of the king, they were to be executed by fire. But before being thrown into the fiery furnace, they were given a second chance to bow to the statue. They could have come up with excuses: (1) We will bow down but not actually worship the idol. (2) We will worship it only once and then ask God for forgiveness. (3) This is a foreign land, so God will forgive us for following its customs. (4) Our ancestors set up idols in God's temple; this isn't half as bad! (5) The Scripture has ordained us to obey the laws of the land, and this is one. (6) If we die, who will deliver God's Word to others? (7) This is clearly a common sense issue; God will not be mad at us for choosing to bow down.

It is possible that the three Hebrew men thought about the above excuses. But did they choose to use any of them? No, they did not. Instead, they chose to take the king's punishment. They were prepared to die if that was what it came to.

When it comes to living a godly life, there are so many things in life that will discourage a person not to try. In recent times, it seems like everything spiritual is becoming obsolete, and perversity is taking over. But like the three Hebrew men, we can choose not to compromise. We can decide not to give in. We can choose to stand for God alone when it is both convenient and inconvenient.

Confession: *Dear Lord, today I decree that I will be Your soldier. Where others may compromise their faith for worldly gain, I will not. I will not find excuses or justifications to live carnally. I will stand for You alone. Give me the grace to do this. Amen.*

MAY 2

•••

CHRIST DOES NOT CONDEMN

And as they continued to ask him, he stood up and said to them, "Let him who is without sin among you be the first to throw a stone at her." ***John 8:7***

While Jesus was on the earth, the Pharisees tried to test Him. They brought in an allegedly promiscuous woman who was caught in the act of adultery. Then they demanded what Jesus' verdict was concerning her "abominable act." Jesus simply turned to them and told them this: "Let him who is without sin among you be the first to throw a stone at her." Not being able to dispute that they were also sinners, the woman's accusers bowed out in shame. Jesus then told the accused that He would not condemn her and that she should go and sin no more (John 8:11). This is a lesson for you and me.

Christ does not condemn, and neither should we. Our mandate on Earth is not to judge others that may not be on par with us morally and spiritually. We are to raise people up, not look down on them with our religious eyes. Christ Himself said He did not come to the world for those who are already perfect but to save those who are not. This means that regardless of other people's lifestyles, we do not have a right to pass sentences on them. Our responsibility is to always reach out to people in love. This is God's commandment to us all.

Confession: *Dear Lord, I know I may have unconsciously passed judgment on others in the past. Please forgive me. My mandate is to love and not condemn people. I desire to do this, but I need Your strength. Help me see people only through Your eyes of love. Amen.*

MAY 3

ACCORDING TO 1 CORINTHIANS 13

Love is patient and kind; love does not envy or boast; it is not arrogant or rude. It does not insist on its own way; it is not irritable or resentful; it does not rejoice at wrongdoing, but rejoices with the truth. Love bears all things, believes all things, hopes all things, endures all things. **1 Corinthians 13:4-7**

One day, a man was discussing his wife with their pastor. The conversation went somewhat like this:

Man: "Pastor, I don't think I love my wife anymore. She has gone from the angel I married to someone I don't even recognize. She never appreciates anything I do. I am frankly running out of ideas on how to make this marriage work."

Pastor: "Then love your wife."

Man: "Pastor, I don't think you understand what I'm saying. I don't feel

anything for her."

Pastor: "Then love her."

They went on and on this way. No matter what the man said, the pastor's response was the same: "Then love her."

I believe what the pastor was trying to get this man to understand is that love goes beyond the way one feels. Also, love should not depend on reciprocation. So if love is not entirely feelings-based, then what is love? What exactly are God's thoughts on this issue? First Corinthians 13 has the answers to all these questions.

Confession: *Lord, love is all that You require. Today, You have revealed Your thoughts on love to me. Now I know that love goes beyond how I feel. Your love is unconditional. I pray that You will help me love like You do. Amen.*

MAY 4

LOVE IS A CHOICE

Greater love has no one than this, that someone lay down his life for his friends.
John 15:13

It was not nails that held Jesus to the cross. It was love. According to Matthew 26:39, Jesus did not feel like dying. Still, He did. He chose to die. You and I can learn so much from this.

The first lesson to be learned here is that love is a decision. It is a decision to do what needs to be done. Love surpasses one's feelings and also requires constant action. The second lesson is that love is a commitment. Love opts to stay and complete a mission, regardless of how tough the process is. Finally, love is selfless. It puts the needs of others first.

Love is a choice to keep seeing the good in others instead of focusing on their weaknesses alone. Love is a choice to accept people for who they are and not try to change them to be who we want them to be. Love is a choice to love as Christ has loved. Love is a choice—choose love today.

Confession: *Dear Jesus, I am grateful for Your death on the cross. Your love for humanity superseded the pain and shame that came with dying. Through Your death, you displayed what it means to love. Today I choose love and choose to love like You do. I choose to put others above myself. Amen.*

MAY 5

LOVE IS NOT A FEELING

Dear children, let us not love with words or speech
but with actions and in truth.
1 John 3:18, NIV

We practice love when we are respectful of one another. We also exercise love when we lift one each other up, open our hands to those in need, and perform other acts of kindness. Love is not jealous, envious, or resentful. In truth, practicing love according to 1 Corinthians 13:4–7 is not something that appeals to the flesh. Nonetheless, love is not just an emotion; it is demonstrated by actions. God's instruction to us is simple. We are to love whether we feel like doing so or not.

In our continual walk with the Lord, we ought to find ourselves dying to self and wanting to be like Christ. Selflessness plays a significant role in living in love. This act also comes with great rewards. Living blissfully here on Earth and qualifying for heaven are examples of such rewards.

If we were to go by flesh alone, we would keep falling short no matter how hard we try. But with the Holy Spirit on our side, this is very much achievable. As we practice love today, let's ask for help from the Holy Spirit. He is ready to walk with us so long as we have yielding hearts.

Confession: *Dear Lord, I am to love regardless of my emotions.*
I know there are moments when my emotions toward others may be far from love.
At this moment, please teach me to love even deeper, Holy Spirit.
Help me to love like You, Jesus. Amen.

MAY 6

LOVE IS KIND

But love your enemies, and do good, and lend, expecting nothing in return, and your reward will be great, and you will be the sons of the Most high, for he is kind to the ungrateful and the evil.
Luke 6:35

If you are helping someone and expecting to be repaid, what you are doing is business and not kindness. True giving entails transferring complete ownership of something to another.

Indeed, many of us give. But the question is, how do we give? Why do we give? Whom do we give to? While many people genuinely give, some give intending to hold people to whatever is being offered. Some give to seek favor. Some give to show off. Others habitually donate things that are of no value to them.

Having searched ourselves, can we say we are among those who give while expecting nothing in return? Or do we know deep within ourselves that our giving usually comes with an ulterior motive? God rewards those who obey His instructions with absolute sincerity. He blesses those who love with a pure heart. When we are kind to others, we will find joy and happiness. The act of kindness makes our world a better place to live in.

Confession: *Lord, Your love is unconditional. It does not carry any motive or hidden agenda. Please teach me how to love others. I want to practice love in its purest form. When I give, I will do so genuinely. So help me, God. Amen.*

MAY 7

LOVE IS PATIENT

Whoever is patient has great understanding, but
one who is quick-tempered displays folly.
Proverbs 14:29, NIV

Patience can be defined as suppressing restlessness or annoyance when confronted with delay. It also means being able to tolerate inconvenience and not complain about it. Patience is not a virtue everyone readily possesses. To some, it comes naturally, but to those that are hot-tempered, not so much. The good news is that patience can be learned regardless of one's temperament.

Christian growth often involves dying to self (Galatians 2:20). Patience is vital in this process. Therefore, those who walk with God are constantly being put through the patience test. If you haven't been put to this test yet, please get ready because you will. At some point, God will deliberately bring people into your life that will push your limit to the extreme. God's expectation of us is that we will exhibit self-restraint. We should be more forgiving toward other's excesses. Failure to do this may lead to the inability to graduate from the school of patience.

Love is patient. It is God's will that all His children love, and this requires us to be patient. Not only is patience a virtue but it is also a sign of spiritual maturity.

Confession: *Lord, in my walk with You, I know I have to grow. As you teach me patience, help me to not rebel against Your training. Give me the patience to be more accommodating of those around me. Please reduce me to love. Amen.*

MAY 8

LOVE DOES NOT ENVY

Love is patient and kind; love does not envy or boast; it is not arrogant.
1 Corinthians 13:4

Sometimes we look at people and only see their beautiful smiles and appealing lifestyles. With one glance, we conclude they have perfect lives. We may even find ourselves longing for everything they have. Worse still, we could begin comparing our lives to theirs. Like many people, I used to be guilty of this too. Over the years, however, I have come to learn that people are not often as "put together" as I assume they are. I also learned that no one has a perfect life. Everyone has his or her own struggle, which are often undisclosed.

We are to love people and not be envious of them. To do this effectively, we need to stop comparing ourselves with others. The ways we struggle are the same ways others do. But when we only compare the good attributes of others with our bad attributes, we are neither being fair to them nor ourselves. Love is not envious. It is content. It is always happy for others. Comparison is one of the root causes of covetousness, but anyone who loves with a pure heart will never feel threatened by others to the point of being envious of them.

Confession: *Dear Jesus, I bring my heart to You today. Please search me. If there is any trace of envy, please deliver me. Help me never to be envious of another again. You have blessed me with much. Help me to always remain content in You. Amen.*

MAY 9

•••

LOVE IS NOT IRRITABLE

The second is this: 'You shall love your neighbor as yourself.'
There is no commandment greater than these.
Mark 12:31

We all have our shortcomings. But why do other people's faults always appear massive next to ours? This is because we tend to look at other's deficiencies through a magnifying lens, yet we find a perfectly reasonable justification for ours. God's commandment is this: Whatever yardstick you use in rating yourself, use the same for your neighbors.

Some folks can be annoying; we all have our share of those around us. In the hope of changing the "irritants" in our lives, many of us have utilized several methods. However, today's reference text has recommended a tested and trusted method—love. We are to love our neighbors as ourselves. In this way, we will be less irritated by their weaknesses.

Bearing with others is not an easy thing to do. In fact, it may be one of the hardest things to practice. But this is God's instruction to us. Matthew 22:38–39 even records that this commandment is the second greatest of all. As we know, God is in the habit of tremendously rewarding those who obey Him.

Confession: *Dear Lord, I confess there are times when I haven't treated others the way I would like to be treated. I repent of this today. Help me to be more tolerant of other people's behavior. Teach me to be more patient in my relationships. Amen.*

MAY 10

•••

LOVE DOESN'T REJOICE AT WRONGDOING BUT REJOICES WITH THE TRUTH

...reprove, rebuke, and exhort,
with complete patience and teaching.
2 Timothy 4:2b

In order not to offend people, I often sat on the fence in the past. How? I'd pretend to be passive about their shortcomings. I did not necessarily celebrate their wrongdoings but kept mute about it. This may sound familiar to you too.

This is a bitter truth: We don't help people by turning a blind eye to their misbehaviors. According to 1 Corinthians 13:6, "Love does not rejoice at wrongdoing but rejoices with the truth." To rejoice with the truth means to only give approval to what is right.

The Bible instructs us to correct other's wrongdoings. This is not the same as quarreling with the wrongdoers. I've realized that there are certain ways we can tell our truth without being offensive. Over the years, the Holy Spirit has revealed ways in which I can gently convey my grievances. Having practiced them, I have enjoyed enormous peace within myself and with God. More importantly, I have witnessed people's lives turn around for the better. We are to give our stamp only to the truth. Today is a good day to begin doing so, but this should be done only in love and with the guidance of the Holy Spirit.

Confession: *Father, Your instruction is that I correct others in love. When I see others going the wrong way, give me the strength and humility to correct them the way You would. Help me to speak Your truth always. Amen.*

MAY 11

•••

LOVE BEARS ALL THINGS; BELIEVES ALL THINGS; HOPES ALL THINGS; ENDURES ALL THINGS

"Your love for one another will prove to the world that you are my disciples."
John 13:35, NLT

Imagine a world where everyone is kind to one another. Imagine a world where everyone believes in and never give up on one another. Imagine a world where patience, optimism, and honesty are the norm. That world would no doubt be safer. It would be a world where the number of broken relationships are reduced, fewer prisons are built, and more geniuses are produced. In short, it would be a world with endless possibilities. This kind of world is very possible, and it begins with you and me.

According to our reference text, there is only one way we can prove to the world that we are Christ's disciples—by displaying compassion. Today we are being called to live with love, especially love for our fellow humans. Let's live to build people up. Let's live to be sources of inspiration to others. Let's be those whose arms are always stretched out, ready to lift others up. This is what God expects from all His children.

Confession: *Dear God, thank You for making me your steward. Today I will be kind, I will believe in others, I will be more accommodating, and I will be an inspiration to others. Amen.*

THE BELIEVER
VS. THE ENEMY

MAY 12

•••

THE DEVIL'S PLAN FOR ALL HUMANS

He was a murderer from the beginning, and does not stand in the truth, because there is no truth in him. When he lies, he speaks out of his own character, for he is a liar and the father of lies.
John 8:44b (ESV)

The beautiful angel, Lucifer, was once close to God. He was eventually cast down because of his greed and pride (Isaiah 14:12–15). His name was then changed to Satan, the adversary. His other names are the devil, tempter, son of destruction, father of lies, murderer, and more.

Who is a human? A human is the being God made in His image and likeness (Genesis 1:27). Perhaps this is one of the many reasons the enemy hates humans. The devil makes it his daily mission to destroy us and all we stand for. And for believers in Jesus, he works extra hard to make sure we miss the mark.

The devil's home is hell, but his plan is not to stay there alone. He also plans to drag as many people as possible with him. Although dragging people to hell is his ultimate scheme, his real-time goal is to make sure we have an awful stay here on Earth. He also plots to make us spend eternity with him in the non-stop, horrendous lake of fire. So he uses ploys, tricks, and appealing temptations to sway us away from the life God has prepared for us. To overcome the enemy, we need to know his exact strategies. To defeat the one who continually wages war against us, we must understand the way he works. But how do we beat the enemy at his own game? How do we win the battle the devil continually wages against our souls? These and more are all we will explore under this new series: THE BELIEVER vs. the enemy.

Confession: *Dear God, thank You for the understanding of Your Word. The devil hates me, and I know this. His plan is to make me miserable here on Earth and to later have me join him in the pit of hell. I rebuke the devil this day. His tricks will never have a hold upon my life. I trample upon him. He is defeated. Amen.*

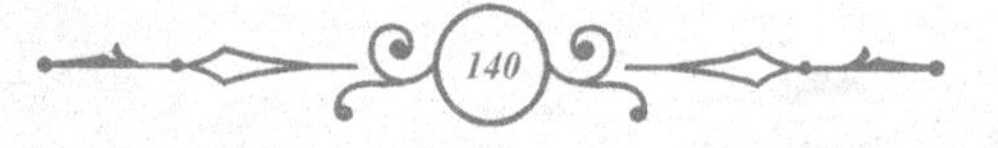

MAY 13

THE BELIEVER vs. the enemy

Behold, I have given you authority to tread on serpents and scorpions, and over all the power of the enemy, and nothing shall hurt you.
Luke 10:19 (ESV)

THE BELIEVER (in uppercase) versus the enemy (in lowercase) has been written exactly the way it should. In the correct realm of things, the human is superior to the devil and all his demons. The devil tries to hide this fact from us, making us believe otherwise. How does he do this? He manipulates us. He uses fear to control us, making us believe and accept his supposed dominance over us.

In defeating the devil, you must come to terms with certain things. First, you need to know where you stand in terms of hierarchy. You have the upper hand here; you have the "God factor," which changes everything. As a believer, you must know your place in Christ Jesus. The devil has already been defeated—you must believe this. You must understand that the life Christ has called you to is one of victory. You must also understand your heritage. Stop letting the devil manipulate you into thinking he is in charge. He is not.

So long as you are a devoted child of God, you are an heir to the throne of grace. As such, the devil has been placed under your feet. Your place is to trample on him and not him on you.

Confession: *Lord, thank You for the authority You have given me. Thank You for giving me power over the enemy. From here on out, I will never again believe the enemy's lies. I am superior to him, and as such, he is under my feet. Amen.*

MAY 14

THE SUPERIORITY OF MAN

The God of peace will soon crush Satan under your feet.
The grace of our Lord Jesus Christ be with you.
Romans 16:20 (ESV)

Some time ago, James's home was attacked. The attacker had a gun, so James felt he had no choice but to comply with all the attacker's demands. The attacker took many of James's possessions but somehow left his gun behind. Upon reaching for the gun, James realized that it was a fake. This trickery made him feel stupid. Why? He was deceived into believing the intruder was armed. James actually had a real gun in the house he could have used to defend his home, but he chose not to use it.

This is the same way the devil works. He is a trickster yet makes it his daily mission to convince humans otherwise. The devil has come to kill, steal, and destroy. He is the thief whose aim is to rob us of the life Christ died for us to enjoy. He sneaks into our hearts to break down our defenses and make us feel powerless. He convinces us that our Great Defender, Jesus, is not on our side. He then establishes his reign over our lives and assumes control. These are some ways the devil carries out his agenda. By understanding this concept, the children of God will be able to defeat the enemy.

Confession: *Heavenly Father, you have made me more than a conqueror. Today I wrap myself in your armor and defend myself against the devil's attacks. I refuse to be an easy target for the enemy to mess with. Jesus, my defender, I cling to you and claim my victory in you. Amen.*

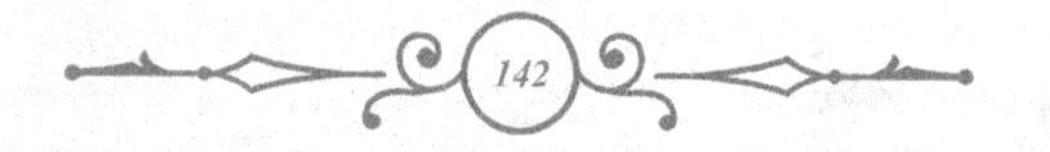

MAY 15

LIKELY TARGETS OF THE DEVIL

Be sober, be vigilant; because your adversary the devil walks about like a roaring lion, seeking whom he may devour.
1 Peter 5:8 (NKJV)

Everyone is a potential target of the devil. So long as you are a human created by God, you are on his watch list. But throughout the scriptures, and even in present times, there are certain people the devil goes after more. Most of these people are believers in Christ Jesus.

The devil hates Christ-followers with a passion because Christians have a good chance of making it to heaven. That they will not be joining him in hell torments him greatly. So he does everything he can to distract them from their final destination of heaven. Those that are not vigilant often end up falling for his traps. They may even end up missing out on eternity with Christ. However, this does not have to be our case.

Jesus' mission and His reason for dying on the cross was to bring us salvation. Salvation could also mean deliverance. As long as we have said yes to Jesus Christ, we have automatically said no to the devil. We have been delivered forever. But even in liberty, the Bible urges us to be vigilant. In doing this, we have to remind ourselves continually that we are not yet "there." We are only on our way. To arrive at our final destination, we need God's grace every step of the way. And this grace is sufficient for us daily if we ask for it.

Confession: *Jesus, I know the devil hates me. All he does is attempt to keep me in captivity. But I thank you for Your deliverance. Though the enemy may come like a flood, You have set a standard over my life. I am a victor. Amen.*

MAY 16

•••

LIKELY TARGETS OF THE DEVIL PART II

Resist him, firm in your faith, knowing that the same kinds of suffering are being experienced by your brotherhood throughout the world.
1 Peter 5:9 (ESV)

I know I am a major target of the devil. Why? Because I am a terror to his kingdom. Not only do I plan on making it to heaven (by the special grace of God) but I also plan on taking as many people as possible with me. Evangelists, ministers, and others who spread the good news are also on his watch list. So if everyone else is being vigilant, we in this group have to be extra vigilant. He will not leave us alone. The devil is not just going to come after us, he will come after us with everything he has.

We can rejoice because, by the grace of God, the devil has already been defeated. He can try, but he will never succeed. The more we work at reducing the number of people he plans on taking to hell, the more he will continually be on our case. The only way to defeat the evil one is to be deeply rooted in Christ. This fight is not ours but God's. We have to be unshaken in God such that nothing can move us.

As we go about our day today, let's take a minute to pray for ourselves and those whom God uses to minister His words to us. Let's pray that God will load them with the power to carry out His assignment diligently.

Confession: *Father, I know the enemy will not stop targeting me. He will keep being on my case because I am an asset to Your kingdom. Alas, You have already defeated him. I will not retreat. I will not surrender to the bullying enemy. I will keep pushing on in You. Thank you for being my fortress. Amen.*

MAY 17

OTHER POTENTIAL TARGETS OF THE DEVIL

"I have said these things to you, that in me you may have peace. In the world, you will have tribulation. But take heart; I have overcome the world." **John 16:33 (ESV)**

There is a particular set of special people that operate at a different level than others. They have gifted minds and can create beautiful content out of nothing. Many know them as extremely talented. These are the inventors, entertainers, writers, and visionaries of this world. Besides creativity, the gifted ones can feel things at a deeper level. Ordinarily, this should be a good thing. However, the devil, being a master manipulator, capitalizes on this trait and uses it to torment them. This is why it would seem that the talented ones are often more prone to depression and melancholy.

Extraordinarily talented or not, no one is invulnerable to the devil and his tricks. The Scriptures make us understand that we will all face trials and temptations. The devil will always come after us, whether we are at our weakest or our strongest. However, as long as we understand our inheritance in Christ Jesus, we are more than conquerors.

When the Holy Spirit is our guardian, He alerts us of the devil's tricks and helps us overcome them. Understanding our standing in Christ gives us the ability and authority to put the devil in his place.

Confession: *Dear Father, thank You for the creative mind You have blessed me with. The devil may plot schemes against me, but he will fail. I know who I am. I am God's heritage. I stand firm in the liberty Christ has availed me. I am unshakeable. The devil may try, but he will never win the battle over my life. I am a victor. Amen.*

MAY 18

THE HUMAN FACTOR

For we do not wrestle against flesh and blood, but against the rulers, against the authorities, against the cosmic powers over this present darkness, against the spiritual forces of evil in the heavenly places
Ephesians 6:12 (ESV)

The enemy works differently with different people. How? He uses something known as the human factor, which are specific traits peculiar to a person. First, the enemy studies individuals well enough to know their strengths and potential. Also, he examines their weaknesses and imperfections. Then he uses their flaws to torment them in a constant attempt to bring about their downfall. For example, the enemy may target those struggling with greed and use this flaw to bring them down. He may also do the same to those who are jealous, prideful, covetous, and more.

There is no perfect human. The only difference is that some have found a way around their shortcomings. Even then, there is still some iota of imperfection no matter how faultless a person tries to be. But in our weaknesses, God's grace is sufficient for us. This is why the God factor cannot be overemphasized.

To navigate through life successfully, we need God. In Him, we will find the strength to overcome the enemy despite our flaws.

Confession: *Dear Lord, You know my shortcomings as a human, and I lay them all at Your feet. Strengthen me, Jesus. Give me the grace to come up higher in my walk with You. Help me so that the devil never uses my weaknesses as ammunition against my life. Amen.*

MAY 19

WEAPONS OF THE ENEMY: OUR WEAKNESSES

Then Jesus was led up by the Spirit into the wilderness to be tempted by the devil. And after fasting forty days and forty nights, he was hungry.
Matthew 4:1–2 (ESV)

Today's scripture reference takes us to Jesus' days on Earth. He had just completed 40 days of fasting and prayer and was fatigued. The enemy chose this time to attack him. We can learn a few lessons from this event:

- As powerful as Jesus was, the devil still tried to reach and tempt Him. This also tells us no one is off limits to the enemy's attempts. He will always try, come what may.
- The devil strategically chose a time when he knew Jesus was physically weak (because of the long fast). When we are most vulnerable is when the devil will see his opportunity.
- The enemy tempted Jesus with that which he thought would meet Jesus' immediate need (Matthew 4:3). After Christ had fasted, he must have been starving. What better way to tempt a man than to mention "turning a stone to bread" to fill his hunger.

Even when Jesus was physically fatigued, one name could chase the devil far away—the name of God (Matthew 4:10). When we at our weakest, we can exchange our weaknesses for God's strength. In doing so, God will fight all battles on our behalf.

Confession: *God, You have given me the authority to trample on snakes and scorpions. I can overcome all the power of the enemy. By no means will the enemy trample upon me. Even at my weakest, I know You will always fight for me. Amen.*

MAY 20

WEAPONS OF THE ENEMY: OUR PAST

Brothers, I do not consider that I have made it my own. But one thing I do: forgetting what lies behind and straining forward to what lies ahead. ***Philippians 3:13 (ESV)***

We can choose to change our names or just about anything about ourselves. Unfortunately, we can do no such thing about our pasts. Past events are those that have happened, and the memory will always stay with us as individuals. The devil knows this all too well, so he uses our pasts as a weapon every opportunity he gets.

I have noticed that whenever I venture into something new, the enemy continually reminds me of all those times I tried and failed. When I am at my lowest, he bombards me with thoughts of past hurt, pain, rejection, and shame. He does all this in an attempt to make me feel defeated and give up on the present. Do you feel the same way?

Today, the Voice of Truth is speaking to us. Our Lord is telling us that our past experiences are in the past. Our Savior does not consult our history before making decisions about our future. Jesus Christ's death on the cross is all about new beginnings. Everyone that has had a terrible past can have a great future by the grace of God. Those who have had fantastic pasts can look forward to an even better future. This is the hope we have in Christ. What voice will we listen to, the voice of defeat or that of hope?

Confession: *Lord, thank you for the gift of a new beginning. Yesterday is gone. All past hurts and failures I leave in the past. I am free from the control of the enemy. The devil has nothing on me. I look forward to the promising future You have for me. Amen.*

MAY 21

WEAPONS OF THE ENEMY: OUR THOUGHTS

Therefore put on the full armor of God, so that when the day of evil comes, you may be able to stand your ground, and after you have done everything, to stand. ***Ephesians 6:13, NIV***

When I was little, I had a wind-up toy car. The car had no power source whatsoever. For the toy car to move, I would have to wind it manually. The more I wound the handle, the farther the car moved when I put it on the ground. When it comes to the human mind, the devil uses this same method. He feeds our minds with strategic thoughts, after which he twists those thoughts until we are in bondage. He loads our minds with depressing, fearful, and upsetting thoughts. Then he spins the thoughts in an attempt to sway us toward the path of destruction. This is why we cannot afford to meditate on all thoughts that drop into our minds. Some of these thoughts are straight from the pit of hell.

Whenever we begin to feel unhappy or depressed, we must understand that the devil is at work. We must learn how to beat the devil at his own game. We should never allow the devil to steal our joy. When negative thoughts come to our minds, we must discard them. Evil thoughts can never be from God.

Naturally, life often throws us punches that sometimes drive us into a low state. But so long as our joy comes from God alone, we can trust Him to give us peace at such times. This peace is all we need to enjoy the good life that God has promised us.

Confession: *Lord, I take captive every thought to make it obedient to You. My mind will no longer be a tool for the devil's use. I declare my mind will only be for the Master's use. Amen.*

MAY 22

RECOGNIZING THE DEVIL IN SPECIFIC FORMS

Now the serpent was more crafty than any other beast of the field that the LORD God had made. He said to the woman, "Did God actually say, 'You shall not eat of any tree in the garden'?"
Genesis 3:1 (ESV)

When the devil was going to mess with Eve in Eden, he disguised himself in the form of a snake. Chances are that if Eve knew precisely who she was dealing with, she would have stayed as far away from him as possible. The devil is smart, but to defeat him, the children of God only need to be smarter.

The devil is not only smart but he is also strategic. When messing with a person, he comes in different forms. He could come through our thoughts and pretend to be the voice of truth when he really is the voice of darkness. He could come through our friends and families with the intent of using them to derail us from God's purpose. Sadly, he could also come in the form of ministers of God. We see so many demonic "men" of God these days that it has become disturbing. The devil can disguise himself in many ways. He especially likes doing so in ways that are less revealing of his intentions.

The Holy Spirit is the One who can help us recognize the devil in his true form. The Spirit of God can also help us win the battle Satan continually wages against our souls. The Holy Spirit can help us discern the enemy no matter how hard he tries to disguise himself.

Confession: *Dear God, thank You for Your victory. Although the enemy comes like a flood, You have raised a standard against him. When the enemy comes to attack me, help me recognize him in his true form. No matter who or what he uses, help me identify and rebuke them. Amen.*

MAY 23

THE CUNNING SNAKE

But I am afraid that as the serpent deceived Eve by his cunning, your thoughts will be led astray from a sincere and pure devotion to Christ.
2 Corinthians 11:3 (ESV)

Some of us think all the thoughts in our minds are our own, but this is not true. Some thoughts are ours, some are from the Holy Spirit, and others are from the devil. How, then, do we recognize which is which? Discerning our thoughts from those of the devil takes a lot of spiritual discipline and maturity.

The devil is very manipulative; things will never appear black or white with him. He uses the process of discovering our thoughts, twisting them into his own, and feeding them back to us. We then begin to think of those thoughts as if they were originally ours when they are not.

The key to winning the battle over negative thoughts is to become one with the Holy Spirit. When we become one with God, we will hear Him clearly when He is trying to communicate with us. We will know it in our gut that it is God speaking to us and not the devil. Also, when we are one with God, the Holy Spirit will help us recognize manipulative thoughts. He will even teach us ways to discard them instantly.

Confession: *Dear God, thank you for making me more than a conqueror. The devil may be manipulative, but I'm thankful that You have given me a discerning spirit. When the evil one speaks to my mind, I will no longer fall victim. My mind is on the alert. The Holy Spirit and not the devil is the authority over my mind. Amen.*

MAY 24

NO MORE FEAR

Submit yourselves therefore to God.
Resist the devil, and he will flee from you.
James 4:7 (ESV)

The devil cannot kill us. He has no such power. What he does, however, is deceive us into thinking he can. I used to hold this belief as well, but through the revelation of the Holy Spirit, that thinking has changed.

I have found my heritage in Christ, and I understand the authority I have in Jesus. Now I know my place in God. I know who I am. I know that I am the King's child. Because of this, I have stopped letting the devil use his manipulative skills on me anymore. The days of being scared are over. In fact, now I do not wait for the enemy to bring the fight to me; instead, I take the fight to him. I find myself using the authority I have in Christ to let the devil and his agents know their boundaries. In the place of prayer, I secure everything and everyone I know under the wings of the Almighty. Instead of being bothered about the enemy and his schemes, I sing praises to God. I ignore the devil, worship God, and go about my daily business.

So long as we are legitimate children of God, this same authority is available for us all if we would only put it to use. No more fear! No more worry! The enemy has already been defeated.

Confession: *Lord, thank you for calling me Your own. Because I am Yours, I know my rights. I understand the authority I have in Christ Jesus. The enemy has no hold on me. He has no grip on my loved ones or my possessions. I am triumphant. I am victorious. Hallelujah.*

MAY 25

ONLY THAT WHICH GOD PERMITS

And the LORD said to Satan, "Have you considered my servant Job, that there is none like him on the earth, a blameless and upright man, who fears God and turns away from evil?"
Job 1:8 (ESV)

The devil can only do to God's children what God permits. In the case of Job in the Scriptures, God was the one who pointed Job out to the devil. God gave the devil permission to do a few things to Job, but this permit also came with boundaries that the devil could never cross. Job's faith, trust, and love for God were tested. At first, it looked like Job lost almost everything. Eventually, however, he was blessed with much more than he ever had before.

In our journey through life, we may encounter certain circumstances that show that the devil is at work. In fact, those situations may look like they will destroy us. We may even find ourselves questioning God's love and His promises. The devil will do everything possible to break us during these times. But through the trials and tribulations, God is there. Just like with Job, God is monitoring the situation. He is the all-knowing, all-seeing God who will never abandon His children. So long as we hold steadfast to him, victory will be ours. The same process that occurs when metals go through the furnace is the same process that occurs with us when we face trials. Eventually, we will come out of our situation stronger, tougher, and refined.

God is in the habit of compensating us for all our troubles. Just like in the case of Job, we can trust that all our lost possessions will be restored and even doubled. The key to victory is to never let go of God. In the end, we will come out better than we were before.

Confession: *Dear Lord, You are aware of everything that happens, and You see everything going on with me right now. You are molding me into all You want me to be. I trust You. I know I will laugh last in the end. Though sorrow may last for the night, I know my joy is on the way. Amen.*

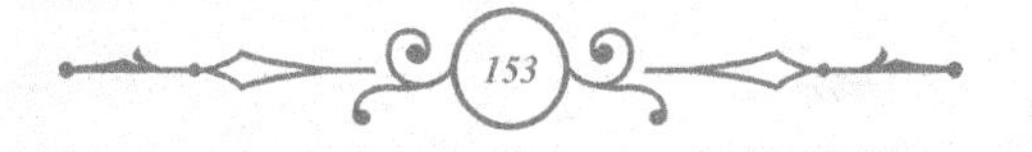

MAY 26

WEAPONS OF THE ENEMY: GUILT AND CONDEMNATION

...holding on to faith and a good conscience, which some have rejected and so have suffered shipwreck with regard to the faith
1 Timothy 1:19 (NIV)

Our conscience helps us distinguish between right and wrong. It also keeps us in check. Every person on Earth has a conscience, but not everyone's conscience carries out the purpose for which it was made. For those whose conscience is still effective, whenever they deviate from doing what is right, they end up with a guilty feeling. According to James 4:17, "Anyone who knows the right thing to do, yet fails to do it, is guilty of sin." No one enjoys feeling guilty. The enemy also understands that no one likes this, so what does he do? He bombards the person with more guilty feelings.

The only way the devil can torment us with guilt is if we sin. All the enemy needs is a crack in the wall to make a huge hole. So how about we stop giving him that little crack by staying away from sin as much as we can? One way to defeat the devil is by living a life of purity and godliness. This way, the devil will have nothing to hold over our heads.

When we stop giving the devil the ammunition he needs to power the guilt weapon, his winning streak over our lives will end.

Confession: *Dear Lord, I submit myself to You today.*
Grant me the power to resist sin so that the devil will no longer have a hold on my life.
I will live in Your light and walk in Your promises.
I will never give the enemy room to mess with my life. Amen.

MAY 27

•••

GOD IS NOT MAD AT YOU

He does not deal with us according to our sins, nor repay us according to our iniquities. For as high as the heavens are above the earth, so great is his steadfast love toward those who fear him.
Psalm 103:10-11 (ESV)

God is a consuming fire. However, this is not all He is to His children. God is also a loving Father. He is a Father who loves us dearly to the extent that He sent His only begotten Son to die on our behalf (John 3:16).

In an attempt to keep God's children in bondage, the enemy convinces them that God is not on their side. He tricks them into believing God is mad at them. Whenever they do something they probably shouldn't, he beats them hard with guilt. The devil's plan is to never let anyone enjoy the special grace found in God that forgives and covers all iniquities.

If you are feeling condemned, ashamed, or guilty, you do not have to anymore. God is calling you into His embrace. Walk into God's outstretched arms today. Ask for and receive His forgiveness. Receive your joy and peace of mind again. Determine to always stay within God's embrace, and never again listen to the devil and his lies. God is not mad at you. Rather, He is madly in love with you. Receive this love today.

Confession: *Heavenly Father, thank You for Your love. Thank You for sending Your Son to die on my behalf. Today I trade my ashes for Your beauty. I trade all my pain and shame for Your glory. The devil will never use my past to put me in captivity again. Amen.*

MAY 28

NO SIN IS TOO BIG

But if we confess our sins to him, he is faithful and just to forgive us our sins and to cleanse us from all wickedness.
1 John 1:9 (NLT)

Many of us believe that some sins are unforgivable. We may also feel that transgressions of a certain magnitude should be unpardonable. Well, although we term them unpardonable, it's a good thing God doesn't abide by man's standards. The scripture explains it all in Romans 8:1: "There is therefore now no condemnation for those who are in Christ Jesus."

There is nothing we have done that can make God stop loving us. He knew us before we were born, and He already loved us even before we existed. You may feel your sins are abominable and unspeakable, but today God is saying to you, "It's okay. Nothing is too big for me to forgive." All you have to do is genuinely ask for His forgiveness. Then exchange your shame and condemnation for His mercy. The moment you do this is the moment your verdict changes from guilty to not guilty. Because of Jesus' death on the cross, you are free. You have been acquitted. Go and live a life of joy and peace.

Confession: *Lord, thank You for Your mercies. I am loved by You, and I know this. No matter what I do, You never let go of Your love. Though the enemy tries to convince me otherwise, I know You deeply care about me. I ask for Your forgiveness for all my past iniquities. I claim my freedom this day. Amen.*

MAY 29

FORGIVE YOURSELF

Put on the whole armor of God, that you may be able to stand against the schemes of the devil.
Ephesians 6:11 (ESV)

After we ask for forgiveness, God forgives. But to enjoy the freedom God's mercy brings, a further step needs to be taken. This step is self-forgiveness.

To forgive oneself means to let go of the past. It also means to put an end to self-blame, shame, and criticism. Truth be told, self-forgiveness is not an easy thing to do. Some may even argue that it's easier to forgive others than to forgive oneself. Yet for true healing to occur, this step is crucial.

Thoughts like "I know I should have done better" or "I wish I could undo all I have done" are haunting, and having to live with these thoughts can be traumatizing. Self-forgiveness is the key to quenching these kinds of thoughts and a living guilt-free life. Now is the time to let go of all your past mistakes and failures. You cannot undo the past. The future, however, is very promising. What you choose to do at this moment will go a long way in determining how promising that future will be. Forgive yourself!

Confession: *Thank You, Jesus, for Your "not guilty" verdict on my life. Your amazing grace has set me free. Today I say yes to self-forgiveness. I forgive myself for my past disappointment and failures. When I let myself down in the future, please help me be quick to forgive. Amen.*

MAY 30

SELF-LOVE

The thief comes only to steal and kill and destroy. I came that they may have life and have it abundantly.
John 10:10 (ESV)

Unknown to many, simply choosing the right lifestyle is sometimes enough to chase the enemy away. One of these lifestyles is loving oneself. Practicing self-love is one way to defeat the devil without having to bind and cast him out. Self-love is also vital to living a happy and fulfilled life.

What does it mean to love myself? It means to appreciate myself for who I am instead of trying so hard to be who I am not. It means to be content with all I have and what I am. It means to let go of all my past shame and resentment. To love myself means that I always take good care of my body by practicing good hygiene and a healthy lifestyle. It means that sometimes I pamper myself just because I feel like it. It means that I only surround myself with those with people with positive energy and stay far from people that exude negativity. To love myself also means that I always give to others.

In loving myself, I choose to be good to myself. I also challenge myself regularly to do everything to the best of my ability. Finally, in loving myself, I conduct my life only to please the One who has made me in His image. God's love is always available, even without asking. But self-love is something one has to pursue intentionally through God's grace.

Confession: *Lord Jesus, thank You for loving me. Today I say no to self-reproach. No more self-blaming and shaming. I want to love myself better. Teach me how to improve my relationship with myself. Help me to stay content with who I am and all I have. Amen.*

MAY 31

THE IMPORTANCE OF SOLID MENTAL HEALTH

Stand firm then, with the belt of truth buckled around your waist, with the breastplate of righteousness in place.
Ephesians 6:14 (NIV)

Troubling circumstances may throw one into depression. However, not all depressions are like this. While some depressions are circumstance induced, others are clinical (hormone related). Regardless of the form and type, depression remains extremely dangerous. When an individual is in a state of depression, that person is also fragile and easily accessible for the enemy to attack.

Who wins when a person commits suicide? The devil. What is one of the primary reasons some decide to end their lives? Depression. Prolonged depression rarely bears any good fruit, and our state of mind influences every aspect of our lives.

Our mental health is important, and we have to pay close attention to it as mental health has been the devil's most recent way of waging his war. We must not let him win this battle over our lives. We must make it our responsibility to care for our mental health if or when we need it. One way to do this is by constantly feeding our minds with more positive things and less negative ones. We must also make God the center of our lives. We take care of the physical part of our bodies. Let's endeavor to do the same, if not more, for our minds.

Confession: *Lord, thank You for blessing me with a sound mind. The mind I have is that of Christ's. Today, I declare that I am not a tool in the devil's hands. Please fix my mind, Jesus. I come against every spirit of suicide. I send the suicide demon far away from me and mine. Amen.*

JUNE 1

CARING FOR OTHERS

Resist him, firm in your faith, knowing that the same kinds of suffering are being experienced by your brotherhood throughout the world.
1 Peter 5:9 (ESV)

Those who have experienced depression describe it as a dark and miserable state. Many of these people say that they pray they never experience such low states again. Folks who struggle with depression go through severe emotional torture that sometimes hurts worse than physical pain. Depression is a disease, a very terrible illness. And it's important that people recognize it for what it truly is.

In waging war against the enemy, we must also care for one another. Not everyone likes to share with others when they are going through difficult times. Still, it is imperative that we regularly check on those around us. We have to be more alert to our environment.

When people talk to us, let's learn how to recognize if there is pain in their voices. If people tell us they are not okay, let's believe them. Let's also help people get to the root of their pain or refer them to people and resources that can help them instead of shutting them out or simply saying we will pray for them. Depression may not have one ultimate cure, but the more we listen to, care for, and love one another, the better things will get for those dealing with it.

Confession: *Dear Lord, thank You for the gift of relationship. For those times when I have been less concerned about my loved ones, please have mercy. For those struggling with depression, please heal them. Should You bring these loved ones my way, give me the right words. Help me be a light to their path. Amen.*

JUNE 2

HE WHO STANDS

Therefore let anyone who thinks that he stands take heed lest he fall.
1 Corinthians 10:12 (ESV)

Although God may choose to bless us, we must not be naive enough to think the enemy will not try to set us up for destruction even in that blessing. I call this the human–enemy setup. No matter how successful we are, the devil will always try to set us up. In fact, the more successful we are, the harder the enemy seeks our downfall.

Anyone who stands is only standing by the grace of God. God is the pillar that holds us. He is the breastplate that defends us against the enemy. The moment anyone begins to feel all-sufficient is the moment that person will start to sink. Once God's breastplate defense is no longer intact, the devil can then be expected to enter into full attack mode.

Let's never feel we have gotten to that point where we no longer need our Maker. God should be our all in all. He should be our beginning and end. God should be all we center our lives around. This way, the enemy will have no fighting chance.

Confession: *Dear Lord, I need You. For the times when I have acted like I don't, I'm sorry. I am only breathing because of Your mercy. You gave me everything I have. You are my all-sufficient Father. Please let me never get to any stage in my life where I feel like I don't need You. Amen.*

JUNE 3

IT'S NOT ALWAYS THE DEVIL'S FAULT

Then Jesus said to him, "Be gone, Satan! For it is written, 'You shall worship the Lord your God and Him only shall you serve.'"
Matthew 4:10 (ESV)

A lot of Christians are quick to excuse their wrongdoings as the devil's fault. Well, this is wrong. It is not always the devil's fault, because the devil can never force humans to do that which they do not want to. Even God does not force man against man's wishes.

During creation, God gave us all the gift of free will. This free will grants us the right to do as we desire. God does not go against our freedom, and neither can the devil. We have absolute authority to do as we please. This is also the reason salvation cannot be forced on us. We all have the right to be saved or not be saved. And should we desire to be, we can ask Jesus individually without going through a third party.

The devil may not be able to force us into doing that which he wants us to do, but he uses his other gift to accomplish his goal. This is the gift of persuasion. When it comes to persuasion, the devil is second to none as it is his area of expertise. But even with the slickest of persuasions, we have the authority to say no to him. Unbelievers can say no to the devil's temptation as well, but as children of God, we have more power. We can rebuke, cast out, and chase the devil far away from us. This is exactly what Jesus did after the devil came to Him in Matthew 4:1-11. The devil can try all he wants. But should we understand our rights in Christ, we would never give him undue authority over us.

Confession: *Dear Lord, today I resist the devil. He has no hold on my life. I say no to him and his temptations. I will never again be a pawn in his hands. Help me. Amen.*

JUNE 4

THE GUESSING GAME

"For I know the plans I have for you," declares the LORD, "plans to prosper you and not to harm you, plans to give you hope and a future."
Jeremiah 29:11 (NIV)

The enemy has certain limitations. One of these is that he cannot see into the future. This may come as a surprise to many Christians, but it is the truth. It is a hidden truth that even scares the devil. He wants no one to be aware of this revelation, so he does everything within his power to distract people from it. The devil knows the past, and he is also aware of the present. But as for the future, he does not know for sure what lies ahead. This is one area where our all-knowing, all-seeing God puts the devil to shame.

What the enemy does is something called the guessing game. Before going after humans, he takes a good look into their past and present. Then he tries to predict what their future may look like. For those whose future looks promising, the devil does everything within his power to derail them from that bright destiny. For those whose future looks bleak, he puts things in their path to make it look even more hopeless.

Now that this particular strategy of the enemy has been revealed to us, we can utilize this to our own benefit. How? First, we can choose to stop giving the devil ammunition for our own ruin. We can also stop listening to the devil's report on how awful our future looks. We can choose to stay on God's course for our lives, refusing all distractions placed in our path. Finally, we can choose to trust and key into the future God alone has prepared for us.

Confession: *Dear Lord, thank You for Your promise of a better tomorrow. Thank You for putting the devil to shame on matters of my future. No matter how hard the enemy may try, I rejoice because You have raised a standard against him. Thank you. Amen.*

JUNE 5

IT'S EITHER GOD OR THE DEVIL

You cannot drink the cup of the Lord and the cup of demons. You cannot partake of the table of the Lord and the table of demons.
1 Corinthians 10:21 (ESV)

In picking sides, there are only two available: God's or the devil's. There is no sitting on the fence as there is no middle ground. The question today is "Which side are you on?"

You can be a regular churchgoer, worker, or big donor in God's vineyard. You can be one who says grace before every meal. You can talk about God and how much you love Him all the time. You can be and do all these and more and still not be on God's side.

There is only one way you can have a true relationship with God. This is by directly asking Jesus to come into your heart. You can do this right now if you so desire. Once you do, you have become a legitimate heir to God's throne. Never has there been a person who regretted entering into a genuine relationship with God. With Him, you can never go wrong. He is the best thing that can ever happen to anyone. If you have fallen away from your relationship with God in times past, now is a good time to get back on track. Spend time with Him, speak to him and acquaint and equip yourself with His Word. Come and experience God for yourself. I assure you that this experience will be worth your while.

Confession: *Lord, I declare this day that I choose You. I denounce the devil. I will no longer stay on the fence. Come into my life, sweet Jesus. Be my all in all. I walk into Your outstretched arms. I am Yours, and You are mine. Hallelujah.*

JUNE 6

AS MANY AS POSSIBLE TO HEAVEN

In My Father's house are many mansions; if it were not so, I would have told you. I go to prepare a place for you. And if I go and prepare a place for you, I will come again and receive you to Myself; that where I am, there you may be also. ***John 14:2-3 (NKJV)***

After being saved, it's our responsibility to help others receive their salvation. The more we invite people into God's kingdom, the more we reduce hell's population. Walking up to people and asking them to accept Jesus into their lives would seem like the popular approach, but there are other ways to minister to people. One of these ways is by living Christ-like ourselves. By living a godly life, we can preach the gospel indirectly. When people see the calm and joy we express everywhere we go, they may also want to partake in the joy.

Inviting people to be partakers of the Christian life is a spiritual journey. It is one that requires the grace of God. It is not something we do just because we have to but because we are led to. For the invitation to yield success, the leading of the Holy Spirit on how to approach people is crucial.

In God's kingdom, there are many mansions. How joyous will it be if all of us can make it? If our relatives, neighbors, friends, colleagues, and everyone we know can make it to heaven, how beautiful will it be? Guiding people to heaven's gate is a gift to God's kingdom. We can be certain sacrifices like these will never go unrewarded.

Confession: *My Lord and Savior, I adore You. Thank You for Your gift of salvation. This day I pray for the grace to populate heaven's kingdom. Please use me for Your glory. Give me the courage to minister to people, and let my lifestyle preach You. When You come back to get Your own, may I and those I know be ready. Amen.*

BEING CONTENT

JUNE 7

LIFE'S MANEUVERS

I can do all this through him who gives me strength.
Philippians 4:13, NIV

When we were babies, the next phase was significantly looked forward to by all. As soon as we started rolling over, we indirectly announced to those around us that we could now move on our own. Then came the teething stage, followed by the sitting and crawling stages. The walking process was a fascinating one for most babies. The running stage was even more exciting. Other developmental milestones naturally took their course after this. As we grew, the schooling and graduation steps were now anticipated. The next expectation after graduation was the working stage. Some then venture into the marriage phase, which brought about raising kids. Many people later become grandparents and/or retire from work. All these tell us how much of a rollercoaster life is. Of course, life stages usually vary from person to person. Still, at some point, everyone will naturally exit one stage of life to move to another. Life is almost like a never-ending race.

Unlike our gadgets that may come with manuals, life doesn't come with any such thing. We get no lesson that prepares us for the series of stages we find ourselves in. A person receives no orientation as to what to expect from life. We just find ourselves living in this big world, and we are supposed to somehow make the best of it.

Nothing guarantees a smooth journey through life's race, but one thing ensures a happy and enjoyable ride. This is called contentment, and this is what our focus will be on as we explore our new series, "Being Content."

Confession: *Dear Lord Jesus, no matter what phase of life I am in, You are always with me. Everything I need, You provide. Help me to always remain content through life's journey. I am exactly where You need me to be; teach me to always remember this. Amen.*

JUNE 8

•••

THE TRUE MEANING OF BEING CONTENT

And people should eat and drink and enjoy the fruits of their labor, for these are gifts from God.
Ecclesiastes 3:13, NLT

Before discussing what contentment is, we should begin by explaining what it is not. Contentment is not complacency. It is not laziness. It is not nonchalance about life or being too comfortable in the same spot for too long. It does not mean not seizing opportunities when they present themselves. It is not settling for a lower quality of life. It is not just taking life as it comes.

Contentment is trusting God through life's seasons. It also implies living with hope. It is praising and worshipping God, even in tough times. It is being okay with today and, at the same time, working toward a better tomorrow. Contentment means being appreciative of every blessing, no matter how big or small. It is rejoicing with those who rejoice. It's living a life of a giver. It is reaching out to those who may need help. This word is also synonymous with being compassionate.

Contentment involves offering ceaseless prayers to God. Contented people are always okay with God saying no or wait to their request. Wherever they go, they radiate joy and happiness regardless of their predicaments. These people never lose their peace over trivial matters. They ultimately believe in God till He fulfills all His promises. The question today is, "Are you a contented person?"

Confession: *Heavenly Father, thank You for Your word today. Thank You for the blessings I see and the ones I don't. Thank you for the hope of a better tomorrow. You've got great plans for my future, and I know this. In my pursuit of a better life, help me so that I never waver from You. I do not want to live a discontented life. Amen.*

JUNE 9

THE WILLINGNESS TO ACCEPT ME

So if we have enough food and clothing, let us be content.
1 Timothy 6:8, NLT

Do you love yourself? Not everyone does. Not everyone even knows that they do not love themselves. All they know is that for them to be happy and complete, certain things must happen. To some, if only they could be taller, slimmer, fairer, or more beautiful, then their life would be so much better. To some, if only they had more money, a better job, or a bigger house, then maybe they would be satisfied. To some, if only they could move to another country or change their location, then they would be most joyful. To some, when they marry or become friends with the rich and famous, their lives will be complete.

To be content means to be happy with who you are, what you have, and where you are. Simply put, it's being okay with being you. Contentment doesn't come from a place of perfection. Rather, it comes from a place of acceptance. Contentment comes from a place of being pleased with the person who stares back at you in the mirror. It comes from a place of having little and still being able to keep your joy. It comes from a place of having abundance and still being humble. Contentment comes from knowing you are the complete package all by yourself. Every other thing or person is supposed to add to you but not complete you.

Finally, contentment comes from a place of self-acceptance. It is all about accepting that which you cannot change but making an effort to improve that which you can. The question today is, "Have you accepted yourself?"

Confession: *Dear God, thank You for creating me the way You have. My weight, height, complexion, and body structure are exactly what I need to fulfill my purpose in life. I do not need to look like or have the things others do. I am perfect in You. I am complete. I accept who I am and all I have. I will no longer compare myself to others, so help me, God. Amen.*

JUNE 10

MONEY IS NOT EVIL

For the love of money is a root of all kinds of evils.
1 Timothy 6:10a

Many Christians have the notion that money is evil. Some even quote Bible texts that speak about money being evil to prove their point. A good example is today's Bible text. The first word to note here is "love." The Bible never connotes money as evil. It says the love of money is what is evil, meaning money by itself carries no danger. Our love for it is usually what causes trouble. Simply put, our attitude toward money is the root of all evil.

The other word to note is "root." According to the scriptures, the love of money is not even evil but rather the "root" of all evil. The word "root" also implies a foundation or origin. Our passion for money is therefore the beginning of problems to come. I believe it was in this context that the Bible text was referring to money. One way to get an accurate meaning of a sensitive scripture verse is to study the surrounding verses. Most importantly, we are to ask the Holy Spirit for the right interpretation.

Ecclesiastics 10:19 says, "money answers everything." The Word of God is never false. Money is needed to make life easier, and it makes dreams come true. It furnishes us with comfort and enjoyment while taking us places we never dreamed of reaching. It opens doors and paves roads. If we would all be honest, we could use a good deal of money. Money is not evil! Our attitude toward it is what makes all the difference.

Confession: *Dear Father, thank You for the understanding of Your Word.*
Thank You for blessing the world with money as a resource.
I pray today that I will have the right attitude toward Your resource.
Help me never to be too overzealous with money issues.
Also, help me understand Your thoughts concerning money

JUNE 11

MONEY ANSWERS ALL THINGS

Bread is made for laughter, and wine gladdens life, and money answers everything.
Ecclesiastes 10:19

A rich man's son was diagnosed with a life-threatening ailment. This man was so wealthy that he could afford any doctor, so he got the best. He was also so well connected that he could get the best treatment facilities, so he got his son into one of the world's finest hospitals. After a long struggle, his son died. His money could not save his child. His words as soon as his child was buried were "My money failed me."

Money can get us the best treatment, but can it cure a disease? Money can buy the best house, but can it buy a home? Money can buy a great companion, but can it buy true love? Money can get us the most comfortable bed, but can it buy us a good night's rest? Indeed, money can grant us temporary happiness, but can it give us prolonged peace of mind? Can money buy manners, integrity, or a good attitude? Can it buy us common sense? Most importantly, can money buy us salvation? The answer to all of these is no.

Money is limited. The rich do not have it all. In fact, some people are so poor, all they have is money. Money is good to have, and it may answer everything, but money is not everything. This is food for thought for us today. May God give us an understanding of His words. Amen.

Confession: *Lord Jesus, I adore You. Today I have learned that money is limited. Only You are limitless. Help me to find my contentment in You and not my possessions. I know You will never fail me, and I know You have all the answers to life's questions. When in need, I will turn to You first. Amen.*

JUNE 12

CONTENTMENT IS A VIRTUE

I am not saying this because I am in need, for I have learned to be content whatever the circumstances.
Philippians 4:11, NIV

Life is a journey. One would think this journey should at least have a specific destination, but not so life. As soon as we have made it through a phase, we are required to change routes. We may do this over and over again until we get to our final destination on Earth— death. Life throws various seasons at us. Some seasons we may be able to control. Other seasons not so much. How then do we navigate through the multiple seasons of "good" and "not so good" and still keep our joy? The secret is contentment.

Paul was incarcerated in the Roman prison when he wrote today's text. Isn't it strange that someone going through difficult challenges is the same person preaching about being content? But Paul didn't just teach about being content alone. He let those who sent him financial aid know that he was okay with or without their gifts. Of course Paul appreciated their gifts, but their contributions were just an addition. He already had what he needed—God. He was content in God and the life he had been called to. Even in prison, Paul was okay.

How many of us can maintain this same attitude when things do not go our way? How many of us can be sources of hope to others when we find ourselves in discouraging situations? How many of us can stay content and happy through life's difficulties? Finally, how many of us will heed Paul's teaching of staying content regardless of the issues we may be facing?

Confession: *Dear Lord, I pray today that You help me. I do not want to live discontented. Because I have You, I have everything I need. In my everyday pursuits, help me to never get hasty. Help me maintain a good attitude even when I am in a lowly state. Help me keep my joy regardless of my circumstances. Amen.*

JUNE 13

IN THE SEASON OF PLENTY

And some people, craving money, have wandered from the true faith and pierced themselves with many sorrows.
1 Timothy 6:10b, NLT

A man earning $5,000 per month may be getting by with his monthly income. Interestingly, as soon as he begins earning $50,000 per month, his new income may not meet his needs anymore. This happens all too often. Perhaps it has also happened to you. But why would a person's increased income become insufficient for his or her needs over time? This is because when a person's income increases, his or her tastes also increases. Also, and most importantly, there is a hunger in humans to always want to have more. This drive to get more, even after having so much, is what pushes many into the problems they face.

Many people blame money (the lack of it or too much of it) for their money issues, yet I have come to realize that money is not usually the problem. The lack of discipline is. A lot of people throw more money at the same problem, thinking it will resolve it, but more money won't. Only contentment will. There is so much money cannot do, such as offer solutions to all of life's problems. This is why the wealthy are not necessarily the happiest people. In fact, many wealthy people out there are even more miserable than those who are not.

In the season of plenty, other factors besides money must also be at work for a happy and peaceful life. Contentment is vital for all seasons of life, even in the season of plenty.

Confession: *Heavenly Father, I thank You for Your provision. All I have is from You. All I am is because of You. Today I ask that You help me understand that money is a tool. In the season of plenty, help me adequately manage the resources You have given me. May I never be wasteful. Help me to be disciplined with Your blessings. Amen.*

JUNE 14

THE SEASON OF LITTLE

I know how to live on almost nothing or with everything.
I have learned the secret of living in every situation,
whether it is with a full stomach or empty, with plenty or little.
Philippians 4:12, NLT

Having greater wealth is not the solution to all money issues. Neither is being poor. Just as the rich man has his problems, so does the poor man. Some may argue that it is easier for a rich man to be content than a poor man since the rich have something on the ground already. But for the poor man who has nothing, what is available for him to be content with? Well, being broke is not an excuse to have a bad attitude. It is very possible to have little and still be satisfied.

The biblical account given of Joseph showed he lived a content life (Genesis 37–50). Despite the various seasons he went through, he remained good-natured. From being the favorite of his father to being betrayed by his brothers, lied about, and sent to prison, Joseph displayed nothing but a good attitude. Even when he became a prominent leader, he was still humble. Also, the Bible mentioned nothing about Joseph not hoping for a better future. In fact, when he got the opportunity to seek a better life, he did so (Genesis 40:14–15). But while he awaited God's promises, Joseph was okay with where God wanted him to be at that moment. No matter how uncomfortable, Joseph was always at peace.

This tells us also that our circumstances do not have to determine our disposition. We alone can decide what our mood will be in every season of life. This is what God requires of us: that we live every season of our lives with contentment. We should do this even as we work toward a better tomorrow.

Confession: *Dear Jesus, You are my one true source of joy. Money does not have the right to control my happiness. In the season of little, I will remain faithful, I will be content, and I will keep my joy. I will never go searching for more outside Your presence. Amen.*

JUNE 15

THE RACE TO GET "THERE"

First, help me never to tell a lie. Second, give me neither poverty nor riches! Give me just enough to satisfy my needs.
Proverbs 30:8, NLT

There is a place called "there" that we humans continually long for. This place is where we hope to find joy and happiness. "There" could mean different things to different people. To some, it could be a dream job. To others, it could be getting married, having kids, and moving to their dream home. For those who got their "there," what was the feeling like? Was it all you hoped it would be and then some? Hopefully so!

There's no doubt that "there" brings us joy. But what happens as soon as we get "there"? Well, tomorrow follows, and then everyday life continues. Before long, we may find ourselves in search of another "there." This is because "there" is never a destination but only the beginning of another journey. It is the start of another phase. This phase will come with its joys as well as its own challenges.

Often people only prepare for the pleasant part of "there." Many people give little to no thought to the unpleasant side that may come with this phase. Upon getting "there," we then realize that as beautiful as it is, it also comes with its own baggage. If we would be willing, I would strongly encourage us to start being happy today. No, we do not have to postpone our happiness to a future moment. Choosing to be content and making the best of everyday life should be our goal. "There" is never as perfect as it looks from a distance. We should endeavor to live our present lives as though we are already "there."

Confession: *Father, I thank You for life. Every day is a gift from You. Today I pray that in my race to get "there," I will not lose sight of the most important thing I need—You. Help me find joy with who I am and all I have at this moment. Help me to always remember to enjoy the present, even as I look forward to a brighter future. Amen.*

JUNE 16

UNDERSTAND YOUR SEASON

Keep your life free from love of money, and be content with what you have, for he has said, "I will never leave you nor forsake you."
Hebrews 13:5

Two major seasons exist in life: planting and harvesting. But after planting, adequate work must be done to yield bountiful returns. This work may include watering, fertilizing, weeding, and more. Some people are currently in their planting season. Others, who may have sown in the past, may now be in their season of harvest.

People at the sowing stage get into trouble when they try to live like those who are at the reaping stage. Success is hardly achieved overnight. Most "overnight" success stories have moments of tenacity in them. Successful people who tell their stories often talk about how they had to work ten times harder. While their friends were sleeping, many of these people were busy burning the midnight oil.

While we are at our planting stage, we must be willing to go through the process and do so diligently. We must be patient to let the seed in the ground germinate and grow before we harvest and enjoy its fruit. We must especially be content with whatever we have at the planting stage, regardless of how little it is. Cutting corners and cheating through the planting stage may yield large harvests but to what to end? Enjoying one's harvest with inner peace brings about a satisfying life. Nothing compares to living a life devoid of regret. We all should aspire for this as it is the life God desires for all His children.

Confession: *Dear Lord Jesus, You love a diligent steward. Thank You for making me one. Thank You for the daily strength You bless me with. As You take me through the process, I pray for Your grace. Please grant me the grace to be honorable in all my dealings. I will not cheat my way through life. Amen.*

JUNE 17

DIFFERENT TRACKS FOR DIFFERENT FOLKS

But those who desire to be rich fall into temptation, into a snare, into many senseless and harmful desires that plunge people into ruin and destruction. ***1 Timothy 6:9***

When someone who usually runs a100m race decides to compete with those who run 10000m races, odds are that this person will fail. The same goes for life. We've all been created with strength and grace to run our specific race, but the moment we deviate from our set track and begin to run other people's races, we are bound to fail.

As one who is somewhat competitive, it took me a long time to understand what it means to run my own race. I love being at the forefront. So when I saw my contemporaries doing better than I was, I would try to catch up with them. The struggle to always catch up continually wore me out until I came to a full understanding of "my journey." This liberated me tremendously.

Everyone is running a different race, therefore life should not be a competition. Unnecessary competition drives people to do what they should not. It makes people live beyond their means. It also makes people do crazy things. Some run themselves into severe debt just because they want to have what everyone else has. Nothing good ever comes out of running a race that is not yours. No two people have identical journeys in life, not even identical twins. One key to enjoying life is understanding the life God has called you into. Focus solely on your set path. Run your own race.

Confession: *Father, thank You for calling me special. Because I am unique, I know I do not have to compare myself with others. Instead, I am to follow the path You have set before me. Help me that I may never go running on another's path and miss mine. Help me stay focused on my calling. Amen.*

JUNE 18

DISCIPLINING THE FLESH

But godliness with contentment is great gain.
1 Timothy 6:6, NIV

Many people believe that so long as you can afford it, then it's okay to go for it. Some may even say that you can do whatever you please with your wealth since it's yours and you earned it. But isn't there more to life than having our way all the time? Also, can the flesh ever be satiated? Wouldn't there always be that desire to have "more"?

People are composed of two major parts: the flesh (external) and the inner man (soul and spirit). The soul is where a man's will lies. Our flesh can be likened to children who believe everything is theirs. Often children will use every means possible to convince their parents to get their way. They may ask politely, throw tantrums, or play tricks until their requests are granted. This sometimes works, but a good parent knows better than to always give in to all a child demands. Occasionally denying a want may leave a child unhappy for a while, but this will end up benefiting them in the long run. Having to say no to the child occasionally is our will, and our will is far stronger than our flesh.

If Christ could have denied Himself of some good things while He was here on Earth, so can we. All it takes is a little discipline. Learning how to say no not only to others but oneself is a high level of maturity in Christ. According to today's text, this act is one that God requires from all His children.

Confession: *Lord Jesus, despite owning everything, You still denied Yourself certain things. This teaches me that I also have to be disciplined. Just because some things are within my reach doesn't mean they have to be mine. For those things You do not want me to have, please give me the grace to resist them. Amen.*

JUNE 19

YOU CAN BE OVERTAKEN

Let us not become conceited, provoking one another, envying one another.
Galatians 5:26

A friend of mine, Mary, seemed to be in an excellent mood for a long time. Then suddenly this mood changed. Unknown to many, Mary's initial good mood was a result of her new house. Among her friends, she was the first to get a house. This gave her so much satisfaction for a long time. But one day, Mary heard that another friend of hers had purchased a brand-new home. Not only did this other friend get a new home but hers was more elegant and expensive than Mary's. This bothered Mary greatly. Mary then decided that she would buy another house, better than her friend's.

Life can be likened to a road trip. When driving on the road, we can overtake anyone at any time. Others can overtake us too. There is simply nothing we can do about this.

Life's journey takes place on a very big road. As such, those coming from behind may pull ahead of us and do better things than we have. Someone, somewhere, will build a more beautiful house than yours. Another person will purchase a car that is trendier than yours. Where one person's success peaks is where another's may begin. Mary will probably not be happy for long. This is because those around her will buy better houses than whatever she decides to buy. Will she then keep changing homes? Please do not be like Mary. Be content. Be happy. Be okay with all that you have. You cannot have it all.

Confession: *Dear Father, thank You for Your provision. All I have is from You. I pray today for the grace to remain content. Help me to be happy with all I have, whether it is big or small. I do not want to live greedily or unappreciative. My inner joy does not come from my possessions but from You. When others around me are prospering, please give me the grace to be happy for them and not envious. Amen.*

JUNE 20

THE JEALOUS AND ENVIOUS SPIRIT

A heart at peace gives life to the body,
but envy rots the bones.
Proverbs 14:30, NIV

"Here comes your neighbor again. Have you noticed how she's always acting all important and perfect when she really isn't? Look at what she's wearing. It looks expensive, but who knows where she gets the money to buy all that stuff. That dress would look lovely on you. If only you could get the exact dress, you'd definitely look prettier in it than she does." Recognize this voice? It is the whispering spirit of jealousy and envy.

To be jealous means to resent someone because of his or her advantages or possessions. To be envious means to secretly covet what another person has. Although these two are somewhat different in definition, they work in combination. Envy and jealousy are both spirits that talk. This spirit may talk to everyone, but it only takes root in the hearts of those that give it room. People whom this spirit possesses will have other traits as well, like bitterness, insecurity, and hate. This is why jealous and envious people rarely go far in life. They are always busy monitoring and desiring other people's lives.

The origin of this spirit is the pit of hell. So should you be one to struggle with envy and jealousy, I implore you today to submit yourself to God for complete deliverance. If you know someone who struggles with this same spirit, please take time out to pray for them today. If experience is anything to go by, the end for these types of people is usually never gratifying.

***Confession:** Dear Lord, please forgive me. For those times when I have consciously or unconsciously envied others, have mercy. Search my heart this day. Should I possess any iota of jealousy, please deal with me. Deliver me from every spirit that is appalling to You. Help me, Jesus. Amen.*

JUNE 21

OVERCOMING JEALOUSY AND ENVY

Love one another with brotherly affection.
Outdo one another in showing honor.
Romans 12:10

We humans have a tendency to be jealous. It comes naturally to us. Some may even argue that a little jealousy is necessary, especially in relationships. Nevertheless, once jealousy takes root in a person's life, it becomes a stronghold, and that person becomes a ticking time bomb. An extremely jealous person is a dangerous person because his or her heart will be filled with bitter thoughts.

Those who let jealousy control them are those who have given up on themselves and God. If this were not the case, why would someone who is God's rightful heir be bitter over other people's successes? The sky is big enough for all the birds to fly. In the same way, the earth is big enough to accommodate everyone's success. That others around a person are succeeding doesn't mean that person's time will not come. It will come in due season.

Until our doors open, God expects us to praise Him in the hallway. We are to have a good attitude while we await God's promises for our lives to manifest. We are to rejoice always with those who may seem to have gone ahead of us in life. This is God's expectation of all His children. It's important we check our minds regularly and make sure that jealousy is not incubating. The jealous spirit is what the devil uses to distract God's children from their blessing to come. Let's decide today to never again be victims of the devil's trick.

Confession: *Heavenly Father, I adore You. Thank You for all You have blessed me with. Whatever I do not have at this moment, it's because You do not want me to. You have given me all I need. I will not be envious of other people's blessings. Instead, I will celebrate with those who celebrate. Amen.*

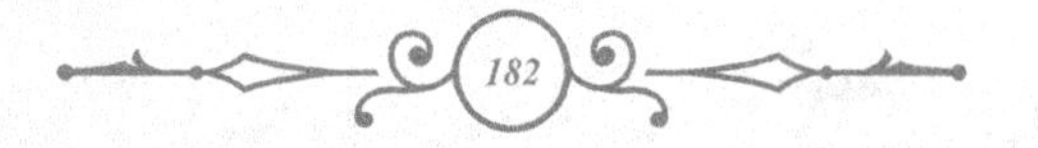

JUNE 22

THE GRACE TO BE GENUINELY HAPPY FOR OTHERS

So let's not get tired of doing what is good. At just the right time we will reap a harvest of blessing if we don't give up.
Galatians 6:9, NLT

It takes grace to be genuinely happy for others. It takes a special kind of grace for one who is not doing well to be truly happy when those around him or her are doing great.

It hurts when those that seem underqualified get things that we (who are highly qualified) don't. Some of us may have been in positions that made us feel unfairly treated. I mean, it's one thing for others to be getting blessed when we are not, but to have to celebrate and be thankful for them just feels like adding salt to our wounds. But like many other instructions God gives, this one, too, is inconvenient. Being happy for others is not just a choice but a must for all children of God. Also, this act has to come sincerely from one's heart.

Personally, life has taught me that those that celebrate others also get celebrated in due time. In fact, they even get honored in more significant ways. By the grace of God, I have learned to be the first to congratulate people on their achievements. While praying, I have learned to first appreciate God for other's successes before asking God for mine. I have learned that other people's successes will not hinder mine in any way. More importantly, I have learned to be content with whatever God blesses me with. Whatever is mine will come to me in due season. And if it does not come to me for any reason, it is because God does not want me to have it. This lifestyle of being happy for others takes the Holy Spirit's dealing to achieve. It is available for you today if you so desire. All you have to do is ask.

Confession: *Dear Jesus, thank You for today's word. I confess that sometimes my spirit gets weighed down when I do not get that which I feel I deserve. But I know I am to keep my joy regardless of my situation. I am also to celebrate others when they are blessed. Please help me remain positive always. Help me keep a joyful attitude through and through. Amen.*

JUNE 23

COUNTING MY BLESSINGS

So if we have enough food and clothing, let us be content
1 Timothy 6:8, NLT

We all have those days when everything just feels wrong. I remember having one of those moments. I felt stuck, irrelevant, and miserable. Everything around me made me feel depressed. This went on for a while until the Holy Spirit unveiled what my problem was. What was the problem? I was looking around instead of looking within. After this revelation, I was further led to look into my life and count all the "rights" against all the "wrongs." I then began counting things like my salvation, children, spouse, ministry, health, shelter, provisions, relatives, and friends. I continued counting all the big and little things until I lost count. When it came to all that was wrong, I could barely count them on my fingers. This revelation changed my life for good. Within minutes, I was in a better mood than I had been in a while.

A good therapy for depression, unhappiness, and hopelessness is gratitude. Living a life of gratitude helps us appreciate life better and reveals to us how much we have been blessed with. It teaches us how to take our gaze from all that is wrong and put it on all that is right. All that surrounds us may or may not bring us the happiness we desire, but looking inward will. We've all been blessed with so much more than we know. It takes purposely counting God's blessings to know how enriched our lives are. Contentment and gratitude go hand in hand. The more we appreciate where we are and what we have, the less we will likely worry about the things we do not have.

Confession: *Dear Lord, when I look around, all I see are Your blessings. You have blessed me with things money can and cannot buy. My being alive is only by Your mercies. Today I focus my attention on all the good in my life. I choose to count Your blessings and name them one by one. You have been amazing to me. Thank you, Jesus.*

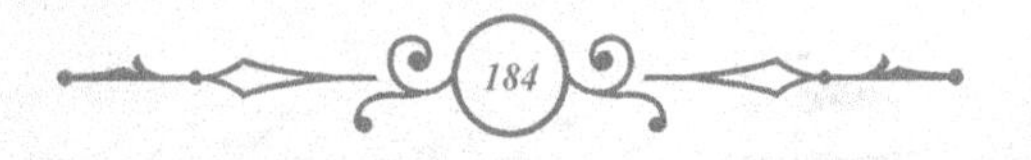

JUNE 24

CONTENTMENT IN RELATIONSHIPS

A new commandment I give to you, that you love one another: just as I have loved you, you also are to love one another.
John 13:34

As established previously, to be content means to be happy with who we are, all we have, and where we are. But being content doesn't just begin and end with us as individuals. It also extends to those around us. Contentment includes loving and accepting people for who they are.

What are your relationships like? Are you in the habit of continually changing friends, spouses, or social groups? Do you always complain and find fault with everyone around you? Today may be a good day to look inward and make some modifications. If only we knew how enriched our lives are as a result of those that surround us, we might be obliged to be more welcoming.

There is some level of good in people if we choose to look for it. Dwelling mostly on the good in people helps us see them in a new light. It helps us reduce our over-the-top expectations of them. When we give people room for their little imperfections, it helps us accept them more. It also helps us minimize our need to change them into versions of them we prefer. No one is without flaws. If flaws are the only thing we choose to see in people, we will find plenty. But if we choose to live with them in understanding, a healthy relationship will likely ensue. To see a change in our relationship with others, we may have to be the ones making some personal adjustments. In doing this, we will begin to see the beautiful sides of those we are in relationships with.

Confession: *Heavenly Father, I appreciate Your gift of relationship. Those You have surrounded me with have their flaws, but they also have good qualities. Please help me see more of their good side than their bad. Help me love and accept them for who they are. If I need to correct them, please help me do so in love. Amen.*

JUNE 25

WHAT'S IN VOGUE

But as for you, O man of God, flee these things. Pursue righteousness, godliness, faith, love, steadfastness, gentleness.
1 Timothy 6:11

My mother was going through her closet one day and found some clothes she forgot she had. These clothes took her down memory lane. She went on to tell me how expensive and trendy the clothes were when she first got them. Unfortunately, they had now gone out of style. After giving it a little thought, she threw the clothes in the waste bin. As she was about to throw them away, she said to herself, "What a waste." This word struck me greatly. Right then and there, I got a change of orientation.

Trends come and go. What's in vogue today goes out of style tomorrow. Trend makers do not consider our financial account or preferences when making their decisions. Why, then, do we have to stretch ourselves so hard to purchase all that is in vogue? Is it just for the need to keep up? Do our lifestyles need to be solely determined by what celebrities use or what is popular?

I believe our lives should be lived based on our own terms, preferences, and budget. Constantly chasing after trendy things may bring temporary satisfaction, but it may also carry some unpleasant consequences in the long run. When it comes to your life, only one person should call the shots—you. Be your brand. Do what works for you. Always remember: Trends will come, and trends will go.

Confession: *I do not need the world's system to complete me. I am already complete in You, Jesus. Henceforth, I refuse to let the world's value dictate my worth. I will no longer permit others to control my life choices. I am a pace-setter. I am a pathfinder. I will live life on my terms. I will set my trend, so help me, God. Amen.*

JUNE 26

THE JOY OF SIMPLICITY

And he answered them, "Whoever has two tunics is to share with him who has none, and whoever has food is to do likewise."
Luke 3:11

One characteristic common to most humans is their attachment to things. Although the degree may vary from person to person, humans tend to cling to things. People hang on to stuff for various reasons. Sometimes these reasons are sentimental, for example, hanging on to things because of the memories attached to them. But there are certain cases of those who never let things go. These people have a compulsive need to keep everything they own.

What level do you fall into when it comes to attachment to your belongings? Do you struggle with parting ways with personal possessions that you hardly use? Do you feel the constant need to acquire more and more things, only to keep stacking them one upon another? Does your home have room enough for you to move around? Or do you feel cluttered as a result of having too many things? Please take a minute to think about these questions. Also check around you and pay attention to those items you haven't used in six months.

Today, intentionally search through your spaces and take note of the clothes, shoes, appliances, furniture, or anything that has not been used in a while. Then rate yourself on how attached you are to your things. On a scale of 1–10, mine is most likely a 4. What about you?

Confession: *Father God, I adore You. I sometimes find it difficult to part with my belongings. I pray for the grace to let things go. I want to enjoy living simply and comfortably. Please help me. Amen.*

JUNE 27

KEEPING IT SIMPLE

But all things should be done decently and in order.
1 Corinthians 14:40

Some time ago, a family was battling severe insect infestation. They complained that they had done everything possible to get rid of the bugs and roaches but all to no avail. One look around the home, however, gave the answer as to what must have caused the infestation crisis: having too many things. With just a single glance, the whole house screamed, "Too busy." A lot of cluttering was happening in this home. This most likely gave the insects multiple places to hide in and many things to feast on. Infestation is just one out of the many disadvantages of cluttering. Another drawback of this habit is suffocation. When things we own begin to drown us, we may need some decluttering.

Developing the habit of only keeping what one needs is not an easy task. However, it is necessary. Only when we periodically part ways with some personal possessions will we know the joy of keeping things simple. This habit makes life easier by making us tidy and organized. On days when I choose to dispose of things I don't need, I find my environment more relaxing. I find my thinking process fresher and more creative.

Cultivating the habit of frequently cleaning out is one we could all use. Those that already practice this habit can assist others around them. Those that have not begun this habit can start today. It may not be easy at first, but with time, it becomes enjoyable. We may even find ourselves looking forward to regularly cleaning out our spaces.

Confession: *Heavenly Father, thank You for Your word that has come my way this day. I long to live simply and enjoy all I have been blessed with. To do this, I know I sometimes may need to part ways with my possessions. Grant me the grace to do this. Please help me find joy in blessing others with my belongings. Amen.*

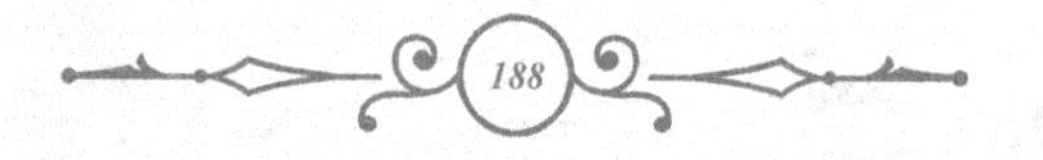

JUNE 28

CONTENTMENT IS LEARNED

Train up a child in the way he should go;
even when he is old he will not depart from it.
Proverbs 22:6

Contentment can be learned at any time. Still, some habits are better cultivated at the foundational level. Today's text establishes that once certain teachings are ingrained in the minds of little children, the lessons follow them throughout their lives. Today parents and guardians are encouraged to instill the virtue of contentment in their kids. Here are a few suggestions on how to do so:

- If a child cannot have something, then he or she should not have it. Period! Should the child throw tantrums, it still shouldn't change the parent's verdict. With time, the child will get over it, and life will go on.
- As a parent, even if it's within your power to grant to your child's desires, say no at times. A child can have most necessities but not all "wants."
- If you cannot afford a particular thing your child desires, explain to the little one why he or she cannot have it. Excessively pressuring yourself to grant all your child's requests is passing a toxic message to his or /her subconscious.
- Finally, the foundation of a child is the most important. This goes a long way in influencing his or her overall outcome. Like the scripture says, if the foundation is destroyed, what can the righteous do? (Psalm 11:3)

Confession: *Dear God, I long for all my children, and all the children I know, to live content lives. Raising godly children entails the discipline of teaching. I know that I will have to be firm. Please teach me how to go about this. Today I pray for all the children that are within my circle of influence. I pray that these ones will grow with the fear of God in their hearts and that they will not be entitled, spoiled children. Rather, they will be disciplined and exceptional. Amen.*

JUNE 29

UNDERSTANDING OUR PLACE IN GOD

You desire and do not have, so you murder. You covet and cannot obtain, so you fight and quarrel. You do not have, because you do not ask.
James 4:2

God owns everything, and every child of His is an heir to His throne. As heirs to the owner and maker of everything, we are entitled to the best things in life by right.

God knows what His children need at every moment. However, today's text tells us that God still expects us to open our mouths and ask. In essence, to receive something from God, we have to talk to God about it. We should do this believing that He will consider our requests.

One crucial point to note is that just because we ask for something doesn't mean we will get it then and there. God sees the end from the beginning. If what we are asking for does not correspond with His plan for our lives, He may withhold it from us. This is why being content is crucial. It is essential for Christian growth. Contentment helps us understand that we won't have our way all the time. On those days when we don't, we have to be okay with the "no" verdict from God. When we fully understand our place in God, we realize that He loves raising disciplined children. At various stages of life, the contentment test is one every child of God will have to excel in to move to the next level.

Confession: *Lord Jesus, my words carry life, so today I decree joy into my situation. I declare prosperity, good health, and increase in my life. I trust that in due time, all You desire for me will come to pass. But in the meantime, I choose to be content. Until You bless me with all You have promised, I will be patient, trusting in Your utmost ability. Amen.*

JUNE 30

BE STILL

"Be still, and know that I am God. I will be exalted among the nations, I will be exalted in the earth!"
Psalm 46:10

I love being on the move. I also love achieving things. This makes me fulfilled. However, in the past, these habits fueled my workaholic tendencies, making it worse. Initially, I got away with drowning myself in work. In my early twenties, I would leave my family for months without looking back. My passion has always been to impact lives, so I would always come up with one idea or the other to make that happen. After a while, I observed that things started changing. God started dealing with me.

At first the lessons were gradual. God started taking things away from me a bit at a time. He took away my audience. Afterward, He took my sponsors, my friends. Finally, he took away my inspiration. It got to a point where the harder I tried, the less inspired I became. This used to get me so frustrated until I handed it all to God. God then brought me to a place of stillness. A place of quiet. A place where I was to do nothing. At first, it was strange and scary. But the more I yielded to God, the more at peace I felt. As soon as I chose to be content with doing nothing and trusting God through that season, I received great joy. In my place of stillness, I eventually received leading for my next life assignment.

Have you ever experienced a place of stillness? Can you remember what your own experience was like? Many Bible examples let us know that at some point, every child of promise will go through this process. These examples and more are what we will consider next.

Confession: *Dear Lord, I trust You. Where I am at the moment is exactly where You need me to be. If and when You take me through a place of stillness, I pray for Your grace through the phase. Help me not to rebel against this process. Please teach me how to remain still while I await Your instructions. Amen.*

JULY 1

BE STILL PART II

"The LORD will fight for you, and all you have to do is keep still."
Exodus 14:14, GNT

The place of stillness is a place where God takes you away from the norm to a place of quiet. Most times the place of stillness is not something that brings comfort. Some even term it as God taking us away from our comfort zone.

Joseph was taken away from the life he knew. Somehow he even found himself in prison (Genesis 39:20). Moses left everything, including his adopted royal family, to flee to a foreign land (Exodus 2:15). The list goes on. Your own place of stillness could be having to leave a big field for a smaller one. It could be your friends and family deserting you. It could be your termination from your place of work. It could be losing somebody close to you.

While he was in prison, Joseph was able to interpret dreams that later propelled him into his breakthrough. Moses also received revelations for his next mission. When God takes things away from us, it's not because He hates us. It's also not because He feels we don't deserve those things anymore. No, not so! More often than not, God takes things away from us for our own good. To hear the tiniest of sounds, we would need to be calm and quiet. To hear God, sometimes He secludes us away from everything and brings us into Himself. In the place of stillness, God deals with us. He also humbles us, gives us peace, and reveals more of Himself to us. In the place of stillness, God eventually gives us instructions for our next mission.

Confession: *Heavenly Father, You are good. In the place of stillness, You reveal Yourself more. You also give us clear directions for our next assignment. Should You bring me to my place of stillness, help me recognize the process. I will come out of this phase transformed and ready for future tasks. Amen.*

JULY 2

BEING STILL: A SPIRITUAL DISCIPLINE

But he said to me, "My grace is sufficient for you,
for my power is made perfect in weakness."
2 Corinthians 12:9a

The place of stillness is not someplace to be dreaded but embraced. Personally, the place of stillness taught me the true meaning of humility. It taught me that I'm not entitled to anything but what God gives. It schooled me on how to appreciate all I am given at every moment. The place of stillness let me know everything can be taken from me at any given time. It also taught me how to pay attention, focus, and listen. Most importantly, it taught me that my life is not mine to control. God can do whatever He wills with it.

How do we recognize the place of stillness? We do this when we notice we are struggling more than usual—that is, when our struggles are more than our successes, especially when we are trying too hard. It then looks like we no longer work in grace but hardship. Hence, we become conflicted internally and lose our inner peace. When all these begin to occur, it may be a good time to stop and ask God exactly what is going on. It would also be a good time to step on the brakes and seek God's face before things get worse.

Being still is a spiritual discipline that all God's children need to learn at some point. One key to excelling at this phase is contentment. Sometimes God wants to bring us to a place where we have nothing. He wants to take all our distractions away. This journey is not an easy one, yet it requires a good attitude. Struggling, fighting, or murmuring won't help in any way. Trusting God is key. Possessing a receiving spirit and a listening heart is also required. God will reveal Himself to us as soon as we make ourselves available for Him.

Confession: *Lord Jesus, thank you for calling me Your own. Because I am Yours, I know You may call me into Yourself and away from anything else. I pray for the grace not to struggle during this process. Please help me remain still and patient enough for You to reveal Yourself to me. Amen.*

JULY 3

WHEN ENOUGH IS ENOUGH

Yes, my soul, find rest in God; my hope comes from him.
Psalm 62:5, NIV

While He was on Earth, Christ sometimes withdrew from the crowd. He did this despite the number of people yet to be reached (Luke 5:16). During creation, God rested on the seventh day. He could have still created more things but chose to rest (Genesis 2:2).

Whether we like it not, there will always be things yet to be done. Sometimes, we just may have to pause and say, "Okay for now."

Certain occasions in life warrant the word "enough." One of these times may be when we are extremely stressed out to the point of becoming miserable. Another example may be when other duties start taking the place of family and God. Also, enough has to be enough when we have done all we humanly can about a particular matter at hand. "Enough" is not a word life tells us. It is what we tell life. In today's text, David said to himself, "Yes, my soul, find rest in God." We, also, can say this to ourselves at times.

Confession: *Heavenly Father, Your instruction to me today is that I find my rest in You. I confess that in the past, I sometimes overwork myself. After doing my best, please grant me the grace to let go and get rest. Help me that I do not overwork myself to the point of total depletion. Amen.*

JULY 4

ENJOY IT WHILE YOU CAN

For we brought nothing into this world,
and it is certain we can carry nothing out.
1 Timothy 6:7, KJV

We brought nothing into this world and will take nothing out of it. This Bible verse may be popular, but most people still do not understand it until they are old. For many older people, their thoughts are overwhelmed by either fulfillment or regret. Sadly, the latter is more common.

There are so many reasons people express regrets on their deathbeds. One of these reasons is that they lived their lives laboring for others alone. These people unconsciously lived with the motto "Labor-Labor-Labor" when they could have chosen "Labor-Enjoy-Labor."

Enjoying life is a good thing. It should be deliberately done regularly. Of course, the need to have more is essential, but it's important that we pause and enjoy the fruits of our labor. Acquiring wealth is good, yet if this is all we do, we may end up only piling up stuff for others around us. Leaving inheritances for those coming behind us is fantastic but not if we spend all our lives working toward that. Continuous acquisition of wealth without enjoyment is a one-sided way to live. You only live once. Occasionally, create time to stop, relax, and savor the works of your hands now that you can. A balanced life is key to a happy life.

Confession: *Dear Lord, thank you for the gift of life. Today I pray for the grace to live a balanced life. I do not want to only labor all the days of my life. I also want to enjoy the fruits of my labor. Teach me how to find pleasure in Your blessings. Help me that I do not live a life of regret but one of fulfillment. Amen.*

JULY 5

THE GIFT OF YOUR PRESENCE

Be very careful, then, how you live—
not as unwise but as wise."
Ephesians 5:15, NIV

A survey was conducted where a group of people was asked why they labored extra hard. Some said they do so to give their family comfortable lives, beautiful houses, and more. Some said they do so to give their children a high-quality education. While a few people in this survey said they labor for themselves alone, many of them do it more for those around them.

I fall into the category of those who love to labor for those around them. I remember when I first had my kids; all I wanted to do was give them the best life had to offer. So I prepared myself to do so. But as soon as I stepped out to begin my pursuit, I noticed God did not quite give me the grace I needed. I encountered so many struggles. "Why?" I asked God. He made me understand that the material things—a good education and a big house—I wanted to give my kids were all great, but He wanted me to first give them something more substantial—the gift of myself. It took me a lot of brokenness to understand this, but as soon as I did, my life's priorities and orientation were redefined.

Money and all that it can buy do not guarantee a happy family or well-raised children. Love does. Many times our time and attention are the primary needs of our loved ones. One of the best gifts we can give anyone is the gift of our presence.

Confession: *Dear Lord, this day I ask for Your mercies. For those times I have least prioritized my primary responsibilities, please have mercy. In my pursuit of a better life for my family, please help me find a balance. Please give me the ability and the grace to be present in the lives of those I care for. Amen.*

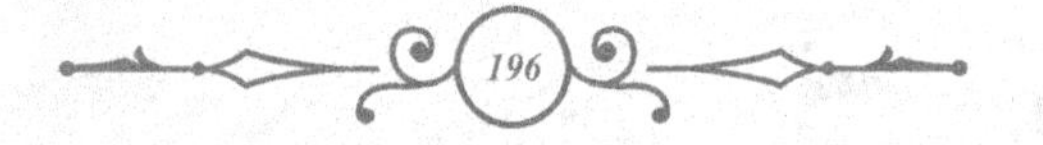

JULY 6

WHERE TRUE CONTENTMENT IS FOUND

For I know the thought that I think towards you, saith the LORD,
thoughts of peace and not evil to give you an expected end.
Jeremiah 29:11, KJV

Material things may fill the void in a human, but this filling will only be temporary. This is the reason man is insatiable and always in search of more. Unfortunately, the more material things we have, the wider the void may become. The void in man can only be filled by God. In grasping this revelation, man can comprehend the need to draw closer to the Maker.

True fulfillment can only be found in God. Material things may bring happiness, but that happiness does not come with a 100% guarantee of wholeness. Only God can ascertain a 100% guarantee on everything. It is in God that we can find satisfaction.

God is interested in every little detail of our lives. His will for us is to live prosperous, peaceful, and joyous lives. His desire is that we live enjoyable and satisfying lives. The only way to key into all that God has for us is by making Him our all in all. God should be the center of our being. The closer we draw to God, the more we will find all we've been searching for. The more we dwell in Him and He in us, the more our emptiness will be filled. Call on Him today. Ask for His leading upon your ways, and watch your life take a turn for the better.

Confession: *Dear Faithful God, I adore You. You are the only true source of contentment. Only in You will I find all I need. In You, I will find wholeness, joy, and abundance. I call on You today. I pray that You will take Your place in my life. I declare that You are the king of my heart. You are my everything. Amen.*

JULY 7

THE BIG PICTURE

Oh, give thanks to the LORD, for he is good,
for his steadfast love endures forever!
Psalm 107:1

A friend of mine was involved in an accident some time ago, and her right hand was injured. For it to heal, she was made to wear a cast on it for a few months. One day, she complained bitterly about how much her left hand hurt. This was because she had to do everything with it as a result of her injured right hand. When I got home, I tried putting myself in my friend's shoes. So I started using my left hand to do most things. In just a few moments, I understood exactly what she was talking about. I was able to relate to how much she must have been hurting from using only one hand. I also went on to try to use one part of my body as opposed to using both. I tried closing one eye and using only the other. I then tried using one leg instead of the two and almost fell, so I had to stop the experiment. That day I realized how blessed I was and how much I had to be thankful for. I also learned to always see the big picture regardless of whatever predicament I may be facing.

The gift of life is a big picture. Being able to walk, read, eat, talk, sit, or use most parts of your body are all big pictures. If you look around you today, I guarantee that you can count ten things to be grateful for—those are the big pictures. We have been blessed with so much. If we would look more at the big picture and less at our everyday worries, we would see that God has been good to us.

Confession: *Dear God, thank you for the gift of life. Today I choose to look at the big picture. I will intentionally count my blessing as I go about my day. You have done so much for me. Even while I'm counting my blessings, I know You will do more. Thank you for Your love. I appreciate You. Amen.*

ATTITUDE

JULY 8

ATTITUDE

So let's not get tired of doing what is good. At just the right time we will reap a harvest of blessing if we don't give up.
Galatians 6:9, NLT

I have studied people for years. Overall, I have observed that there is a certain link between one's attitude and quality of life. Attitude is a person's viewpoint or temper. It can also be defined as the attribute that sustains a person's altitude.

Life is filled with ups and downs as well as smooth and rough times. No one knows what will happen next, and a lot of things in life are beyond our control. A good number of times, nothing prepares us for what life may throw our way. Nonetheless, life is 10% what happens to us and 90% how we react to it. Our attitude toward life will significantly determine our quality of life. Regardless of the hiccups life throws at us, our response makes all the difference.

Now that we have established what attitude means, a few questions still need to be considered: How are attitudes formed in the first place? Is it ever too late to change one's conduct? What do the Scriptures say about this matter? How has attitude been able to break or make individuals in today's world? All these and more are what we will discuss in this series on attitude.

Confession: *Dear Lord, thank You for Your word that has come my way today. Without the right attitude, I cannot go far. Please help me build the right attitude in my work with You and in my daily life. Amen.*

JULY 9

HOW ATTITUDES ARE FORMED

...to be made new in the attitude of your minds.
Ephesians 4:23, NIV

Attitude and behavior are often thought of as being interchangeable. However, there are significant differences between the two terms. Attitude is about what goes on within, while behavior is how the individual expresses that attitude. In short, we could say attitude has a lot to do with the mind, and behavior has much to do with actions. Attitude is originally chosen by observation. This is why an innocent little child will most likely act as he sees others around him or her acting. As humans, it's only natural to feed off our environment. Other attitude-influencing factors include one's beliefs, culture, exposure, temperament, education, and personal experiences.

Today's discussion aims to draw a link between our minds and our behavior. To do this, we need to answer a few somewhat personal questions: What is your own character like as of today? How has your upbringing, environment, or faith influenced your behavior and lifestyle? Has your thinking pattern been a continual source of growth or regression for you? But for your constant thoughts, what heights could you have attained? How have your daily thoughts affected your overall life? What correlation can you draw between your perception toward life and how you act out? These are questions we need to ask ourselves today and always.

According to Proverbs 23:7, "as a man thinks in his heart, so is he." In essence, one's attitude is primarily formed in one's mind.

Confession: *Dear Lord, I am grateful for the gift of another day. As I conduct an attitude check, help me to do so honestly. Search me this day, and help me identify those behaviors that I need to work on. Amen.*

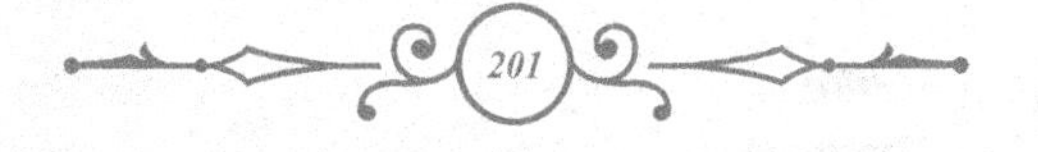

JULY 10

ATTITUDE VS. SUCCESS

You have loved righteousness and hated wickedness. Therefore God, your God, has anointed you with oil of gladness beyond your companions. **Psalm 45:7**

One definition of success is the achievement of something attempted. To attain success, a person doesn't necessarily need to have a positive attitude or be upright. This is why some cheat, liars, thieves, racists, rapists, and even murderers have been able to climb to the top. But the inevitable thing about this set of people is that they eventually come down.

Attitude can sustain someone at the top or drag them down in the future. A bad attitude will catch up with us at some point. A successful person with an ugly character is a time bomb waiting to self-destruct. The greater the success conjoined with a terrible attitude, the greater the fall will be.

God desires that we prosper and be in good health even as our souls prosper (3 John1:2). Today's reference text also describes God's promise to those who live righteously. This promise is gladness. The Bible is all about keeping the right attitude no matter what. The more we do this, the more we will key into heaven's blessings for our lives.

Confession: *Lord, I appreciate Your Word that has come as a reminder of how important attitude is. You have mandated that I keep a good attitude no matter what. Please forgive me for times when I have negatively maneuvered my way in search of success and help me to do better. Amen.*

JULY 11

ATTITUDE VS. TALENT

Do you see a man skillful in his work? He will stand before King; he will not stand before obscure men.
Proverbs 22:29

Talent is God's gift to a person. Naturally, talented people should have some edge over their contemporaries, but I have observed that this is not usually the case. Ironically, the one voted most likely to succeed isn't always the one who is most successful. Several factors can be attributed to this. One of these is attitude. The gifted person who is arrogant, wayward, and lazy is no better than those not as talented with the same traits. In fact, what is being observed is that the average people with great attitudes are taking over in life's races.

It's one thing to be talented. However, how that talent is managed will make all the difference. This is what today's scripture reference pointed out by using the word "skillful." Potential is never and can never be enough. As a talented person, if you wonder why you are not progressing, an attitude change may be all you need. Our attitude will affect every aspect of our lives. Attitude plays a massive role in how high we will soar in life.

Confession: *Lord Jesus, I appreciate Your gifts. I also thank You for how You have been able to help me utilize them. In ways where I have been arrogant and wayward with Your blessings, please forgive me. Teach me to be skillful. Amen.*

JULY 12

ATTITUDE AS A CHOICE

For you have been called to live in freedom, my brothers and sisters. But don't use your freedom to satisfy your sinful nature. Instead, use your freedom to serve one another in love.
Galatians 5:13, NLT

We cannot control all life throws at us, but there is one thing that will always be within our control: our choices. Life is an equal opportunity giver. This fact has been proven by those who have faced awful experiences but still turned out great. This has also been established by those who have had the best things in life yet turned out to be a mess.

Within us lies the power to be whoever we want to be, and this overrides any negative or positive yesterday we might have had. How a person turns out boils down to his or her life choices.

We cannot change yesterday. What we do have within our jurisdiction, however, is the ability to choose the present and future we want. Every day, life presents us with a fresh start. The question is, what kind of today and tomorrow do we desire—an outstanding one or a chaotic one? Our daily attitude will be a significant determinant of that.

Confession: *Father, thank You for the blessings of life. Thank You for the present. I also appreciate yesterday's ordeal. You have used this to mold me into who You want me to be. I know that with You, my future is secure. Amen.*

JULY 13

THE NEED TO CHANGE

...and to be renewed in the spirit of your minds.
Ephesians 4:23

Many factors promote progress in a person's life. Some of these are favorable opportunities, family affluence, education, and more. So why would folks who have all these factors at their fingertips still not progress in life? Perhaps it's because they have a particular defect that keeps pulling them down—a bad attitude.

A bad attitude will not sustain anyone's progress in life. Having established this fact, now is a good time to do some personal soul searching. What are those attitudes you exhibit that have likely held you back in life? What are those things you were born with or picked up that you know are unattractive or can be better? Personally, I would say stubbornness and being too set in my ways, among many things. What about you?

Our attitudes go a long way in defining what our overall lives will turn out to be. We all have aspects of our character that could use some adjustments. The earlier we attempt to get the unpleasant aspects of ourselves fixed, the better it will be for us. Let's look within today and begin noting those distasteful things. Who knows? Maybe an attitude change is all the answered prayers we need for that great life we have been trusting God for.

Confession: *Dear Lord, thank You for all You have surrounded me with. Search me, Jesus. If there are any adjustments I need to make to progress or help my path to heaven, please help me recognize them. As I reflect on my life, help me identify and begin working on my shortcomings. Amen.*

JULY 14

WHAT DO OTHERS SAY?

Work at living in peace with everyone, and work at living a holy life, for those who are not holy will not see the Lord.
Hebrews 12:14, NLT

When it comes to self-examination, most people prefer to do this themselves. However, a better approach would be for others to examine you. The truth is, there is a limit to what we can see ourselves. God designed us like that. Where we cannot see ourselves, we are expected to use a mirror. The people that surround us are our mirrors. They help us see things about us that we may not. We may know ourselves, but we can never know ourselves 100%. There are certain ugly sides of ours that we unintentionally close our eyes to.

Sometimes we have awful habits that we are not conscious of. So when people complain about them, they may have a right to. Besides, everyone cannot be wrong at the same time. If there is a behavior that more than two people keep pointing out, there may be some truth to their claim. Often the problem is not others but you and I. There are times when other people's opinions of us will be inaccurate, but in some cases, others will be correct even if we may not see it that way.

Before disregarding people's opinions about our annoying attitude, let's first check within. Let's carefully search our hearts and determine if there is some truth to it. If there is, then we need to acknowledge the habit and make the needed adjustments.

Confession: *Dear Jesus, Your thoughts toward me are good to give me an expected end. Sometimes I am quick to examine myself, leaving room for my ego. You put people in my life for a reason. Use them to teach me and deal with my heart. Amen.*

JULY 15

CHANGE BRINGS ABOUT CHANGE

For I can do everything through Christ, who gives me strength.
Philippians 4:13, NLT

We have all had insufferable people we feel stuck with. These may include our parents, siblings, friends, or anyone we cannot easily ignore. It may even appear like these people have made it their mission to drain our energy as they keep doing things that upset us. No matter how much we complain and ask them to change their attitude, they just seem to keep it up. We pray and hope people change their irritating attitudes, but they don't. What do we do then? Well, we may have to be the ones to change.

I used to get so worked up by the attitudes of some of my loved ones. On some days, I could get so agitated that I would let their annoying ways ruin my entire day. But at some point, the Holy Spirit made me realize that my approach was not the best. Letting other's negative attitudes infuriate me won't make them change. The Holy Spirit also made me understand that for there to be any difference, I would have to change my approach. So I did. I stopped my usual yelling and nagging. I chose not to get worked up as I used to. If I had something to say, I did so calmly. I resolved to be more patient and understanding. I also started praying to God for peace and tranquility. Then things began changing as I started seeing significant changes in those I never thought could do so.

Sometimes all it takes for others to improve is devising a different course of action. Change brings about change. If you long to see a transformation in others, begin by being the change. Nothing changes if nothing changes.

Confession: Lord, thank You for Your word that has come my way today. I acknowledge that sometimes I find change difficult. Strengthen me to improve where I need to. Teach me how to relate better with those around me. Amen.

JULY 16

BAD COMPANY CORRUPTS

Do not be misled: "Bad company corrupts good character."
1 Corinthians 15:33, NIV

I met someone who seemed very impressive at upon first meeting her. After a while, I noticed that whenever I knew I was going to see her or speak with her, I would start getting anxious. The reason was simple: This lady, although charming, was also an energy drainer. She would complain about everything and everyone. She would always insist on having the last say. Nothing could ever pass her by. She was so sensitive that even a little joke would come off as offensive to her. She just had this negative energy around her that was contagious. Whenever I spent time with her, I ended up feeling tired from overexplaining and pleading. One day I decided to shift from "hoping not to see her" to deliberately exempting her from my plans.

Show me your friend, and I'll tell you who you are. Some may call this saying a cliché, and it may be, but it still holds true. Anyone who chooses to become friends with a crazy person may likely end up crazy too. Life really is too short to waste around those with negative attitudes and vibes. We may be obligated to put up with some unbearable ones with whom we are stuck with, like our family members. But for those who are not that close, we are not obliged to keep them within our circle of influence. In fact, if all they do is provoke us, we are to run away from them as far as our legs can take us.

The Bible is clear on this issue: Evil communication corrupts good manners. Simply put, bad company can ruin the goodness of a man.

Confession: *Lord, I thank You for today's words. In this life's journey, please channel the right people in my direction. May those who surround me challenge me to succeed. Grant me the grace to discern bad company that will derail me from Your purpose. Amen.*

JULY 17

KEEP YOUR ATTITUDE

Do not be conformed to this world, but be transformed by the renewal of your mind, that by testing you may discern what is the will of God, what is good and acceptable and perfect. **Romans 12:2**

There are certain things that life or other people should never be able to take from us. One of these is our good attitude. Life is in the habit of throwing us difficult punches. This tends to make us question whether being kind is really worth it. As a matter of fact, it would seem that those with vile attitudes are the ones making it further in life. Also, it's no longer common for good manners to be rewarded or celebrated by the world. Why, then, does one still need to maintain a good attitude?

We are to be virtuous because, first, this is what God wants from us. More so, every day we display our good character, we win against the world. Should we let the world corrupt and change us, then the world wins. Yes, we may look gullible, and others may even call us naive. But the moment we give in to the pressure is the moment we begin to lose parts of ourselves. In truth, it's easier to keep a lousy character than a good one. But will taking the easy way out bring us the joy and fulfillment found in Christ Jesus? Certainly not. Never let people change you from being the upright person you are. Always aim to be the best version of yourself. In due time, your outstanding character will speak for you. A good attitude will yield worthy fruits in the long run.

Confession: *Dear Holy Spirit, I appreciate Your dealings with me. You see my heart. You know I always want to do right by God, but sometimes I find it challenging to do so. Today I receive the grace for righteousness no matter what the world celebrates. Amen.*

JULY 18

THE PRUNING PROCESS

He cuts off every branch of mine that doesn't produce fruit, and he prunes the branches that do bear fruit so they will produce even more.
John 15:2, NLT

Not everyone is meant to be in our lives for a prolonged time. While a few people are destined to stay with us for a lifetime, others are supposed to be with us for a season. The mistake people make is offering seasonal people permanent roles. One way to live satisfactorily is by regularly checking our lives. We need to prune those who hold spots in them often. Some of those we need to prune are time-wasters and those that bring little or no value to our existence. Also, folks with negative energy and leeches should be clipped off. Finally, those that wish to exit our lives should be free to do so.

The pruning process involves cutting away unproductive, weak, and dying branches. It also involves deliberately shedding all unnecessary weight. When we regularly trim whom and what we give our attention to, we become lighter. Frequent pruning helps us maintain focus. That way, we can keep our eyes on essential assignments as opposed to flimsy ones. This act helps us value our time more. It also helps us fully understand our own worth. We do not need others to complete us, for we are already complete in Christ Jesus. The more we practice pruning in our relationships, the more we will find ourselves living a life of peace.

Confession: *Dear Lord, I love You, and I only want to live for You. Please prune every branch that is not bearing good fruit. I want to fulfill all I have been assigned to on Earth. Help me shed off all unnecessary weight that is tying me down. Amen.*

JULY 19

THE PROUD ATTITUDE

And he gives grace generously. As the Scriptures say,
"God opposes the proud but gives grace to the humble."
James 4:6, NLT

A proud person is a know-it-all, fault-finding, self-absorbed, and defensive person. A proud person feels he or she is better than everyone and answerable to no one. Also, one prominent trait of this person is overconfidence. God encourages us to be confident. However, what irritates Him is pride. Proverbs 8:13b says, "Pride and arrogance and the way of evil and perverted speech I hate."

The word "opposes," as used in today's reference text, means to disapprove of or resist someone. Therefore, we can conclude that God doesn't just hate proud people. He is very much at war with them. A good example is Nebuchadnezzar's story as described in Daniel 4.

Today's devotional is a wake-up call to some of us who honestly acknowledge that we exhibit arrogance. From time to time, our flesh naturally may swing in the pride direction, even if we do not mean for it to. Today let us go back to God in humility. Let's ask for His forgiveness. Once we do this, God will hear us and draw us into His embrace once again.

Confession: *Dear God, thank You for the gift of another day.*
You hate the proud and bless the humble. Please search my heart today.
Should I exhibit pride-like attitudes, please help me deal with them.
Let me never display habits that will make you be at war with me. Amen.

JULY 20

THE CONFIDENT PERSON

For God hath not given us the spirit of fear;
but of power, and of love and of a sound mind.
2 Timothy 1:7, KJV

To gain respect and attention, one doesn't necessarily have to be smart, honest, or likable. Sometimes just one thing is required: confidence. The devil has a good understanding of how confidence or the lack of confidence impacts human beings. No wonder it seems like unbelievers manipulate this skill in promoting worldliness. In fact, it would appear that believers are being bullied into the shadows while perversion is taking over.

Being confident is all about calm and composure. It is about confronting unacceptable situations with wisdom. It is about taking a stand, apologizing when wrong, and being responsible. It is also about being decisive and standing by our beliefs no matter what. Confidence involves trusting God to see us through every junction of our lives. The confident ones listen more and speak with intelligence.

If we haven't yet, it's high time we developed this attitude. This will help us push forward in our daily endeavors and our service to Christ.

Confession: *Dear Jesus, thank You for all that You have deposited in me. My confidence is in You. Help me find this confidence today. Henceforth, I refuse to be timid. I choose to hold my head high and take hold of all that is mine. Amen.*

JULY 21

THE CONTENTMENT ATTITUDE

But godliness with contentment is great gain.
1 Timothy 6:6

Envy is longing to have something belonging to another. Jealousy can be defined as hostility toward another who may be more successful. Jealousy and envy are often accompanied by bitterness and covetousness. A jealous person may not necessarily want what another has, but an envious person may not be able to take his or her eyes off the possessions of another.

A life of envy and jealousy is one lived in bondage. I have seen it ruin lives—the rich, educated, powerful, and even Christians. So I pray daily for grace never to indulge in such thoughts. By the special grace of God, I am growing into one who is always happy for others. Through the dealing of the Holy Spirit, I have learned that what others have belongs to them. God will give me whatever is mine in due season.

No one has a perfect life. We all have our battles. When we compare other people's good to our own bad, we are not being fair to ourselves. Today let's choose to ask for God's mercies to help us remain content and appreciative of all that we have. A contented person is a happy person, and a heart filled with contentment is a liberated one.

Confession: *Dear God, thank You for Your blessings. You have given so much, even more than I have asked. My life is a miracle, so I should not be jealous or envious of other's blessings. I am content in You, and I'm thankful for all You've done. Amen.*

JULY 22

PARENTS TO KIDS ON ATTITUDE

Train up a child in the way he should go;
even when he is old, he will not depart from it.
Proverbs 22:6

One of the best gifts anyone can give a child is the gift of proper training. Proper training goes hand in hand with having a good attitude. Kids love recitations. Below is an attitude definition by Amanda Morin we can have our kids read often. Before reading each sentence of the ATTITUDE acronym, the child who is reciting should say his or her name. For instance, "Tony, always sees the good in a situation."

Always sees the good in a situation
Tries to find solutions to problems
Takes time to appreciate the little things
Is happy with what he/she has
Takes responsibility for his/her actions
Understands the need to listen to other people's opinions and thoughts
Does not complain too often
Enjoys life

Inheritances, an expensive education, and fun experiences are great, but the gift of a positive attitude sticks with children throughout their lifetimes. Let's teach our young ones to be the salt of their world. As their guardians, let's also show them by example what it means to have a positive attitude always. In doing this, we will create a better world.

Confession: *Thank you for the children you have placed in my path. Teach me how to coach these precious ones. Open their hearts to receive the instructions You have for them through me. Amen.*

LIFE IS BEAUTIFUL

JULY 23

LIFE IS BEAUTIFUL

...casting all your anxieties on him,
because he cares for you.
1 Peter 5:7

Life can assume so many things. More importantly, life assumes whatever name is given to it. Some see life as a boxing ring, so they go about in their gloves, ready to throw punches. Some see life as tough, hard, complicated, depressing, and unfair, and they have found life responding to them in the same manner. Many, however, see life as friendly, exciting, and favorable. Life in return has never failed to smile at them. More often than not, what we perceive life to be is exactly what we get from life.

What is life to you as an individual? When you think about man and existence in general, what comes to mind? What exactly does it mean that one gets from life what one expects from life? Is it possible for one to live a life completely free from hiccups? Does life play fair? If life is truly beautiful, how can one key into this? What are certain vital things one needs to watch for in this adventure called life? All these and more are what we will explore under the new theme, "Life Is Beautiful."

Confession: *Dear Lord, thank you for the gift of life.*
I owe everything I am to You. Today I declare life as awesome and beautiful.
I no longer see life as a struggle. I am joyous.
I will enjoy my life to the fullest, so help me, God. Amen.

JULY 24

INNER PEACE

For unto us a Child is born, to us a son is given; and the government shall be upon his shoulder, and his name shall be called Wonderful Counselor, Mighty God, Everlasting Father, Prince of Peace.
Isaiah 9:6

Every person is made up of a spirit, soul, and body. In every person, a void is also present. This space was put there by God. The primary purpose of this void is spiritual communication, but how we fill this void is what brings about a peaceful or turbulent mind.

Inner peace can be described as a state of calmness and deep contentment. It is a state of wholeness. This is one attribute that even life's challenges can never take away. Inner peace is what every human aspires to have. However, in the everyday pursuit of this peace, many don't even know that this is what they are looking for. Many have searched all over for this peace. But because they've been searching in the wrong places, they have yet to find it.

True inner peace has only one source. According to today's text, this source is our Lord Jesus, who is the Prince of Peace. But how can we fully obtain this peace from Jesus? What kind of peace does Jesus have in store for His beloved? This and more is what we will discuss next.

Confession: *Lord Jesus, You are great. I have searched far and wide for peace but have found nothing satisfying. You are the only true source of peace. Today I take hold of the calm and inner joy found in You. Amen.*

JULY 25

INNER PEACE PART II

Peace I leave with you; my peace I give you. I do not give to you as the world gives. Do not let your hearts be troubled and do not be afraid.
John 14:27, NIV

Today's text was Jesus' words to those around Him moments before His death on the cross. For one facing a death sentence, what would be expected are fear and anxiety. Instead, Jesus was at peace. He also promised to give His kind of peace to the world.

People are naturally calm when everything is going well. What Jesus is promising is quite different. Jesus' peace is a deeper kind. It is a permanent kind of peace. Regardless of circumstances, it never wavers. It's joy during difficulties and calm during life's storm.

There is a level of joy that comes with being at peace. It's the joy that can only be given by the Lord Himself. This joy can be yours too, should you desire it. All you have to do is accept Jesus into your life if you haven't already. If you've already accepted Christ into your life but still desire inner peace, ask Him today. Jesus is always willing to give beyond what you seek. Attaining inner peace is possible, and so many believers are living witnesses to this.

Confession: *Lord Jesus, Your peace passes all understanding. Thank you for blessing the world with Your rest. I ask that You come into my life today. Please be my peace and joy. Amen.*

JULY 26

BLESSINGS WITHHELD

Two things I request of You (Deprive me not before I die): Remove falsehood and lies far from me; Give me neither poverty nor riches – feed me with the food You prescribe for me; Lest I be full and deny You, And say, "Who is the LORD?" Or lest I be poor and steal, And profane the name of my God. **Proverbs 30:7–9, NKJV**

Sometimes it may seem as if God is not answering our prayers for being blessed with more material things. The reason for this may be because of today's text. Not many of us can handle God's big blessings. Therefore, God may choose to withhold them.

How do you react when God blesses you? Do we see a different person with a different attitude altogether? To see some in their pure element, just wait until they come by extra wealth. These people may become completely unrecognizable. They may even become inaccessible. They may talk differently, walk differently, and act like they own the world. Every shred of humility flies out the window! Some won't even attend church anymore because of answered prayers. Are you someone like this? Please search yourself today.

The Bible explains in Luke 16:10 that he that is faithful in little will be faithful in much. Eventually, you may realize that the reason God has yet to grant your heart's desire is for your own good. He may not want to give you that which you cannot handle yet. So are you one who has exhibited arrogant attitudes toward God's blessings in the past? Please ask for God's mercy today. Ask that the Holy Spirit will teach you to have a better attitude toward God's provisions. May heaven's gate open, and may God's blessings continually pour upon us all. Amen.

Confession: *Dear Lord, please have mercy on me. For those times when I have distanced myself from You, please forgive me. Your blessings should draw me closer and not away from You. Give me the grace to handle all the blessings that come my way. Holy Spirit, help me remain humble no matter how successful I become. Amen.*

JULY 27

PERFECT?

He who is of a proud heart stirs up strife,
but he who trusts in the LORD will be prospered.
Proverbs 28:25, NKJV

Are we perfect? Although our answer is probably no, don't we all act like we are?

Some time ago, I had a misunderstanding with someone. However, I refused to reason with the person or consider that I might be the one at fault. This was because I was "his benefactor" (or so I thought). I wouldn't hear of any grievance he had. In fact, I took offense to the fact that this young man would dare say that I offended him after all I had done for him. I wasn't even concerned with what caused the misunderstanding in the first place. I was just mad at him for being ungrateful.

Many of us act like this—like we can never be wrong. We only see things our way, and if we have people benefiting from us, we feel we should be their small god. We believe that others have no right to pick offenses or express their hurt feelings. This is wrong. We are not perfect, and we can never be right 100% of the time. Sometimes we offend people, and they have every right to express their feelings. We should actually encourage them to. Our assistants, employees, kids, and others may be under us, but that doesn't make us their god. When people express their grievances, let's attempt to look into the issue. If wrong, let's apologize and move on. This is the maturity expected of us as Christians. This act also promotes healthy relationships.

Confession: *Lord Jesus, no one is perfect but You. As a human, I know I have my flaws and weaknesses. When others complain about my attitude, I pray that I will be humble enough to say I'm sorry. Amen.*

JULY 28

EXISTING VS. LIVING

You make known to me the path of life; in your presence there is fullness of joy; at your right hand are pleasures forevermore.
Psalm 16:11

The words living and existing are often seen as interchangeable. However, there are significant differences between them.

- To exist means to be present on Earth like every other thing. It means to occupy space, use up resources, and spend every day observing the same routine. To live, on the other hand, means to be alive and excited about life. It means to contribute to the planet, explore it, and impact the world.
- People who exist merely kill time by doing nothing or mundane things. They hardly have a vision for the future. All they work toward is getting by each day, putting no plan in motion for a better tomorrow. These people are passive and would settle for anything and everything. But those who live do so to the fullest. They possess directions to ensure a progressive life. These people always strive to make a difference.
- For the ones who exist, everything begins and ends in this world. But those who live do so with heaven in view.

Life is more beautiful and exciting when we live and don't just exist. Life is more fulfilling when we choose to live to the fullest, holding nothing back. Let's begin living today.

Confession: *Heavenly Father, You created me not to only exist but to live. I matter. I am not just in the world to occupy space. I pray today that my life will count for much. I will live fully to Your glory. My days here on Earth will be fruitful. I will live daily with heaven in view. Amen.*

JULY 29

NOTHING TO HIDE, NOTHING TO FEAR

The LORD will keep you from all harm—he will watch over your life.
Psalm 121:7, NIV

Those who need heavy artillery for protection may be those in power, the wealthy ones, celebrities, or those who have something to hide. Why are those who have something to hide often scared of being harmed by others? Maybe it's because these people feel like others are out to get them. Or maybe it's because they have directly or indirectly done harm to another.

It is a wicked world, no doubt. The innocent get hurt and killed every day. But something I have come to observe is that our God is just, especially toward His elect. Those that worship God in truth, love their neighbors, and do right by others will always have heaven's backing.

Are you one who does your best in living right but easily gets frightened? Please be assured today that evil will not prevail against you. Your fears are only tools the devil is using to keep you in bondage. This bondage will be broken once you commit your fears into the hands of God. But if you still carry guilt as a result of past wrongdoings, now would be a good time to make amends. Finally, for those that do not fall into any of these categories, please continue enjoying the beautiful life God has blessed you with.

Confession: *Dear Lord, You are my shield and fortress. Only in You will I find absolute protection. Please have mercy on me for the times I have done things that have stolen my peace. I long for a free mind. I do not want to live with the thought of people being after me. Give me the grace to make restitution where I need to. Amen.*

JULY 30

DECLUTTERING YOUR LIFE

John replied, "If you have two shirts, give one to the poor. If you have food, share it with those who are hungry."
Luke 3:11, NLT

Many of us have what we need, what we want, and duplicates. We may even term some stuff as "just in case" or "that will be useful in the future." Some of us have gadgets, clothing, accessories, and stuff we haven't touched in months or even years. If we haven't used them in a long time, chances are that we may never use them. Accumulation of unused things is what primarily causes clutter.

Today we are being encouraged to declutter our lives. Having too many things can sometimes choke us, leading to suffocation. And suffocation may lead to death. A person may not die physically, but they may just stop loving life. This is similar to dying inside. If you are one who doesn't enjoy going to your home or office, please check again to be sure it is not because you feel choked. Choking may also arise from having too many friends, engagements, meetings, and so on.

I suggest you keep the needed but shove the "just in case" and duplicates into a box and throw them away. You may also choose to sell them or give them away because you really do not need them (even if you feel you do). In doing this, you create more breathing space for yourself. You also provide a more refreshed and peaceful life for yourself.

Confession: *Lord Jesus, thank You for Your blessings. One way I know I can live freely is by decluttering my spaces. But I sometimes find this challenging. I do not want to be choked by stuff I own anymore. I want to live every day with a refreshed mindset and environment. Help me, Lord. Amen.*

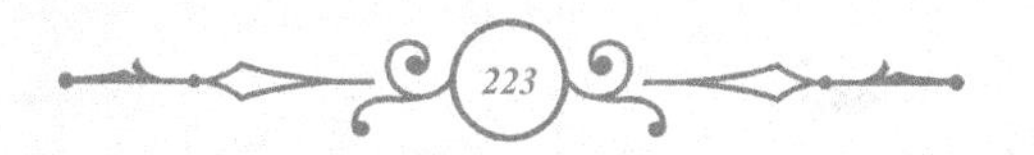

JULY 31

MEDDLING

He who passes by and meddles in a quarrel not his own is like one who takes a dog by the ears.
Proverbs 26:17, NKJV

To meddle means to interfere in something that is none of our business! A good percentage of the problems we face in this life is because of meddling.

It may be difficult sometimes not to help others solve their problems. However, we must understand that not all fights are our fight. There are some issues that require us to intervene. Yet there are other situations where completely staying away from the situation is the best thing to do. To emphasize today's text, if you pull a dog's ear, he may bite you. Even innocent-looking dogs do that. In essence, let sleeping dogs lie.

In our consistent work with the Holy Spirit, we sometimes hear Him tell us to keep quiet and stay away from some issues. Yes, we mean well and feel like we can help fix that person's situation. We may also feel we can help two people settle their issues. However, we need God at all times to help us discern between helping out and meddling. Besides those already mentioned, there are other reasons why we shouldn't always stick our noses in other people's issues. One is because our interference may worsen an already terrible situation. Another is that one shouldn't be too nosy or engrossed with other people's problems. We've all got our issues, and these should be dealt with first.

Confession: *I know I should be a source of help, but I also know that it is not every issue that I need to meddle in. Lord Jesus, please grant me a discerning spirit. From here on out, help me never to get ahead of myself with other people's issues. Help me learn how to mind my own businesses when the situation calls for it. Amen.*

AUGUST 1

TRAVELING LIGHT

Don't you realize that in a race everyone runs,
but only one person gets the prize? So run to win!
1 Corinthians 9:24, NLT

I have heard people say it's wise to travel light when taking a trip. The same advice may be applicable to life. Life is a journey. We may all have similar destinations, but we likely take different routes. Whatever route we take, it is vital that we journey light. We need not overburden ourselves with unnecessary weight. Examples of burdens may include little things like an overstuffed kitchen or closet. It could also include having time-wasting friends, unproductive engagements, or excessive social media usage.

Events can be categorized into four basic groups: (1) urgent, (2) urgent but unimportant, (3) important but not urgent, (4) not important and not urgent. Before giving time, money, and energy to something, first categorize it. After this, you can give the matter the appropriate attention it deserves.

If it's urgent, then deal with it is as such. If it's important but not urgent, then it can wait while you deal with the urgent stuff. If it is not important and not urgent, you may choose not to even attend to it at all. Things that do not concern us should be paid little or no attention. Things we feel we want but may not necessarily need should be carefully considered. Let's always remember that how far we travel in life depends on our everyday choices. If you want a smooth trip through life, I suggest you keep it simple.

Confession: *Heavenly Father, You have blessed me with a beautiful life. I want to live purposefully. My time is precious, and I will treat it as such. Time wasters and unimportant things will no longer steal my energy. I will strive to engage in fruitful activities. Amen.*

AUGUST 2

WHAT WE PERMIT WILL CONTINUE

Then, going over to the people who sold doves, he told them, "Get these things out of here. Stop turning my Father's house into a marketplace!"
John 2:16, NIV

Many folks would rather murmur and complain about a situation than do something about it. Until we take a stand and decide to stop accepting certain things, those things may never change. Life is beautiful, but permitting improper attitudes from others all in the name of "keeping the peace" or "being polite" won't let us enjoy life to the fullest.

Employees won't stop acting unprofessionally if their jobs keep permitting them to. Many people in relationships will be treated poorly until they demand otherwise. Sometimes those paid to provide services may not do so efficiently until it is demanded of them. The list goes on.

Today's discussion hardly suggests that we should be unaccommodating because of a few inconveniences. Far from it! We should be very accommodating. Nonetheless, we shouldn't have to subject our everyday life to unnecessary hardships. According to today's text, Jesus put His foot down and demanded better from those who disregarded His Father's house. We also can and should demand better from unacceptable situations. Let's never forget that what we permit will continue.

Confession: *Dear Father, thank You for Your word today. I decree henceforth that I will no longer tolerate unacceptable behaviors. Lead me, Holy Spirit. Please give the right words that will evoke positive changes in others. Teach me when and how to put my feet down and demand better from others as the situation calls for it. Amen.*

AUGUST 3

SAYING NO

Let what you say be simply 'Yes' or 'No';
anything more than this comes from evil.
Matthew 5:37

I have observed from daily interactions that it is easier to say yes than no. Some people say yes as opposed to saying no because they always want to appear nice. Some say yes to every request because they do not want to be impolite or offensive. Some always say yes because of their need for approval and also because they cannot bear to disappoint others. Many people say yes because they cannot stand the guilt that often follows saying no. And others say yes because they are people-pleasers. These are just some of the reasons people say yes with their mouths but no with their hearts.

One of the most liberating experiences anyone can have in this life is mastering how to say no. As simple as the two-letter word "no" sounds, it is a powerful word. I believe this word exists to simplify every individual's existence and manage life's stress. A good number of people that claim to be under pressure are not always there by necessity. Many put themselves in this situation by giving others permission to pressure them.

Saying no to others means saying yes to yourself. Saying no to unnecessary stress and people means saying yes to your happiness. Saying no to mediocre things means saying yes to greater things. Mastering this act is not as terrifying as it often seems. How to go about saying no is what we will consider next.

Confession: *Dear Lord, thank You for today's word of wisdom. I don't need to engage in every activity. Also, I don't have to say yes to every request. I confess that I sometimes struggle with saying no. I pray that You will grant me the strength to say no when I need to. Give me a better understanding of the appropriate usage of this word. Amen.*

AUGUST 4

WHEN TO SAY NO

I can do all things through Christ who strengthens me.
Philippians 4:13, NKJV

There are times when you may want to think about a matter or get back to someone concerning something. But there are other times when you must say no without mincing words. These times include: (1) when your niceness is being taken for granted; (2) when you are feeling unduly stressed, abused, or smothered; (3) when you are being asked to go against your beliefs; and (4) when you know that the path is clearly not God's plan for your life.

The word "no" should be said to bad people with bad intentions. It should also be said to good people with bad intentions. More so, you should say no to good people with good intentions that do not fit into your plans. Prophecies and counsels should be weighed and tested before being accepted.

After your relationship with God, the next most important relationship is the one you have with yourself. The constant habit of saying yes to others to your own detriment could have a crippling effect on your relationship with yourself. This is why many people do not like themselves. There is a time for everything in life. Certain occasions will arise where the only befitting response is NO.

Confession: *Dear Lord, with You, I can do everything. Today I ask for the power to be firm. I no longer want to say yes to requests that do not serve me or Your purpose for my life. To fulfill my purpose here on Earth, I know I must say no to some requests brought my way. To hear You, I know I may need to close my ears to others. Please help me. Amen.*

AUGUST 5

HOW TO SAY NO

But above all, my brothers, do not swear, either by heaven or by earth or by any other oath, but let your "yes" be yes and your "no"" be no, so that you may not fall under condemnation. **James 5:12**

Today's devotional is dedicated to those of us who have a phobia of confrontation or saying no to others. Previously, we established instances where we certainly must say no. But how do we go about this and still maintain amicable relationships with others? The following points should be able to furnish us with some ideas. If we truly must say no, then we should:

- First, listen attentively without interruption to all that is being said.
- Say no with reasons (if need be), but be brief about it.
- Say no politely and gracefully.
- Never lie or make unrealistic promises in an attempt to redeem the relationship.
- Entertain no room for guilt, especially if you have done the right thing.

Another thing that could further assist us in saying no is being selectively available. Let's understand that saying no is okay. At the end of the day, it's our lives. Whatever we make of it is up to us. We are the only ones who will give account for our lives when we return to God.

Confession: F*ather, I know I sometimes have to say no. Please grant me the courage to do so as the occasion demands it. Saying no to others helps me say yes to You and Your will for my life. Irrelevant activities will no longer have priority in my life. Whatever does not favor Your plans for my life, I will say no to from now on. Amen.*

AUGUST 6

SELF-CARE

Beloved, I pray that you may prosper in all things
and be in health, just as your soul prospers.
3 John 1:2, NKJV

Many women work tirelessly taking care of their families. They allocate 99% of their resources and life to making sure everyone around them is happy. A lot of men also do likewise. These people make it a duty to do nice things for others, which is great. But do they also do nice things for themselves? Rarely.

Many are quick to care for everyone but themselves. All they do is fix other people's problems and make certain others are well nurtured. A lot of these people assume their absence would only result in everything falling apart, so they are always doing everything by themselves, making sure nothing is out of place. Are you like this as well?

Those who usually feel indispensable are not, because humans adapt. As soon as a person is out of the picture, those around that person somehow adjust to living fully again. Adjusting may take a while, but once they have been able to acclimate well, they will continue living their lives. This lets us know that no one is all-powerful but God. No one is indispensable. Serving others is important, but let's also seek to find a balance. Let's care for ourselves too. Only when we are well taken care of will we be able to effectively care for others. Do for yourself as you do for others. You also deserve nice things.

Confession: *Heavenly Father, thank you for making me in Your image. You call me Your temple. Please have mercy for the times when I have neglected to care for Your temple adequately. While I am to care for others, I know I am also to care for myself. Teach me how to live a balanced life. Amen.*

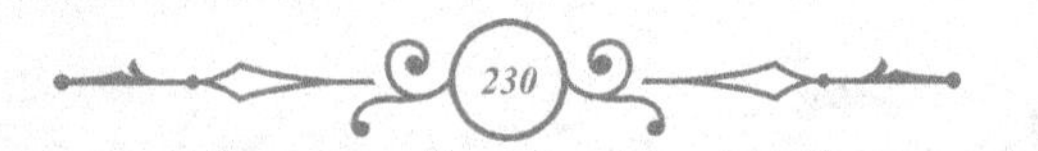

AUGUST 7

SELF-ACCEPTANCE

And we know that in all things God works for the good of those who love him, who have been called according to his purpose.
Romans 8:28, NIV

Not everyone is equal in life, and not everyone can be. This was done on purpose so a balance can be created. For instance, if everyone were to be CEOs, then there would be no one to be secretaries, janitors, reporters, soldiers, and all the other careers that support the community. Life is more like a jigsaw puzzle. For it to make any kind of sense, the different edges with various sizes must be filled in accurately.

The first step for anyone who desires the best out of life is self-acceptance. Long ago, I accepted who I was and what I was. I wasn't going to be anyone else besides who God had created me to be. I wasn't going to be this person or that person no matter how hard I tried, so why not just be me? The more I accepted "me," the easier life became. I remember feeling so relieved as soon as I started dropping all of the unnecessary weight that came with wanting to be another.

The question today is, who are you? Remember the jigsaw puzzle? You can only fit into the scheme of life when you bring in the correct edge and size of "you." Trying so hard to be someone else only builds pressure. Believe me, it's not worth it. Every other person is taken, so why not accept the only person left—you. Give yourself the chance to be who God has truly created you to be. Close your ears to the external noise, and search deep within you to find out what God's calling on your life is. Then pursue that calling with all your might, and watch the joy and fulfillment that will follow you.

Confession: *Dear God, thank you for making me exactly the way I am. I am content with who I am in you. As You reveal your calling on my life to me, give me the strength to pursue and achieve all I have been created to do. Amen.*

AUGUST 8

•••

CHECK YOUR COUNSELOR'S LIFE AGAIN

Whoever walks with the wise becomes wise,
but the companion of fools will suffer harm.
Proverbs 13:20

Of course we should receive counsel. The question is, from whom?

I remember a particular day when someone who meant well gave me counsel. I thought the counsel was excellent and was about to carry it out only for the Holy Spirit to stop me. The Holy Spirit asked me to look at my counselor's life. He asked me if that's where I would like to be in the near future. After thinking hard, I realized that this counselor and I were not headed toward the same path. Heeding her advice would most likely be detrimental to my journey in life. So I repented and asked God for the right path. Then God showed me the way—my way. Thank goodness!

In the multitude of counsel, there is safety, no doubt. There are times when we need to confide in or receive advice from someone. But at those moments, we need to be very careful that we don't go seeking counsel in the wrong places. At the least, let's try to turn to those who are trusted leaders in society or those with whom we share the same faith. Married folks should be careful about receiving counsel from those who are not. They should be especially cautious of advice from those whose marriages are in chaos. Christians should also be cautious about receiving counsel from unbelievers.

Confession: *Dear Lord, thank You for Your wisdom. When seeking counsel, help me to never look for it in the wrong place and with the wrong person. May I never carry out foolish counsel that would negatively impact my life. Please order my steps. Teach me how to discern and disregard counsel that is wrong for me. Amen.*

AUGUST 9

THE HOLY SPIRIT IS THE BEST COUNSELOR

But the Helper (Comforter, Advocate, Intercessor – Counselor, Strengthener, Standby), the Holy Spirit, whom the Father will send in My name (in My place to represent Me and act on My behalf), He will teach you all things. And He will help you remember everything I have told you. ***John 14:26, AMP***

God speaks through people to us, but the purest, unedited, and most authentic counsel can only come from the Holy Spirit. If we desire to receive satisfying counsel, then it would be in our best interests to make the Holy Spirit our primary counselor.

When we make the Holy Spirit our primary counselor, wrong counsel will be countered. Furthermore, counsel from others will only act as confirmation of what has been previously laid on our hearts by the Holy Spirit. So instead of just blindly doing all that our counselor has asked us to do, we will do what God is leading us to do.

Are you wondering how you can directly receive from the Holy Spirit? Well, first you must understand God's method of communicating with you. God uses various means to interact with different people. So which method do you think God uses to speak to you? Always remember, the Holy Spirit is accessible and never judges. The Holy Spirit advises accurately. Let's endeavor to primarily seek God's face for sensitive and life-changing matters. Even little issues should always be brought to God's attention first.

Confession: *Holy Spirit, You are the one true counselor. In seeking You, I know I will get the necessary and life-promoting counsel I need. Please come into my life today. Teach me how to hear from You. Give me a listening ear and a yielding heart to Your instruction. Amen.*

AUGUST 10

RELATIONSHIPS TO AVOID

And now, dear brothers and sisters, we give you this command in the name of our Lord Jesus Christ: Stay away from all believers who live idle lives and don't follow the tradition they received from us.
2 Thessalonians 3:6, NLT

Some time ago I met someone who was incredibly charming upon first meeting. But upon getting to know him, I noticed he possessed one undeniable trait: self-absorption. This man was basically in love with himself and himself alone. It was like the world revolved around him. Everything was all about him. This person exhibited habits common to those with narcissistic personality disorder.

What are narcissists? Narcissists are the rather self-absorbed, self-centered ones. These people can also be called takers. They are parasites, and like true parasites, they feed on their host and damage them. They like to be on top, so they do everything they can to pull down those they are in relationships with. They lack empathy and also possess insane needs for admiration. Those that get close to these people end up feeling exhausted. I, for one, ended up being drained from being friends with a narcissist. I eventually had to end the relationship.

It is true that God says to love everybody. However, there are certain people we must love from afar for the sake of our peace of mind. We must be cautious with those we move close to or those we let come close to us. People whose attitudes tilt too much to the extreme may be tolerated but not so much that they end up draining the life out of us. People whose primary job is to pull us down so they can be on top should be kept at arm's length. People that only take and never give back should not be prioritized in our relationships. We must also stay away from people whose sole purpose is to derail us from making it to heaven. Life is beautiful, but to enjoy it to the fullest, some people must be avoided. Period!

Confession: *Dear Lord, thank you for Your word that has come my way today. I want to live happily. But in doing so, I know that I may have to stay away from damaging relationships. Teach me how to love everyone. Also, teach me how to stay away from those that will only fill my life with hurt and pain. Amen.*

AUGUST 11

SAFETY IS OF THE LORD

So neither he who plants nor he who waters is anything,
but only God who gives the growth.
1 Corinthians 3:7

It's interesting the lengths to which we'll go to provide security for ourselves only for that same security to be breached. Despite letdowns, many of us still don't learn that safety is of the Lord.

Death takes the poor and also the rich. Sickness befalls both the privileged and the less privileged. But for God, no one is off limits to harm. No matter what class a person falls under, that person is still subject to life's challenges. No one has been created that cannot be brought down in this life.

That child, car, home, job, or position is only safely kept by the Lord. Of course we are to play our own role by obtaining appropriate security measures but not so much that we place our faith primarily in our own man-made safety measures. Where a man's strength stops is where God's begin. The only one that can guarantee a man's complete well-being is God, our Maker. With Him, we are preserved. In Him, we are protected.

Confession: *Father, only in You will I find absolute safety. It is only You who can guard me and mine. For those times when I have taken matters of my safety into my hands, leaving You out of it, I repent today. Please protect me and my household. Amen.*

AUGUST 12

THE GIVING ACT

The generous man [is a source of blessing and] shall be prosperous and enriched, And he who waters will himself be watered [reaping the generosity he has sown].
Proverbs 11:25, AMP

Many people are in the habit of demanding. They continually ask what their parents, government, society, and everyone around them can do for them. These people live overly entitled, as if asking and receiving is a right. They also live like everyone owes them something. This is one way to live, but there is another way to live. In fact, this other way guarantees a more fulfilling, joyous, and thrilling journey through life. This way is what today's scripture describes. It is the "giving" kind of life.

Unfortunately, many people do not understand the giving principle. So, when they are asked to donate their resources, they become defensive. The act of giving is a deep spiritual exercise that brings about great returns. There is great power and reward attached to this act. Giving also helps one feel better. It brings one joy. It is an act God is pleased with. Genuine givers never lack the good things of life.

What can you do for your community? How can you make the world better than you found it? How can you be of service to those around you? Great satisfaction comes with helping the poor, sick, elderly, or others who have special needs. Look around you; there are many opportunities to be a blessing. Get in the habit of giving rather than receiving, and watch your life turn around for the better.

Confession: *Dear Lord, I'm thankful for all I have been blessed with. I pray for a deeper understanding of the giving act. Open my eyes to the plight of those around me. Everywhere I go, please make me a source of blessing. Amen.*

AUGUST 13

THE CONFIDENT ATTITUDE

For God has not given us a spirit of fear,
but of power and of love and of a sound mind.
2 Timothy 1:7, NKJV

To be confident means to believe in one's abilities. It also means to be bold and courageous.

It took me a while to understand why some people always get away with doing bad things. I also had a hard time figuring out why those that are not half as good trick others into accepting them as superb. Then it occurred to me that most of these people are not necessarily more intelligent. They have just mastered the art of manipulating people with their confidence. Having understood the power being confident carries, many unbelievers use this tool for their own advantage. We see them talking and bluffing their way through everything. Many even use the confidence tool to acquire prosperity. So if other people can use this good thing to gain a good life, why not we children of God?

If we would be honest, a lot of us still need to work on being confident. If you feel this is you too, you could begin today by having a little more faith in yourself. You can do it. You can make it. There is so much more deposited in you than you give yourself credit for. Believe in yourself. Whenever you feel your human strength will disappoint you, believe in God. Confidence commands respect. Life will always be beautiful to those that possess confidence in themselves and in God.

Confession: *Dear Lord, You have given me a sound mind, not a timid spirit. You live in me. I decree this day that from here on out, I will start behaving like one who carries God. I will no longer hide my face or shy away from things. I will walk in God's pride. I will talk like a confident child of God. My confidence is renewed in You. Amen.*

AUGUST 14

YOU ONLY KNOW WHAT YOU KNOW

"Judge not, that you be not judged."
Matthew 7:1

You meet someone, spend a few moments with them, and then summarize them according to what you feel you know. You listen to a one-sided story and then judge based on only the information you have. You look down your nose on a person because he or she doesn't live up to your supposed expectations. I do not know about you, but I used to be very guilty of this.

It took me a long time to understand that there is always more to people than I know. Just because I met an individual some time ago doesn't mean I know all about that person. That individual is made up of a lifetime I may know almost nothing about. That person is also composed of a different temperament, experience, and background. All these are what inspired the person's life choices. The only thing I know about the individual is what I know now. I do not know his or her entire story.

As Christians, we have been called to love and not judge others. In loving people, we are to follow Christ's example by caring for people and never condemning them. We are also to let others be themselves and not just who we want them to be. When we genuinely love others, our actions will push them toward God and not pull them away from Him. When we love, we do not look down on people. God knows them inside and out. Let God alone be their judge.

Confession: *Heavenly Father, today I humbly come to Your throne and ask for mercy. In times past, I have judged others and even secretly condemned them. This is not what You desire of me. I am to love and never judge others. I am to be an example of what a true Christian is. Help me love genuinely. Amen.*

AUGUST 15

AFTER YOU'VE DONE ALL YOU CAN

And on the seventh day God ended His work which He had done, and He rested on the seventh day from all His work which He had done. Then God blessed the seventh day and sanctified it, because in it He rested from all His work which God had created and made. **Genesis 2:2–3, NKJV**

God worked for six days. On the seventh day, He rested. The Bible did not say that God needed to rest on the seventh day. Instead, He chose to rest. The Bible did not say God was fatigued, hence this was His sole reason to pause. Rather, He opted for a break. Some writers call this the "Purposeful Stop."

There are so many lessons to be learned from God taking a rest after Creation. One of them is the important role stopping and relaxing plays. When you stop and relax, you refuel. Also, you are refreshed and able to view things with a clearer vision. If God in all His supremacy could cease work after He had done all He needed to, how much more should you and I? After you've given your best at work, school, and other daily endeavors, stop and relax. Yes, persist as hard as you can, but also understand that you have limits. Don't let your body completely break down before you realize this. Anything done in excess never bears good fruit. The same goes for overworking our bodies. After you've done all you know you can humanly possibly do, call it a day.

Confession: *Dear Father, thank You for the gift of life. I know I sometimes overwork myself, and I repent of this today. Help me to never get my body to a point where it shuts down on its own. As You grant me Your strength daily, help me to never overdo things. Amen.*

AUGUST 16

STOP AND PRAY

"Ask and it will be given to you; seek and you will find; knock and the door will be opened to you."
Matthew 7:7, NIV

I remember one particular day when things went from bad to worse. I just felt disjointed, disconnected, and muddled. I had a lot to do, but the more I tried, the more things took a turn for the worst. A friend asked what the matter was, so I explained, telling him I couldn't understand it myself. He then went on to ask me this life-changing question: "Have you prayed about it?" I replied, "Yes, I prayed this morning, asking God to order my steps and grant me a productive day." Seeming not to be satisfied with my response, he asked, "Have you told God right here exactly how you feel and how you would love Him to help you?" My response was that I had not. So I did as prompted. Immediately, things started working out on their own. That day I achieved much more than I would have on an average day. It also turned out to be one of the best days for me. Every day after that, I applied the same approach, and this had always yielded the exact result or better.

Just like my friend suggested this approach to me then, permit me to also recommend the same to you today. Two to five minutes of secluded prayer time may be all you need sometimes. Talk to God. Tell Him everything, and humbly request His help. After doing this, go ahead with your day. God will turn things around for your good. Whatever it is, wherever you are, and however horrible your day may be going, just stop and pray about it. Prayer works.

Confession: *Dear ever-present God, I adore You. Whenever I call on You, You always hear me. You are ever attentive to my needs. I lay all my worries at Your feet. I exchange my weakness for Your strength. When I am at my lowest, help me to always remember that Your grace is sufficient for me. Amen.*

LIVING
CONFLICT-FREE

AUGUST 17

AN OPEN MIND

And it is my prayer that your love may abound more and more, with knowledge and all discernment.
Philippians 1:9

As humans, most times we see things the way we want to see them and not necessarily how they really are. In essence, we naturally observe things from our own perspective. This is why some argue that there is really no difference between wrong and right.

Today's devotion is mostly dedicated to the opinionated ones out there, including me. We opinionated ones believe our way is always right. During conversations, some of us unknowingly shove our opinions down other's throats. Should they disagree with us in any way, we are quick to pick a quarrel with them. We believe our methods are always the best. It's either our way or no way at all.

Two plus two equals four, but so does three plus one. Others don't always have incorrect perspectives on things. Sometimes other people are not outright wrong. The only dissimilarity is that we often see things from different angles. At the very least, let's endeavor to be objective and have an open mind. Let's hear others out too. Let's listen attentively when others present their ideas. More often than not, they also have good points.

Confession: *Dear Lord, help me be levelheaded. Help me be more understanding and accommodating of other people's points of view. Your will is that I live in peace with all men. Help me achieve this. Amen.*

AUGUST 18

ASSUMPTION RUINS

Don't jump to conclusions—there may be a perfectly good explanation for what you just saw.
Proverbs 25:8, MSG

To assume means to accept something as the truth without proof. It could also mean to act based on inaccurate information and not pure facts. People fond of this habit think they "know," but they don't. They may also think they are correct but are often greatly misled. Assumption stirs up strife. It causes errors in judgment and paranoia. These are just a few downsides of assuming.

Seven out of ten times, the person assuming is wrong. I know this for a fact because I have been in close contact with people who exhibit assuming habits. I have also witnessed firsthand how relationships have crumbled to pieces because of this. There is a lot of danger that comes with assuming. It is a chronic disease that eats deeply into relationships.

Assumption ruins relationships, and the devil is fully aware of this. Over time, he has turned this into a tool he often uses to play his demonic tricks with our lives. He does this for the sole purpose of messing with us and the relationships we've built up. But the devil can only do this to those who permit him to. So if this is the case, then it's high time we believers stopped allowing him. How to go about this is what we will be considering next.

Confession: *The scripture says that I will know the truth and the truth will set me free. Holy Spirit, help me. Teach me how to gather facts and examine them before jumping to conclusions. Amen.*

AUGUST 19

AS OPPOSED TO ASSUMING

...but test everything; hold fast what is good.
1 Thessalonians 5:21

Life is simple. It is our actions and/or inactions that complicate it. Assumption is the root of many relationships gone sour. Below are points worth noting:

- Do you want to have the right opinion? Work with precise information and facts from the actual source.
- Do you want to judge a matter correctly? Listen to all the parties involved with an unbiased mind.
- Do you want a great relationship? Be humble enough to apologize when you've assumed wrongly.
- Do you want to be understood? Be direct with your words.
- Do you want to understand? Ask and ask again until it is fully clear.

When we stop assuming, we will begin to enjoy the happy and peaceful life Christ has made available for us. The devil then won't be able to raise his ugly head as we won't be leaving cracks in the wall for him to penetrate.

Confession: *Heavenly Father, henceforth I only want to deal with the truth and the facts. I want to have a better relationship with those around me. Help me to apply the above principles to my daily life. Teach me how to stop assuming or jumping to the wrong conclusions. Amen.*

AUGUST 20

BECAUSE YOU MAY BE QUOTED

Whoever guards his mouth preserves his life;
he who opens wide his lips comes to ruin.
Proverbs 13:3

It's amazing how words, once uttered, can come back to haunt one. Sadly, many have ruined today's opportunities because of words they uttered in the past. Some of these words they probably didn't even mean at the time they said them. This is one reason why spoken words are delicate.

Another good reason it is necessary to be graceful with our words is that people often quote them. Sometimes they quote them back to us. Other times, they relay them to others. This makes it paramount that we do not just voice the first thing that comes to mind. It's imperative we think about the impact of our words before letting them out.

Many people have had to learn this the hard way. Hopefully this won't be you and I. Henceforth, let's try to strictly say what we mean and mean what we say. Let's desist from side talks that could erupt controversies. Also, let's only say behind people's backs words we can say in front of them. Let's always remember that we may not be there to defend ourselves whenever we are quoted or misquoted. Therefore, we should try to avoid disputable statements that could cause strife.

Confession: *As a believer, my words are supposed to be seasoned with grace and wisdom. My words are supposed to inspire others. For all those times I have fallen short, please have mercy. Teach me how to speak with wisdom. Holy Spirit, please caution my tongue. Help me to always say the right things. Amen.*

AUGUST 21

DON'T GO LOOKING FOR TROUBLE

When you see trouble coming, don't be stupid and walk right into it—be smart and hide.
Proverbs 22:3, CEV

A good number of unfortunate situations that happen to people are self-inflicted. For those who believe in God's name, the Bible says that when they drink deadly poison, it will not harm them (Mark 16:18). However, does this give one the go-ahead to purposely drink poison, hoping harm will not come to him or her? Absolutely not! Some people would call that stupidity. If anyone intentionally drinks poison, chances are high that the person will be harmed.

As powerful as Jesus was when He was on Earth, the Bible never once recorded that He went looking for trouble. At some point, Jesus even left for other countries. He did this in a bid to avoid trouble (Luke 9:51–56). Whatever we do, we mustn't go poking the bear. If we poke the bear, we are asking for trouble. It's imperative also that we avoid conflicts as much as we can in our daily lives. In fact, we should endeavor to run far from unnecessary controversies. This doesn't make us cowards; it only makes us wise. If a person drinks poison, it will likely harm him or her. In the same way, if we go looking for trouble, we will probably find it. Let's leave room for peace in our lives. One of the best ways to do this is by avoiding anything that would rob us of our joy.

Confession: Jesus, please order my steps. Help me remain where You need me to be. May I not use my hands to ruin my future. Teach me how to let sleeping dogs lie. Help me so I never go looking for trouble. Amen.

AUGUST 22

DON'T SWEAT THE SMALL STUFF

Turn my eyes from looking at worthless things;
and give me life in your ways.
Psalm 119:37

In life, there are issues, and there are Issues. While many issues are important, consequential, and life-altering, others are merely flimsy. Before addressing life issues, it is important that we label them first. For instance, we can ask ourselves the following questions: Are the issues crucial? Are they serious? Can they wait? Are the matters timewasters or pertinent? Once matters are labeled, it's easier to attend to them with the appropriate approach. Things often seem bigger than they really are when we first learn about them. When we calmly look again, we will likely see the issues for what they are and not what we assumed them to be.

When situations arise, a lot of them are not worth the stress and energy we give to them. A lot of the everyday matters that arise are really "the small stuff." The small stuff engages us in irrelevant activities. This keeps us distracted from the relevant things that really require our focus. Five-, twenty-, or thirty-minute problems should be addressed as such. These small, straightforward issues should be treated with a matching degree of attention. No more, no less.

Confession: *Dear Jesus, please help me so I will not get caught up in unnecessary distractions. Teach me to always give issues the attention they deserve. Help me recognize every timewaster in my life. Amen.*

AUGUST 23

HOW YOU SAY IT MATTERS

Again the king sent the captain of a third fifty with his fifty. And the third captain of fifty went up and came and fell on his knees before Elijah and entreated him, "O man of God, please let my life, and the life of these fifty servants of yours, be precious in your sight." **2 Kings 1:13**

Most often it's not what we say that matters but how we say it. Two people could imply the same things but voice this with different words and tones.

According to 2 Kings 1, the king summoned Elijah to the palace, and the order was to be carried out by his captains. Upon meeting Elijah, the first captain bluntly delivered the message, saying, "O man of God, the king says 'Come down.'" This provoked Elijah, and in response, he called out fire from heaven that burned the captain and his men to ashes. The second captain did likewise and met the same fate. The third, upon arriving, decided to use a more subtle approach. This is what today's text explains. Not only was the third captain able to get Elijah to the palace but he was also able to save his own life and the lives of the fifty men with him.

Communication goes beyond talking. A well-meaning statement could end up causing severe damage because of a wrong word choice. Words are sensitive. This is why it is crucial we use appropriate words at all times during conversations. Appropriate body language, eye contact, and proper tone also aid excellent communication.

Confession: *Precious Lord, Your will is that I live in peace with all. My words matter. Give me an understanding of this, and teach me how to communicate with people better. May my words bring life and progress. May they bring healing. May my words never get me in trouble. Amen.*

AUGUST 24

LOUDER DOESN'T MAKE US RIGHT

Don't have anything to do with foolish and stupid arguments, because you know they produce quarrels.
2 Timothy 2:23, NIV

Arguments are natural. No matter how we try to avoid arguing, we still find ourselves doing it at some point. Some would even say that any relationship in which those that are involved never argue or disagree is not a healthy one. Arguments come in different forms. Our focus today will center on both the destructive and constructive kinds.

A destructive argument is a type of dispute that involves belittling, degrading, and attacking. It is often followed by threats, insults, and name-calling, among others. This behavior births sour relationships. However, constructive arguing is when those involved resolve matters amicably. They do not add (for instance, what happened in the past) or subtract from the issue at hand. They keep their emotions in check while addressing their dispute. Those who argue constructively do so without passing blames. They take turns to listen to all that the other party has to say before calmly responding.

Shouting doesn't make us right. No, we do not always have to yell to make a point. We can do so constructively and still keep our peace with our fellow men (Hebrews 12:14). Arguments and disagreements are not necessarily bad things. How we go about them makes all the difference.

Confession: Jesus, Your instruction is that I avoid unnecessary arguments.
I know I will always encounter those whose only aim is to engage me in quarrels.
At such times, please give me the wisdom to keep my cool.
If ever I need to engage in a dispute with others, help me to do so constructively.
Help me to always maintain my calm and composure. Amen.

AUGUST 25

NOTHING TO LOSE?

And what do you benefit if you gain the whole world but lose your own soul? Is anything worth more than your soul?
Matthew 16:26, NLT

The person who has nothing to lose does not stand to suffer any consequence by taking an action.

"What do I stand to lose?" "What do I stand to gain?" These are questions that can assist you in making good decisions at every junction in life. For example, if after asking these questions, what you stand to lose from a relationship is of great value, you may want to reconsider working hard on it. But if what you stand to gain is of little significance, you may just want to let it go. This is especially crucial for toxic relationships. By practicing this habit, negative and harmful people get cut off from our lives easier. This practice also makes both major and minor decisions easier to make.

For many of us who prioritize heaven, this constant self-check will help us keep heaven in view. Certainly, nothing on Earth is worth losing heaven over. Asking what we stand to gain or lose avails us the opportunity to analyze the impact of any action before taking it. It helps us to refrain from doing things that will put our relationships in jeopardy. It also helps us rank things according to their importance in our lives.

Confession: *Dear Lord, thank You for Your word of wisdom this day. Today I declare that heaven is my top priority. My peace of mind and joy are also my priorities. Before I take actions, please teach me to weigh their consequences first. May I never replace important things in life for flimsy ones. Amen.*

AUGUST 26

WHAT CAN PEOPLE SAY ABOUT YOU?

If possible, so far as it depends on you,
live peaceably with all.
Romans 12:18

Not everyone will like us or have good things to say about us. In fact, a handful of people may have their misgivings about us. This is okay. But when everyone tends to point a negative finger at us, it may be time for some self-introspection. Yes, people will see what they want to see. Some people even intentionally only see the faults in people. Still, everybody cannot be wrong at the same time. If everyone feels we have certain habits that are unpleasant, we most likely have that habit.

Is there a particular character trait of yours most people complain about? Is there something about your attitude that turns others off? Please recognize that habit today and consider making some self-adjustments. Of course you mean well, and everyone just misunderstands you. Many people feel like that too. Maybe you genuinely do not mean to come off as offensive, but people say you are anyway. Well, how about considering changing your approach to things?

Today's scripture reference did not ask us to do our best to make sure everyone likes us. Rather, we are being asked to live at peace with ALL. It may not be possible to be everyone's favorite, but it is within our power to have cordial relationships with others.

Confession: *Lord, as I reflect on my life and my attitude this day, help me to do so honestly. In areas where I need to improve, please help me to be humble enough to do so. When people point out my faults, help me to be mature enough to listen and make adjustments. Amen.*

AUGUST 27

THE OFFENDER AND THE OFFENSE

A person's wisdom yields patience;
it is to one's glory to overlook an offense.
Proverbs 19:11, NIV

There is a big difference between the offender and the offense. The offender is the one who commits the wrongdoing. The offense is the crime committed. There are so many surprising reasons people do hurtful things to their fellow men. Some do so out of spite, envy, jealousy, or vengeance. Some do it because they feel it's their most suitable option at that particular time. Some do it to make themselves feel better. Some do it to selfishly save their own heads. But often offenders are just tools in the hands of the devil. The enemy's primary aim is to steal, kill, and destroy beautiful relationships.

Those who don't love us can hurt us. Those who love us can hurt us even deeper. Granted, some crimes are absolutely inexcusable. But everyday little misunderstandings can be resolved amicably. When our spouse, friends, kids, parents, and colleagues upset us, let's try to deal with their offense graciously.

Not everyone who hurts us does so intentionally. When an offense is placed on one side and the "offender" on another, chances are that the issue will be resolved. This is better than when the two are muddled together. Not all misunderstandings have to cripple relationships. Some can be salvaged and others revived. Give beautiful relationships and remorseful offenders another chance today.

Confession: *Dear Lord, Your instruction is that I live in peace with all men. To do this, I know I will sometimes have to be the bigger person. I may even need to apologize when I am not wrong. Jesus, please grant me the wisdom to always settle matters amicably. Help my relationships flourish. Amen.*

AUGUST 28

SILENCE IS GOLDEN

Too much talk leads to sin. Be sensible and keep your mouth shut.
Proverbs 10:19, NLT

Ecclesiastes 3 records that there is a time to speak and a time to be quiet. Sometimes certain things need to be said, and say them we must! Other times the best thing to do is to be quiet.

Some situations arise that demand our silence since doing otherwise may cause severe damage. A good instance is when we are upset. When we are angry, a considerable percentage of what we say will be regretted later. An angry person is a dangerous person. But with silence, we can curtail the damage that could have resulted. Other instances when silence may suffice may be when asked self-implicating questions.

Maintaining our silence has its rewards. For one, it creates some kind of mystery around you. It also suggests you are an outstanding listener and a great thinker. In truth, maintaining silence can be difficult, especially for the outspoken people. But always remember, silence is golden. Words you don't say can never be used against you. Also, words said can never be unsaid. Once a word is out, it is out. Even if you apologize or try to walk your words back, it will never be the same as not saying them in the first place. So instead of saying words that could later set a trap for you, why not liberate yourself by not saying them at all? Silence in itself speaks volumes.

Confession: *Father, on my tongue, You have placed life and death. Today I choose life. In moments when I absolutely need to be quiet, please help me hold my tongue. The words I say cannot be unsaid. Help me to never say things that would leave long-lasting scars on others. Amen.*

AUGUST 29

WHEN YOU LEAVE THE BATTLE TO HIM

But as for you, you meant evil against me; but God meant it for good, in order to bring it about as it is this day, to save many people alive. **Genesis 50:20**

The battle is the Lord's. Some of us already know this in our hearts, yet as soon as an unacceptable event occurs, we find ourselves swinging into full action. Many of us deal with our issues before asking the Holy Spirit for direction.

Should others unjustly accuse, betray, jilt, or connive against you, please put it all in God's hands. Should they even intentionally hurt you, embarrass you, or set you up, choose to give it to God. When you leave folks who hurt you in God's hands and keep a positive attitude, God will reward you.

You shouldn't leave things in God's hands because you cannot do something to change that situation. You should do so because you have chosen to completely trust God. When you put offenders in God's hands instead of repaying evil for evil, God honors that trust. He also handles the situation a million times better than you would have. This is exactly what God did for Joseph in the scripture above. Joseph was good to his brothers, but they were not good to him and even sold him into slavery. Eventually, the Lord fought for Joseph and made him ruler of Egypt When we leave the battle to the Lord, He will take care of business on our behalf. Our God is always in the habit of giving us double blessings for our troubles.

Confession: *Dear Lord, I am in awe of Your love for me. You are my defender. You fight even those battles You do not reveal to me. I long to trust You, but my flesh keeps getting in the way. Please grant me the grace to always put things in Your care. Amen.*

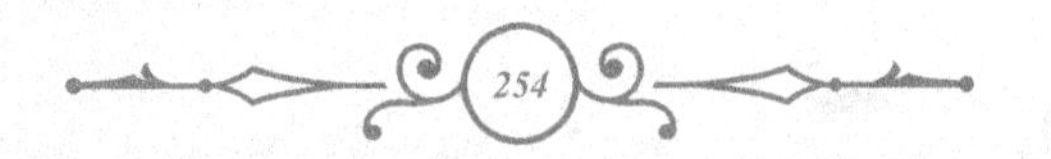

LIFE BEYOND OUR FEELINGS

AUGUST 30

LIFE BEYOND OUR FEELINGS

The heart is deceitful above all things,
and desperately sick; who can understand it?
Jeremiah 17:9

When our skin itches a little, we will most likely scratch it. We may also choose to ignore it if the itch is not a severe one. But there is a particular itch that drives a person crazy. Have you ever experienced such an itch? This itch seems nearly impossible not to touch, and as soon as we scratch it, we may feel temporary relief. But to get more comfort, we may have to scratch the surface some more. As soon as we begin scratching, we may even find ourselves enjoying the pleasure that comes with it. What the itch is to the skin can be likened to what our feelings are to our lives.

Feelings are what make us humans. Those who have no emotion are said to be "dead on the inside." Feelings are great as they help us express our dispositions at a particular time. Feelings are also compelling. Our feelings represent what we crave. It is like an itch on the skin that begs to be scratched. While we may choose to sometimes scratch an itchy surface, we may occasionally decide not to. Not many people know that it is within their power not to scratch their skin no matter how strong the urge is to do so. In the same way, we do not have to give in to everything we feel at every moment. We can say no to our desires from time to time. Of course, expressing one's feelings should be encouraged. But excessively giving into feelings is one of the unfortunate reasons many never go far in life. When we live solely based on emotions, sentiment, and impulse, we will most likely not get the best from life.

Feelings are important and should be acknowledged. We have already established this. The question is, to what extent? Is it even possible not to live driven by our feelings? And where do feelings originate from? These questions and more are what we will explore in the new series, "Life Beyond Our Feelings."

Confession: *Dear Jesus, thank You for today's word. I acknowledge that in times past, I have let my feelings control my actions. But I know that I am to live a God-driven, not a feelings-driven, life. Please bestow upon me the grace to do this. Amen.*

AUGUST 31

ESPECIALLY WHEN YOU DON'T FEEL LIKE IT

Hear, my son, and be wise, and direct your heart in the way.
Proverbs 23:19

In the past, when we did not feel like doing something, we would not do it. But from now on, whether we feel like doing a particular thing or not, we will (especially if it's the right thing to do). Here is why and how:

WHY: Feelings are subjective and change. They are not steady. They are temporary. You can feel one way one minute and feel another way the next. Feelings come and go. Feelings can manipulate you if you give them the power to do so. But if you take charge and do that which you know you should, your feelings will follow suit.

HOW: When you wake up in the morning and feel like doing absolutely nothing, ignore that feeling and go about your daily activities. Do only that which you know you should at that point. Whenever you set out to do something, discard all negative and unproductive thoughts.

Yes, feelings are important, but they should never be our reasons for not achieving all we know we can and should. Our feelings do not have to dictate our actions. Our feelings do not have the power to command us. Rather, it is the other way around. Our feelings are subject to our command. Only when we understand this will we begin to win the battle over our minds.

Confession: *My feelings do not have authority over me. My will is stronger than my emotions. I declare today that I will always do what is right, regardless of how I feel. My feelings will not be a hindrance to me in my life. I will set out to achieve all I have been destined to, in Jesus' name. Amen.*

SEPTEMBER 1

WHAT OUR SKIN REPRESENTS

For the mind that is set on the flesh is hostile to God,
for it does not submit to God's law; indeed, it cannot.
Romans 8:7

Our flesh can be likened to a child. Just as a child's desires are limitless, so also is our flesh. Our flesh desires those things that are beneficial, but it also sometimes crave those things that are not. Our flesh may even hunger for those things that are not God's will for us.

Good parents grant some of their children's desires, but they also know that it will not be in their children's best interests to give in to every request being made. In the same way parents know what's best for their children, we know what is best for us. We have authority over our flesh. Regardless of how we feel, we must always do the right thing. Of course, it is not every time we will feel like doing that which needs to be done. But as masters over our bodies, we should always aspire to do what is right and not just what is felt.

As we continue to grow in the things of the Spirit, maturity will be required of us. We may even hear God instruct us to deny ourselves of certain things. When the flesh throws tantrums like a typical child, maturity knows better than to give in. Maturity understands that the body will get over it after a while, especially if it is not much of a necessity. The more we mature, the better we get at doing things because they are right and not just because of our emotions.

Confession: *Father, my emotions are a part of my life but do not have to dictate my life. My feelings do not have the right to dictate what I will or will not do. My will has authority over my emotions. From here on out, help me never live solely based on how I feel. Amen.*

SEPTEMBER 2

WANTS AND NEEDS

Once I was young, and now I am old. Yet I have never seen the godly abandoned or their children begging for bread.
Psalm 37:25, NLT

Need can be defined as life's necessities that are crucial for living. Want is more like a desire or wish. It is that which we crave but may not be necessary. Needs (like shelter, food, water, and more) are essential for survival. Wants, not so much.

We often mistake wants for needs. For instance, a homeless man may desire a mansion to live in when all he needs is a place to lay his head. Another instance may be an individual in desperate need of a car to move around with that longs for a luxury car.

When God wants to provide for us, He gives us our immediate needs. But most of what we pray for are wants. To this, God says a "yes," "no," or "not yet." There are certain times also when God may grant us even better than what we crave. All these He does in His own timing. Today's reference text assures us that as God's children, we will never go hungry. In essence, God makes it His priority to always meet our daily needs but not necessarily give us all we desire.

Confession: *Heavenly Father, thank You for all You have blessed me with. For those times when You have said yes, no, or wait, I appreciate You. All You do is for my good. In Your timing, You will give me all that is mine. Help me stay content. May I never go looking for "more" away from Your presence. Amen.*

SEPTEMBER 3

DO I NEED THIS?

And he went on to say to them all, "Watch out and guard yourselves from every kind of greed; because your true life is not made up of the things you own, no matter how rich you may be."
Luke 12:15, GNT

Do I need this? Can I afford this? Would acquiring this have a future consequence? What is my reason for desiring this in the first place—is it out of want or need? These are questions we need to ask ourselves when we get a strong urge or craving for something. Our desires are insatiable. There is seldom a limit to human longings.

It's only natural for us to want nice things for ourselves. But people do not usually run up debt because of their immediate needs. It is often because of unnecessary expenditures. Many would go out of their way just to impress people or feel as equals. Many would also spend more than they earn and, as a result, run into huge problems.

One of the best ways to live debt free is to stay within your means. Also, prioritizing pressing needs over frivolous, extravagant, or unimportant spending is crucial. Purchasing a house is a good investment, but buying a $5,000 piece of clothing may not be a smart idea if you cannot conveniently afford it. There is a certain peace of mind that comes with not having money problems. This peace of mind can be yours too if you decide to stay within your means.

Confession: *Lord Jesus, I'm sorry. For those times when I have mishandled Your blessings, please forgive me. Teach me how to stay within my means and all You have provided. Please reveal to me how to be a better resource manager. Amen.*

SEPTEMBER 4

LIFE BEYOND OUR WANTS

For the moment all discipline seems painful rather than pleasant, but later it yields the peaceful fruit of righteousness to those who have been trained by it. ***Hebrews 12:11***

It's one thing to be unable to afford something and not acquire it. It's another to be able to afford a certain thing and still not purchase it. According to today's text, discipline is needed for a peaceful life. Sometimes discipline entails being tough on ourselves and our excesses. It also involves saying no to ourselves and our imprudent wants.

Today's text further points out that discipline isn't always pleasant at the initial state. This means that our flesh may not be happy with choosing to deny ourselves that which we can afford.

Discipline is not something that comes naturally to everyone. But should we desire a blissful life, discipline has to be our watchword. In essence, it's not about being able to afford a thing but sometimes choosing not to acquire it. It's not about struggling to say no to our desires but doing so and walking away with our heads held high. It's about knowing where to draw the line. It's about being satisfied with what we have at every moment as we work toward a better future. It's about setting priorities and not putting important things at the mercy of unimportant ones. These are the "disciplines" today's scripture describes. Yes, it may not be easy at first, but with practice, it gets better.

Confession: *Jesus, while You were on earth, You lived a disciplined life. You had everything within reach, yet You denied Yourself certain things. Please help me be like You. That You have blessed me with so much does not mean I should be excessive with my spending. Teach me how to live with contentment. Amen.*

SEPTEMBER 5

COUNT THE COST

But don't begin until you count the cost. For who would begin construction of a building without first calculating the cost to see if there is enough money to finish it? **Luke 14:28, NLT**

Big things ruin lives, but so do little things. Sadly, many have let thirty minutes of enjoyment bring their lives to a halt. Today's focus is on those desires that occasionally tempt us.

It takes effort, resources, and time to erect a structure. Destroying it, however, takes much less time. No matter how enticing some things may look, we need to first count the cost of doing those things. Before giving in to that inane thought, please endeavor to take a good look at your life and how far you have come. Then determine if that thing really matters. Determine if that few moments of pleasure is worth losing all you have spent your life building. Ask yourself if that silliness is worth throwing your faith away for.

Sometimes certain actions may initially look harmless, but their repercussions are devastating. If there is even a slight chance that this temptation will bring about damaging consequences, wisdom dictates that you stay far away. First count the cost. Then make your choice.

Confession: *Dear Lord, Your instruction is that I should only begin after I have counted the cost of my actions. Before undertaking any life-ruining action, Holy Spirit, please stop me in my tracks. May I not lose all I have spent my life gathering because of a few minutes of pleasure. Amen.*

SEPTEMBER 6

•••

IT CAN'T ALWAYS BE ABOUT YOU

Do nothing out of selfish ambition or vain conceit.
Rather, in humility value others above yourselves.
Philippians 2:3, NIV

Many people live their lives expecting everything and everyone to revolve around them. These people live life expecting others to understand that they are weak and feeble. They may also expect those around them to be sympathetic to their shortcomings. Their conversations often begin and end with what they want, how they feel, and what they desire. They pay little or no attention to other's feelings or interests. If you honestly know you are like this, with all due respect, this is a self-centered way to live. It can't always be about you. Whether you know it or not, your behavior affects others.

Before taking an action, we would do well to at least consider how much it would affect those around us. Scandal, adultery, incarceration, and defamation cases don't just affect those in it. In fact, those who are not directly involved often suffer significantly more fallout than the transgressors. Spouses, children, parents, relatives, and friends bear the brunt of our actions.

Let's seek to consider others when we feel the urge to do something foolish. Let's also endeavor to protect those that surround us. One way to do this is by staying away from anything that will hurt them. Considering other's feelings alongside ours is a sign of maturity in Christ.

Confession: *Heavenly Father, I ask for Your mercy. For those times I have been self-centered, please forgive me. It can't always be all about me. Holy Spirit, please teach me how to put other's needs ahead of mine. Help me live Jesus-centered. Amen.*

SEPTEMBER 7

MOOD SWINGS

Why are you cast down, O my soul, and why are you in turmoil within me? Hope in God; for I shall again praise him, my salvation and my God. **Psalm 42:11**

Life is a roller coaster. Sometimes we may find ourselves in situations that make us excited. Other times we may encounter things that make us downcast. This is only natural as emotions are part of the human makeup. Now, it's one thing to have occasional moodiness. Constant moodiness, however, is a different thing. Moody people usually alternate between hot and cold. You just never know what you will get next. One minute they are excited about life. Then, for no apparent reason, they could switch to being gloomy. I have associated with many moody people, so I know firsthand the pain that comes with doing so.

If you are a moody person, today you are being encouraged to step up. You see, when you have people who care about you, whatever way you feel rubs off on them. Your family members, colleagues, and friends care about you. You may not know this, but your unhappiness is their unhappiness too. Your depressed state is theirs as well. Of course, you may not mean to put them in an uncomfortable position, but your unconscious grumpy attitude does just that.

Please do not let things get to a point where people around you become numb to your mood swings. Decide on your own that you will do better and deal with your moody issues, if only for the sake of your loved ones. Exactly how to deal with this is what we will consider next.

Confession: *Dear Jesus, You are the one true source of joy. Today I desire to act better with my emotions. I do not want to be known as the moody, unstable person. I want others around me to be comfortable in my presence. I want to exude happiness everywhere I go. Please grant me the grace to achieve this. Amen.*

SEPTEMBER 8

MOOD SWINGS PART II

You will keep in perfect peace those whose minds are steadfast, because they trust in you.
Isaiah 26:3, NIV

Previously we established that moody people tend to drag others into their downcast state. But not many moody people do this on purpose. Moodiness varies with temperament. It is a state a lot of people fall into, not necessarily because they want to but because that is how they are wired. The good news is that we can all choose to live life on our own terms and not just how our emotions dictate. Here are a few tips on how to address moodiness.

As a moody person:

- Whenever you feel the need to go back into your shell, take time to identify what triggered it in the first place. It could be stress from work or other things.
- Communicate your feelings to those around you. Let them know they did nothing wrong but that you are dealing with a few things that may make you withdrawn.
- Decide on your own that you will not entirely give into your "not being in the mood" feeling. Moods tend to dissipate once you take purposeful actions.

Remember, moodiness is a product of the mind. The trick is to not submit to how you would love to be in your own world, all by yourself. Begin doing all you would have done if you were not feeling moody at that moment. When you do this, everyone is happy, including those around you.

Confession: *Lord, thank You for opening my eyes to how my mood affects others. I pray today that You will walk with me through this change process. Help me be a better version of myself. Help me change from the inside-out. Help me to never give into extreme moody feelings anymore. Amen.*

SEPTEMBER 9

A FEW MORE FACTS ABOUT OUR FEELINGS

...but they who wait for the LORD shall renew their strength; they shall mount up with wings like eagles; they shall run and not be weary; they shall walk and not faint. ***Isaiah 40:31***

Feelings are a thing of the mind that may also affect an individual's physical state. But how are feelings formed over time? Feelings can arise from prior or present happenings. For instance, a woman may be super excited because she just won the lottery. Feelings can also result from visual stimuli. For example, a man may wake up feeling irritated because of what he watched on TV the previous night. Hormones running wild may make one jolly one minute and gloomy the next. There are also certain cases when our feelings cannot be explained. These are moments when we may just feel like doing nothing, talking to no one, or not going anywhere.

Our feelings are powerful, yet they are only as powerful as we let them be. Feelings can be controlling, but their controlling power depends on whatever permission we give them. Should we decide to live based on feelings alone, chances are that we will not live to our full potential in life.

Whether we feel like it or not, let's always do the right things. Naturally, our feelings always try to take the easy way out. But we can decide not to if it is not the right choice at that moment. Our feelings are subject to change. So long as we choose to be in command, our feelings are subject to our will.

Confession: *I may not be able to control my feelings, but I know that I can choose not to let them control me. Lord, You have made me a master over my emotions, so I will act like one. I refuse to strictly live by just how I feel. Henceforth, I will be intentional. Even if my feelings suggest otherwise, I will push on and achieve all. Amen.*

SEPTEMBER 10

TEACHING THE UPCOMING GENERATION

Train up a child in the way he should go;
even when he is old he will not depart from it.
Proverbs 22:6

I read about a wealthy woman who would occasionally pretend her car was broken down. She would then present her kids with the option of reaching their destination by foot, bus, or train. When asked her reason behind this act, she stated, "My motive is to show my kids that there exists another world outside the comfortable one they live in." She further explained, "That way, they get to feel what other children, who are not so as privileged as they are, feel. They also learn to be grateful for all the luxuries that life and their parents provide. From their young age, it sinks in deep that they are simply favored and all they enjoy is not a right. It teaches them how to deal with little inconveniences. More importantly, it teaches them from an early stage that they won't always get their way all the time."

We may or may not agree with this woman's approach to things, but she makes a good point. Kids these days are smarter than we give them credit for. They know when they are being unnecessarily spoiled by their guardians and when they are not. So they act accordingly.

More often than not, who we train kids to be is who they'll grow up to be. Let's provide the proper teaching for our kids. Even when they get old and their parents are no more, they will still remember and live by those good teachings.

Confession: *Dear Jesus, I commit all the children I am acquainted with to Your hands. I pray that these children will grow in Your wisdom. May they be those that never take life for granted. Help them know the value of everything they have been blessed with. Teach me how to be a role model for these little ones. Amen.*

SEPTEMBER 11

ENCOURAGE YOURSELF IN THE LORD

And David was greatly distressed; for the people spoke of stoning him, because the soul of all the people was grieved, every man for his sons and for his daughters: but David encouraged himself in the LORD his God. **1 Samuel 30:6, NKJV**

As married couples, it's not every day we get that warm, fuzzy feeling toward our spouses. The same goes for parent–child, employee–employer, and other relationships. It's not always that we feel delighted toward others. As a matter of fact, it's not always we feel that loving feeling toward ourselves. There are also times when we may not feel especially happy toward God.

Some situations may make you question what you thought you felt in the first place. The death of a loved one might make you reevaluate God's love for you. After all, He is the all-knowing, all-seeing God. You may feel God could have stopped the death if He wanted to. A misbehaving spouse may make you feel like you made a mistake and said your "I do" to the wrong person. Sometimes, for no reason, you may not just feel excited about those things you used to.

It's only natural to encounter certain times when you don't have much to fuel your happy feelings. At such times, determine on your own how you will react to all you feel. When you are at your lowest, please encourage yourself in the Lord. Trust in the Holy Spirit to help you get through those periods. The Lord will come through for you.

Confession: *Dear God, You are my all in all. It is only in You that I can find reassurance. When everything does not go according to my plan, help me to always remember that I have You. You are aware of all the happenings in my life. You will see me through it all. You will never leave me. Amen.*

SEPTEMBER 12

OUR APPEARANCE MATTERS

Do you not know that you are God's temple
and that God's Spirit dwells in you?
1 Corinthians 3:16

Have you noticed that on days when you take time out to look gorgeous, you hardly meet anyone you would love to impress? But on days when you decide to be carefree about your appearance, it's almost like a reunion. Somehow you begin to meet everyone that matters. I do not know about you, but for me, it's always like people see me more when I am at my worst.

Having embarrassed myself more times than I can imagine, I have come to this simple conclusion—God wants us to be excellent always. This shouldn't be just an "important occasion" thing. Whether we feel like it or not is inconsequential. We have to be presentable everywhere we go. When we are outdoors, we may need to interact with strangers. We may also be impressed by the Holy Spirit to introduce Jesus to someone. But if we are looking scruffy, effective interaction may be hindered.

Today's scripture reminds us that we carry God with us. Therefore, we represent Him everywhere we go. Our God is excellent. We, in turn, should never look short of being at our best, as the occasion demands. Whether you are going to the house next door, a grocery store, work, church, or an event with the high and mighty, always look presentable.

Confession: *Lord, thank You for making me Your temple.*
Your will is that I represent You well at all times. Please help me achieve this.
From now on, I will appear decently and as the occasion calls for.
My appearance will not cripple my relationships. Amen.

SEPTEMBER 13

THE POWER OF OPPOSITION THINKING

Finally, brothers, whatever is true, whatever is honorable, whatever is just, whatever is pure, whatever is lovely, whatever is commendable, if there is any excellence, if there is anything worthy of praise, think about these things. **Philippians 4:8**

The mind is everything. More often than not, what we think is what we become. A good number of the things we experience are planned by us. How? The Bible states that as a man thinks, so is he (Proverbs 23:7). In essence, our thoughts can set us up for either good or bad things.

Opposition thinking involves substituting limiting thoughts with positive ones to keep yourself focused. This also helps you set your mind in the right place for the next event. For example, on a Sunday evening, instead of voicing out depressing thoughts like "I wish I did not have to return to work tomorrow," you may want to immediately replace this with "I cannot wait to return to the office. Even if I may need to put in extra effort, I love accomplishing things. I enjoy being productive." You may also say things like "I am thankful I have a job at the very least. Many would be more than happy to be in my shoes right now. I will put my best foot forward and trust God to see me through." Upon doing this, discouraging thoughts that would have followed you through the week will be dismissed.

Please develop the habit of countering negative thoughts with positive ones. It works wonders!

Confession: *Dear Lord, You have blessed me with so much. You have been good to me. Please have mercy on me for those times I have been less appreciative of Your blessings. From here on out, I want to think positively. I do not want to think depressing thoughts anymore. Please help me. Amen.*

FEARS AND UNCERTAINTY

SEPTEMBER 14

FALSE EVIDENCE APPEARING REAL

The LORD is my light and my salvation—so why should I be afraid? The LORD is my fortress, protecting me from danger, so why should I tremble? ***Psalm 27:1, NLT***

We all have fears. Whether or not we admit it, we all have certain things that scare us. While many have a few, others have a lot. Using a mnemonic, fear can be defined as False Evidence Appearing Real.

Fear works this way: First, our minds picture a possibly bad scenario. This can also be termed as a seed. Once that seed is sown and not immediately uprooted, it germinates and begins to grow. As it grows, we begin to unconsciously align our lives, thoughts, and actions to that pattern. This is how fear gets its nourishment. Then one day we realize, that which we fear most is happening. Things will likely get worse from there.

Our greatest fears don't necessarily have to come to pass if we don't let them. Initially, when fear thoughts are formed, they are not real. They are only mere illusions that may or may not come to pass, depending on how we handle them. The more we nurse and feed our fear thoughts, the more life we give them. The more life our fears get, the higher their chance of actually occurring. How, then, do we stop feeding our fear thoughts? What are the various fears? These and more are what we will explore under the new theme, "Fears & Uncertainty."

Confession: *Lord Jesus, You have not given me a spirit of fear but that of courage. I lay all my worries at Your feet today. I exchange them for Your peace. I do not want to live tormented anymore. Help me stop giving life to my fears. Amen.*

SEPTEMBER 15

FEAR OF THE UNKNOWN

Don't be afraid, for I am with you. Don't be discouraged, for I am your God. I will strengthen you and help you. I will hold you up with my victorious right hand. **Isaiah 41:10, NLT**

Life is filled with many fearful circumstances. In truth, no one knows what exactly will happen in the next minute. No one can accurately foretell all that will happen tomorrow. The best we can do is hope.

A typical fear is the fear of the unknown. Countless people suffer from this, and this fear has kept so many from going far in life. It is also one reason many never leave a bad situation, for instance, abusive relationships. The fear of the unknown is why many people hold back and run away from things they should ideally face head on. They do this mainly because they are not sure of what the outcome will be. So instead of venturing out with even the slightest chance of things succeeding, they take the easy way out and do not delve into it at all. Not many people are aware that they have a phobia of the unknown. All they know is that they feel uneasy whenever something unfamiliar arises or whenever their comfort zone is threatened.

What would you and I do differently if we got a 100% guarantee that our aspirations would work out? My guess is that we would most likely venture into them without reservations. Unfortunately, life does not always avail us guarantees. So how, then, do we tackle our fear of the unknown? We do so by trusting God. Of course, the unknown tends to be overpowering. But what is even more powerful is having a God who knows it all. This is the power we Christians have in Christ Jesus.

Confession: *Lord, You see my heart. Sometimes the unknown scares me. I find myself worrying about what is to come. Help me with this. I do not want to hold back anymore. Please give the strength to always push through. Help me overcome my fear of the unknown. Amen.*

SEPTEMBER 16

FEAR VS. FAITH

But when he saw the wind, he was afraid, and beginning to sink he cried out, "Lord, save me."
Matthew 14:30

While God works with faith, the devil works with fear. When angels addressed humans in the Bible, many times they began by first saying, "Fear not." Have we ever thought about why this is so? This may be because God cannot work effectively in a life filled with fear.

In the scripture above, Peter was doing fine walking on water until he started doubting the power of God. Peter may have been fearful before he asked Jesus to join him on the water. However, as soon as Peter gave in to his fear thoughts, he started to sink.

God created us, so He has first-hand knowledge of how we function. He knows that sometimes the devil will trick us into doubting our beliefs, and this is fine by Him. He isn't expecting us not to feel fear but rather to trust Him through our fears (Psalm 34:4). Should God decide to use us, He will make up for our inadequacies. Our total confidence should always be in God. It should especially be in God when we find ourselves performing exploits, like walking on water. As long as our gaze is on God, we will never sink.

Confession: *Lord, You cannot perform exploits with someone who doesn't have faith. I want to be mightily used by You, so please help me. Regardless of my fears, help me push through all I need to, trusting You. Help me to only keep my eyes on You despite all the surrounding turmoil. Amen.*

SEPTEMBER 17

LEVELS AND TYPES OF FEAR

God is our refuge and strength,
a very present help in trouble.
Psalm 46:1

The first step to overcoming fear is to recognize it. Today we will analyze various types and forms of fear. Please take the time to acknowledge your kind of fear as we will examine many.

Fear can be grouped into two types: conscious and unconscious fear. The former is that which we are probably aware of and the latter, not so much. Conscious fears may include fear of water, heights, crowds, animals, fire, ghosts, or even death. Unconscious fear includes fear of failure, success, rejection, not living up to expectations, being alone, and the unknown. Fear also has different depths. To some, their fear is on the surface, hence they handle it effortlessly. But for others, their fear has eaten deep within them and even crippled their lives. They live each day with the weight of their fear continually pulling them down.

Having explained the types and depth of fears, where would you say you fall? What kind of fear do you exhibit and at what level? Even if yours is not listed above, please still search within and identify your type of fear today. You may also go further by writing it down. Once you do this, the process of fear elimination has begun. One of the gifts God promises His children is peace. This gift can be yours too should you let go of all your fears.

Confession: *Dear Lord, I bring my fears to You this day. As I reflect on those things that terrify me, help me deal with them. Help me overcome all my conscious and unconscious fears. Give me the courage to look past my fear and set my gaze more on Your promises. Amen.*

SEPTEMBER 18

ROOT CHECK

Search me, O God, and know my heart;
test me and know my anxious thoughts.
Psalm 139:23, NLT

Every fear has its origin. To overcome fear, one has to do what is called the "background check." Some fears have their source as far back as decades ago. Perhaps your fear has resurfaced because of some recent events that triggered the buried memory.

For many people, their fears go back to as early as their childhood. For instance, a woman once struggling with the fear of failure was able to trace its origin to her early years. While she was growing up, her father harbored unrealistic expectations of her. When his wishes were not met, he abused her emotionally and physically. This experience only fed her fear of failure, and this thinking process followed her into her adult life. But as soon as she could recognize the origin of her issues, she successfully utilized all the help she was receiving. Shortly after this, she got her deliverance.

Today we are being encouraged to trace whatever fear we face to what we think started it. It could be a word from someone. It could be a horrifying sight. It could be from a terrible experience or just about anything else. Every time we find ourselves struggling with fear, let's try to figure out its origin first. Once we do this, we can then proceed to the next stages, which we will be exploring subsequently.

Confession: *As I reflect back on the roots of my fears, Holy Spirit, please open my inner eyes. Lord, help me identify all the sources of my fear and overcome them. Please give me complete liberty from all that frightens me. Amen.*

SEPTEMBER 19

HANDLING FEARS

Guard your heart above all else, for it
determines the course of your life.
Proverbs 4:23, NLT

Everyone has fears. While some can handle their fears better than others, it still doesn't change the fact that we all have our fears. Previously, we explored the different types of fear. Today we will discuss various ways to overcome them.

Fear is powerful. It can hold a person captive for decades or a lifetime if this person permits it. Therefore, there is a need to emphasize today's text, which admonishes us to guard our minds. Another word for guard is shield. In essence, we are to barricade our minds against anything that would harm them, most notably fear.

Barricading one's mind is one of the best ways to overcome fear. We can do this first, fortifying our minds with the Word of God. We can also barricade our minds by meditating more on positive and inspiring materials. We can barricade our minds by choosing only to dwell on good news and hopeful thoughts. For many of us, everything we want is on the other side of fear. Let's endeavor to get to that other side today.

Confession: *Lord, today I barricade my mind with Your Word, which says You have given me a sound mind. Help my mind to work for me and not against me. Fear will not cripple me. Help me to always feed my mind with uplifting things. Amen.*

SEPTEMBER 20

SHAKE IT OFF

We destroy arguments and every lofty opinion raised against the knowledge of God, and take every thought captive to obey Christ.
2 Corinthians 10:5

The devil knows us well enough and understands how we humans work. He has studied you and me well enough to recognize how we function. Have we noticed that once we open our eyes in the morning, thoughts pour into our minds, especially negative ones? Whatever we open our hearts to lingers. This guides our actions throughout the day.

Weeds are destructive. They can destroy the garden and other plants if the planter does not pull them out at their developing stages. The same goes for the negative thoughts we permit to take root in our lives. Every negative thought that grows in our minds has a high chance of corrupting our inner person.

The devil is cunning. He first plants seeds of deception in our hearts. After this, he watches from a distance to see what our response will be. Perhaps our usual response in the past has been to give these thoughts life. We may also have unconsciously let those thoughts take root until they become a stronghold. Before long, those thoughts may become a reality. Whenever a pessimistic thought comes across our minds, let's shake it off that instant. Let's determine to never allow ridiculous thoughts to take root in our minds. Let's also resolve to never give room for the devil to play tricks with our minds.

Confession: *Today I decree that all foul thoughts are under the captivity of Christ. I function with the mind of Christ. I will no longer take the bait of the enemy. From here on out, my thoughts will be productive. They will be thoughts that promote my creativity. Amen.*

SEPTEMBER 21

THE POWER OF A MENTAL IMAGE

...(as it is written, "I have made you a father of many nations") in the presence of Him whom he believed—God, who gives life to the dead and calls those things which do not exist as though they did.
Romans 4:17, NKJV

One reason some of us avoid envisioning our goals is so we won't be disappointed when we don't reach them. We feel we will be able to handle it better if we haven't been too hopeful.

Peak performers attract success. This is because they see success first. When you look for something, you will find it. If you continuously expect success, you will likely get it eventually. But if all you expect is bad news, chances are that struggles are all you will get. You get what you expect; this is the power a mental image carries. Having a mental image doesn't mean things will go as you have pictured them in your mind. Still, it is imperative that "you see those things that are not as though they are." This is what the Bible commands in Romans 4:17.

What are you trusting God for? What are your dreams and aspirations? If you desire that they come to pass, endeavor to keep putting them at the forefront of your mind. Also, constantly remind yourself and God about what you are expecting. Then go ahead and live life with the joy and hope of things to come. As long as God has sanctioned what you are trusting Him for, it will surely come to pass.

Confession: *Dear Jesus, thank you for blessing me with a sound mind. Today I choose to be optimistic about my dreams. I will envision my aspirations even as I plan them. All things are possible with You. I know You can make all my ambitions come to pass. I will live with hope and positivity because I know my tomorrow is blessed. Amen.*

SEPTEMBER 22

A COUNTERRESPONSE

The thief comes only to steal and kill and destroy.
I came that they may have life and have it abundantly.
John 10:10

Many people think it is impossible to keep a positive frame of mind. Some ask whether maintaining a godly mind frame is within everyone's reach. For those who may still ask, the answer is yes. Chasing fear far from our minds may not be attainable overnight, but with constant practice and help from the Holy Spirit, this habit is achievable. It's not enough to shake off negative thoughts that pour into our hearts. Those imaginings must be replaced with positive thoughts. Only then can there be a balance. When we choose to maintain a positive frame of mind, our fears will be crippled and will no longer have bearings to hold on to. In the past, our thoughts may have been thoughts of death, sickness, rejection, and poverty. Henceforth, these should be replaced with thoughts of life, excellent health, acceptance, and prosperity.

Today's text admonishes us to be alert. The devil is working overtime. He is not messing around. Today's text also lets us know that Jesus is the only source of peace. Only in Him can we find rest. For God's peace to reign in our lives, every fearful frame of mind needs to be replaced with faith.

Confession: *Dear Lord, thank You for Your word today. The devil's mission is to keep me depressed and frustrated. Every opportunity he gets, he feeds my mind with terrifying thoughts. Today I say, "No more," to him. My mind is on alert. Every awful thought that comes pouring in will be replaced with thoughts of hope and joy. Help me, Holy Spirit. Amen.*

SEPTEMBER 23

DO IT ANYWAY

You keep him in perfect peace whose mind
is stayed on you, because he trusts in you.
Isaiah 26:3

Yes, fear is powerful. It can cripple a person, both mentally and physically. However, we can overcome fear. One of the best ways to overcome fear is to look it right in the eyes and face it head on.

Whatever scares you or makes you nervous, do it! For instance, if you are one who has a phobia of crowds, heights, or animals, deliberately put yourself in situations that will make you face them. Granted, the first few attempts probably won't be easy. In fact, you may even embarrass yourself. But with continuous practice, it gets better.

You do not just outgrow fear. You have to face it head on. Action is a great restorer and builder of confidence. Inaction is not only the result but a cause of fear. Fear is not going anywhere until you take action. That action has to start now. There is so much fight in you than you know. A good way to fight fear is to do that which scares you anyway. Do what you fear most, and the death of fear is certain. Also, never forget who the source of peace is—God. Ask Him for His perfect peace today.

Confession: *Lord, as I face my fears head on today, please give me Your strength. With my human might, I know it will not be easy. But I can do all things through You who give me the power. Through this process, please grant me Your peace that passes all understanding. Amen.*

SEPTEMBER 24

THE TIME IS NOW

For God has not given us a spirit of fear,
but of power and of love and of a sound mind.
2 Timothy 1:7, NKJV

We can pray, fast, read our Bibles, and go to church every day of the week. Still, this won't yield any results until we start practicing all we have learned. In essence, it's not enough to know things but rather it's the application of these things that will make a difference.

Now is the time to act on all that has been previously addressed about fear. This moment is the best time to face your fears. Today, look fear in the eyes and stand your ground. Determine at this time to resist the devil and his tricks. Now is the time to break yourself free from strongholds. Forge ahead, and take all life has to offer without holding back. Now is the time to start living your life to the fullest.

As Christians, we cannot afford to be laid back and nonchalant about issues of our own lives. According to today's text, fear is not one of God's promises to us. Rather, power, love, and a sound mind are. These and more are what Christians should enjoy.

Confession: *Dear Lord, I thank You for the gift of the present moment. I decree this day that my former fears no longer have a hold on my life. I am free. I am no longer held in captivity of the mind. I am taking hold of the beautiful present and future Jesus has made available for me. Amen.*

THE COST OF CHRISTIANITY

SEPTEMBER 25

IT ALL COMES WITH A PRICE

"...but God said, 'You shall not eat of the fruit of the tree that is in the midst of the garden, neither shall you touch it, lest you die.'"
Genesis 3:3

To live in the Garden of Eden, Adam and Eve had to pay the price of obedience, but they failed to do this. Before long, they were kicked out of the garden. God is organized, and for there to be a balanced world, He has put in place measures that will keep us in check. He started this with the first man and woman He created.

The easiest things to do in life are ones that require little or no sacrifice on our paths. Some of us like it easy-breezy. If given a choice, many of us would likely select a world where no rules exist—no guidelines, no checkpoints, just a world where we can all do as we please without being questioned. Where there are no rules, there is no sin. Everyone then gets to act as they wish. This is why various societies have guiding rules that keep everyone in check. If not for checks and balances, the world would be one big mess.

Under this new theme "The Cost of Being a Christian," we will be exploring how much God expects from us, His children. We will also be discussing the kinds of sacrifices that may be required of us as Christians. We will be checking and balancing our lives with God's Word. We will also be giving an answer to the question, "Does living a righteous life come easily?" Furthermore, we will be discussing the price (if any) we have to pay for our daily Christian walk.

Confession: *Dear Jesus, thank You for blessing the world with order. You have put systems in place to make life less chaotic. As a believer, please give me the grace to abide by all Your instructions. Amen.*

SEPTEMBER 26

YOU WANT THE LIFE? YOU PAY THE PRICE

The soul of the sluggard craves and gets nothing,
while the soul of the diligent is richly supplied.
Proverbs 13:4

Sometimes we look at people and their appealing lifestyles and then conclude in our hearts that these people must be lucky or fortunate. We may even infer that these people were probably presented with more opportunities in life. For many of us, when we look at the highly prosperous people in our society, most of what we see is the end product. What we don't see is what happens behind the scenes in their lives. When successful people tell their stories, many of them talk about their sacrifices. They also speak of the discipline, hard work, and other positive things they did that propelled their success.

Is overnight success possible? Yes, it is. However, this only happens to a handful of people. Not everyone who plays the lottery wins; only a small fraction does. The same goes for overnight successes. Many that crave overnight success without wanting to put in the work end up cutting corners. Many of them also cheat their way through life. In desperation for success, many end up losing their way.

Everything in life comes with a price. Success does not just fall into people's laps. We cannot wish our way into prosperity. Hard work will be required on our part. Sometimes even extra hard work. Do you want a good life? You need to pay the price.

Confession: *Dear Jesus, thank You for Your blessings. Today I pray for Your mercy. In the race for success, I do not want to miss You. Please order my steps. Empower me to keep pushing until I attain all You desire for me. I will not be a lazy Christian. Amen.*

SEPTEMBER 27

YES, IT WOULD BE CHALLENGING

Indeed, all who desire to live a godly life
in Christ Jesus will be persecuted.
2 Timothy 3:12

It seems easier to tell a lie than the truth. There are times when those who lie and cheat get promoted while we Christians may remain in the same spot. Some believers may even get demoted for choosing honesty.

For those starting out their Christian walk, please note that in living godly, you will be challenged. Our flesh will be required to go through continuous brokenness. So, no, it won't come easily, at least not at first. Living righteously will involve some pruning, trimming, breaking, and restructuring. It's a walk that will require sacrifices, like biting our tongues and giving when it is not convenient. We may even be obliged to pray for our enemies.

The good news is that it gets easier. In our devoted work with God, the initial discomforts will stop appearing as such. As we progress in our walk with Christ, we will begin to place more value on the joy that comes from living righteously. We may just find that those things we used to struggle with have become things of the past. We will also be less interested in our former way of life. We will find ourselves needing and longing for more of God. Gradually, we will be made to understand that it is only God we need. So long as we have Him, we are all right. God is enough for us. Living Christ-like is the best way to enjoy life to the fullest.

Confession: *Heavenly Father, living Christ-like is difficult in today's world. People do not even celebrate righteousness anymore. But I do not want to live for people. I long to live for You. Please hold my hands. The journey may be tough, but I have Your strength. With You, I know I can do all things. Amen.*

SEPTEMBER 28

BE ALL YOU WANT TO BE

I can do all things through him who strengthens me.
Philippians 4:13

At the back of our minds, most of us have a picture of whom we would love to be. That person we long to be has such a put-together life that it may look as though the person is out of our reach. To some of us, getting to that place we dream of looks impossible.

When you think about where you are now and where you would love to be, what discourages you from going for it? Is it how far you have to go? Is it the discipline you would have to adopt? Or the fear that you are not enough or hoping for too much? Maybe it's the habit and people you would have to give up. Or perhaps it's because nobody believes you can account for much. Is this you?

In this life, you can be all you want to be. You can achieve anything you set out to do. This may sound cliché, but it is the absolute truth. The reason you have that picture in your head is because it is achievable. But to do this, you will have to quit settling for your current comfortable life. Yes, it may seem far off, and there will be costs to pay along the way. Start paying them today, and begin reaching out to the one on the inside of you. Everything you need to succeed has already been deposited on the inside of you. Give yourself that push today.

Confession: *Father, thank You for Your strength. Also, thank You for the promise of a better tomorrow. You have placed so much on my heart. Please help me never to undervalue all You can do through me. Please give me the courage to pursue until I achieve all You have destined me to. Amen.*

SEPTEMBER 29

GIVE TO CAESAR WHAT IS DUE HIM

"Well, then," Jesus said, "give to Caesar what belongs to Caesar, and give to God what belongs to God." His reply completely amazed them.
Mark 12:17, NLT

According to today's text, Jesus encouraged those who were with Him to give to Caesar all that was Caesar's. I believe giving to Caesar as used in this context wasn't just referring to paying taxes to Caesar alone. It also meant giving respect to the authorities in the secular world. This includes submitting to the rules that have been placed around us.

God is the overall authority. Still, from jurisdiction to jurisdiction, some people have been appointed as leaders. Sometimes these leaders assume big roles and other times small roles. As Christians, we are never to look down on authority figures, even if they may not control as much as we do in our own world. We must abide by the guiding rules of the land. As we do this, we also obey God, who has placed these people in charge over us.

The traffic warden, the usher in church, and your supervisors are examples of those in authority. Jesus encourages us to obey authority figures. So long as their instructions do not contradict God's Word and are right within the context of their authority, then we have to do as Jesus mandates. Titus 3:1 says, "Remind them to be submissive to rulers and authorities, to be obedient, to be ready for every good work."

Confession: *Lord, You love an obedient child. You even promised many beautiful things to those who abide by Your instructions. From now on, please teach me how to give Caesar what is due to Caesar. In obeying those You have placed in authority over me, I am obeying You. Please give me a submissive and humble heart. Amen.*

SEPTEMBER 30

OUR LIVES: THE PRESENT-DAY BIBLE

In the same way, let your light shine before others, so that they may see your good works and give glory to your Father who is in heaven. **Matthew 5:16**

Show me a man who is diligent, compassionate, full of wisdom, and impacts lives, and I'll show you a likely child of God. It's not enough to own ten Bibles or have Jesus stickers on your vehicle. It's also not enough to attend church daily or preach the gospel. The question is, how has God's Word changed you? How have you exemplified all you have gained in Christ? Can your spouse, colleagues, friends, and those around you testify that you are a believer? Has someone ever asked you about makes you distinct? Has your life ever preached Christ to others? Has your conduct and composure ever made others certain that, indeed, you are a Christian?

You see, in this present time, your life and mine are the Bibles people read. Your lifestyle is what unbelievers may study to understand if this "Jesus thing" is real. Our words and conduct are what unbelievers may use as a manual to the "Christian lifestyle." I wonder if my life and yours preach Jesus or crucify Him more. It's not too late to make the necessary adjustments. Today is another opportunity to make Jesus proud through our attitudes.

Confession: *Lord, thank You for calling me Yours. Today I ask for mercy. Please forgive me for those times I have been a negative review for the kingdom. Henceforth, let my life and conduct reflect You positively. When people see me, let them see You. Amen.*

OCTOBER 1

OVERANALYZING THINGS

Woe to those who are wise in their own eyes,
and shrewd in their own sight!
Isaiah 5:21

I used to be a devout worrier. In the past, I worried when things were not good. I even worried when they were. My thoughts were constantly questioning: Am I doing the right thing? Is God in this? Doesn't this look too good to be true? What if I'm wrong? What if I miss it? What if I miss God? Could this be God's blessing? After pondering on these thoughts, I would go ahead to check and doublecheck things. I did this until I almost drove myself crazy. Are you like this too? If yes, has this held you back from achieving the great things you know you could have? It did in the past for me.

It's one thing to live one's life on the surface. But it's equally detrimental to be too rigid and calculating. Sometimes things looking too good to be true is God's grace at work. Sometimes not being in control is not a bad thing.

Just let yourself go, and let yourself go in the Lord. Enjoy the blessings of God that make you rich and add no sorrow. You are not being tested. You are only enjoying the benefits that come with serving a God who is all sufficient.

Confession: *Dear miracle-working Father, Your ways are not my ways. Your thoughts are not my thoughts. Please give me a deeper understanding of You. Open the eyes of my understanding that I may see You in Your simplicity. Teach me how to stop overthinking and complicating things. Amen.*

OCTOBER 2

PERSISTENCE

And I tell you, ask, and it will be given to you;
seek, and you will find; knock, and it will be opened to you.
Luke 11:9

To persist means to keep at something until the desired result is seen. Persistence is what keeps us going. It's what drives us when others quit. One of the prices we have to pay to enjoy all Christ has provided for us is to stop being "fast food" Christians. To be persistent, we must be required to stop living our lives for the here and now alone. We also need to understand that things may not always go as expected.

Today God is calling us to lives of tenacity. We are being urged to lives that persist despite all odds. We are also being invited to lives that see things through, despite our surrounding challenges. This is the same kind of life Christ demonstrated while He was here on Earth. He was pushed, humiliated, betrayed, falsely accused, and devalued. If He had given up, He would have certainly been justified, especially seeing that those He suffered for were the same ones putting more coal in His fire of torment. Instead, Jesus kept His gaze strictly on the goal at hand. He never let go until the end. We all can learn from this.

When we feel like we can't take one more step and would rather concede, let's choose to take yet another step. Despite oppositions and frustration, let's keep pushing forward. Eventually we will conquer.

Confession: *Lord Jesus, I am grateful for the strength You have given me. Every day You empower me with the grace to keep pushing on until I have attained all. Help me walk in this grace. Help me know that even when I am tired and feel like giving up, I can find deeper strength in You. Amen.*

OCTOBER 3

PERSEVERANCE

Count it all joy, my brothers, when you meet trials of various kinds, for you know the testing of your faith produces steadfastness. **James 1:2–3**

Previously we discussed persistence. Today we will be discussing something similar yet different—perseverance. To persist and to persevere entail reaching a goal. While persistence is about not giving up before reaching one's destination, perseverance is about one's attitude through the journey. Perseverance encompasses endurance, steadfastness, and keeping calm during adversities.

Anybody can persist, but only a few can persevere. In the same way, anybody can set a goal and keep at it, but only a few can power through with a good attitude. Anybody can work toward success, but only a few can do so without compromising their faith. Anyone can go through hardship, but only a few can do so and still remain noble.

Today's reference scripture informs us that our faith will be tested. We will face various trials that will stretch our limits. We would be pushed, shoved around, cheated on, taken for granted, and looked down on. A major reason we go through these tests is so that we become even more steadfast. While we await God's promise, we are to endure the challenges that may precede it. Not only are we to bear the hurdles but we are also to count it all joy while we do so. In spite of the obstacles and stress that comes with "the process," please persevere. At the end of the tunnel, you will be glad you did.

Confession: *Dear God, Your expectation of me is that I keep a good attitude no matter what. This might be difficult in today's world, but I know that despite the challenges, You have already given me the grace to persevere. Today I choose to endure all the trials that will come at me on my journey to success. I will not compromise. I will not give in to my frustration. Amen.*

OCTOBER 4

SACRIFICIAL LIVING

Jesus said to him, "If you would be perfect, go, sell what you possess and give it to the poor and you will have treasure in heaven and come and follow me." **Matthew 19:21**

To live sacrificially means putting other's needs ahead of one's own. This act involves a lot of selflessness. As Christians, we cannot run away from living sacrificially. This lifestyle is in fact one way we show that we are God's children. Sacrifices will be required of us in our everyday lives. Not only will this act be requested of us but we will also be tested regularly by this. To get more rooted in our walk with God, we will have to pass this test daily.

Living a sacrificial life is not easy. It is not a habit our flesh will readily adhere to. During Jesus' ordeal at the cross of Calvary, He did not walk majestically to the cross and ask to be crucified. This act took everything out of Him. He had to die to self first before dying for all. This selflessness is what Christ asks us to exude today.

As we continue our walk with God, we will be required to do things that we will not directly benefit from. We will be obliged to reach out in kindness to others that may have no means of repaying us. Things may be taken from us to add to others that may or may not have as much as we do. Those that rebel against this process of selflessness have found themselves stagnating. Many remain spiritually and financially stagnant until they carry out the selfless acts God instructs them to. Let's not be one of those people. Today let's be selfless as Christ pulls us to where He is.

Confession: *Dear Jesus, thank You for dying on my behalf. You made Yourself a sacrificial lamb for the world. I know that in my walk with You, I will be required to make certain sacrifices. I pray that You will give me the grace to do so at such moments. I do not want my life to revolve around me alone. Help me be like You, Jesus. Amen.*

OCTOBER 5

SACRIFICIAL LIVING PART II

Then God said, "Take your son, your only son, whom you love—Isaac—and go to the region of Moriah. Sacrifice him there as a burnt offering on a mountain I will show you."
Genesis 22:2, NIV

We benefit from sacrificial living in two ways. First, giving helps us understand the value of all we have been blessed with. Also, this act helps us put our trust only in God and not in our possessions. In the scripture above, God told Abraham to sacrifice his only son, who was born very late in Abraham's life.

Abraham cared deeply for his son. Even while he heeded God's request and was going to sacrifice Isaac, he must have done so with a heavy heart. Abraham's love for his son ran very deep. However, his trust in God ran even deeper. Else, what other reason could one have for wanting to give up something as important as one's child? No wonder Abraham was referred to as the father of faith. Well, his faith paid off in the end as he was given a ram to sacrifice in place of his son.

One lesson you and I can learn from Abraham's story is that God may not use our sacrifices. Sometimes the message God may be trying to pass across to us is that He alone should come first. We should never hold on to anything or anyone more tightly than we do Him. God may not require us to sacrifice our children, but He may occasionally ask us to let go of those things we care for. We then have to trust Him enough to drop it all at the altar without looking back.

Confession: *Father, throughout Abraham's life, he trusted You. Everything You asked him to do, he did without questioning You. And because of this, You blessed him abundantly. I pray today that You will help me understand that You are my all in all. Without You, I am nothing. In You, I have everything. Amen.*

OCTOBER 6

STOP LISTENING TO THE VOICE

Submit yourselves therefore to God.
Resist the devil, and he will flee from you.
James 4:7

Certain voices speak to our minds. These voices may come from our conscience or the Holy Spirit. However, another voice speaks to us as well. This voice continually reminds us of all the times we have tried and failed and also gives us many reasons why things won't work out. It constantly nags us about how we have messed up as it sows condemning seeds about how God is mad at us. It does this with the hopes of demoralizing us into giving up as opposed to aspiring for better in life. This voice never lets us forget all our past wrongs and mistakes. Do you recognize this voice? I do. It is the voice that comes at me full force as soon as I open my eyes in the morning. It is the voice that follows me all day, hoping to distract me from my daily mission. It is the voice of the devil.

The devil knows our weaknesses. He also knows our greatest fears. He uses these to torment us at every opportunity he gets. But today the voice of truth is telling us to stop listening to him. We are to resist his lies and deceit.

How do we resist the devil? According to today's text, we do so by submitting to God. We also do so by yielding ourselves to the leading of the Holy Spirit. Once we begin doing this, we will start becoming less bothered about the evil one. Whenever he comes at us, we will find ourselves just shaking him off, ignoring him, and going on our way. Before long, that which used to hold us in bondage will no longer have power over us.

Confession: *Today I resist the devil. He no longer has a hold on my life and thoughts. I submit myself to You, Lord. From now on, I will only listen to the voice of truth. I will only pay attention to the voice of hope and peace. Never again will the enemy torment me. Amen.*

OCTOBER 7

WHAT WILL HEAVEN'S RECORD BE OF YOU?

Now there happened to be there a worthless man, whose name was Sheba, the son of Bichri, a Benjamite. And he blew the trumpet and said, we have no portion in David, and we have no portion in David, and we have no inheritance in the son of Jesse; every man to his tents, O Israel! ***2 Samuel 20:1***

As Christians, our character matters. Many people in the Bible were defined by their lifestyles and attitudes. Abraham was called the father of faith (Romans 4:11), David was characterized as the man after God's heart (Acts 13:22), and Daniel was described as a wise man (Daniel 1:20). However, in today's text, Sheba was described as worthless. A worthless person is one whose life accounts for little or nothing. So on this note, what would you and I be described as? Would we be characterized as faithful, excellent, diligent, or otherwise?

It's one thing for humans to have a beautiful record of our existence here on Earth. The question is, will heaven have the same record? What will heaven document about you? You see, humans will always see what is made visible to them. But heaven cannot be fooled. All that has been done in the dark will come to light eventually.

Today we are being encouraged to do an inner check. With the way we conduct our life's affairs, what do we think heaven's account of us will be? This exercise is not so we can praise or condemn ourselves. This is so that we can appraise our lives and come up stronger in areas where we may be falling short.

Confession: *Dear Lord, thank You for making me a vessel for honor. On occasions when my way of life has been appalling, I pray You have mercy. Please forgive me and give me a fresh start. May my life not be recorded as worthless. May I be remembered as one who stood for righteousness, and may my life be a blessing to the world. Amen.*

COMMITMENT

OCTOBER 8

COMMITMENT

So let it grow, for when your endurance is fully developed, you will be perfect and complete, needing nothing.
James 1:4, NLT

To be committed means to pledge to do something. But commitment goes beyond making promises. It entails deliberately executing all that has been promised. This is regardless of whether it is convenient or not. The difference between a committed person and one who isn't may not be noticeable at first. Eventually, however, it will be glaring. So many attitudes can be observed in the life of the non-committal person, some of which may include being evasive, cagey, and cunning. Some may even exude a nonchalant, "I don't care" attitude.

Commitment or a lack of it affects all aspects of life. It most especially affects our relationships (marriage, friendship, work, family, and God). So how can the commitment attitude catapult us into living triumphantly? How can the application of this principle make all the difference in our everyday life? What significant impact can it have on our lives? This is what we will explore in the new series, "Commitment."

***Confession:** Lord Jesus, thank You for Your word this day. In all I do, help me stay committed. Give me the strength to endure and persevere until I achieve all I am destined to. Amen.*

OCTOBER 9

COMMITMENT VS FEELINGS

Just say a simple, 'Yes, I will,' or 'No, I won't.'
Anything beyond this is from the evil one.
Matthew 5:37, NLT

An individual can be talented, motivated, and educated and still not achieve all that he or she is capable of. This may be because this individual keeps failing the commitment test. Of all the advice I have been given, there are two I hold on to dearly. The first is, no matter how you feel, get up, dress up, show up, and never give up. The second is, commitment is the foundation of great accomplishments. These two quotes have been life-changing for all who have put it to use, me included.

Commitment goes beyond how we feel. It is 0% feelings compliant and 100% intentional-effort compliant. While commitment stays no matter what, feelings come and go. Commitment endures, but feelings change when circumstances are no longer favorable. Commitments are ties that bind, but feelings break free at will. Commitment makes one honorable, but feelings make one unstable. Finally, commitment keeps one accountable, and feelings...not so much. Does this then mean we should never consider our feelings when making decisions? No, not so! We are human and are naturally feelings-driven. Today, we are only being encouraged to place our commitments above our feelings.

There are certain demands a successful life will place on us; one of them is a full commitment to all our endeavors. We have to do this whether we feeling like it or not.

Confession: *Dear Lord, I appreciate all I have been blessed with. Many times I have been too feelings-driven and have let my emotions cloud my judgment. Please forgive me. Help me act better from this day. Amen.*

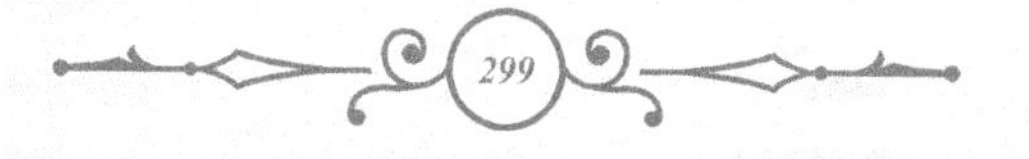

OCTOBER 10

ALLOWANCE FOR ERRORS

Make allowance for each other's faults, and forgive anyone who offends you. Remember, the Lord forgave you, so you must forgive others.
Colossians 3:13, NLT

A man once said to his wife, "I have forgiven you for all you have done in the past and all you will do." How realistic this would be in the long run is still up for debate. However, one thing can be said of this man. He was willing to work out a way to deal with his wife's wrongdoings even before she committed them.

We are not yet perfect. For this reason, it would only be to our own good to have a prepared mind toward other's excesses. As a matter of fact, I would encourage us to anticipate these. This entails leaving room for people's mistakes even before they commit them. Those we are in relationships with have their own weaknesses, as do we. When they begin to manifest, we must have an inbuilt shock absorber that absolves their offenses.

The shock-absorbing principle can also be applied to every sphere of life. Having some way to accommodate unplanned eventualities will save us from plenty of frustration. The more we practice this, the more we will glide through life with grace and maturity.

Confession: *Dear Jesus, I'm thankful for my relationships. As a human, it's hard not to be offended by others. But with You, Lord, I know I can do all things. Help me this day to be more like You. Amen.*

OCTOBER 11

EMBRACING THE NOT SO GOOD

Indeed, there is no one on earth who is righteous,
no one who does what is right and never sins.
Ecclesiastes 7:20, NIV

God has made everyone in such a way that there will always be a black spot on their white linen. Here is what I mean: God never creates anyone and then hands him or her perfection in all areas of life. Frankly, I have never met a perfect person with perfect everything. And if I were to take a guess, I would say neither have you.

There will always be that thing we can tag as the "not so good" in people's lives. This may also be called weaknesses, disorder, or shortcomings. Everyone on Earth has a default of some sort. For some, it can be seen on the surface. But for many, it may not be quite noticeable at first glance until one gets very close and intimate with them.

Some vows carry a "for better or worse" clause. Today we are talking about that worse, meaning those nauseating attitudes people exhibit that upset us. We are also talking about accommodating other's imperfections. We are to love people through their good, bad, and worse.

Confession: *Dear Lord, thank you for loving me through my good and not so good. Give me the grace to do the same for others. Give me the grace to see more of the right and less of the wrong in people. Amen.*

OCTOBER 12

REDUCED EXPECTATIONS

Love prospers when a fault is forgiven, but dwelling on it separates close friends
Proverbs 17:9, NLT

There is no doubt those we are in relationships with can frustrate us. To become less provoked by their actions, there are certain things we may need to work on. One of these is our expectations of them. Having some level of expectations of people is a good thing, but when these expectations are too high or unrealistic, frustration is inevitable. People are different, and so they will act differently. We, in turn, need to accept those around us for who they are instead of trying to change them into who we want them to be. That you groomed your child in all you believe in doesn't mean your child will end up being anything like you. That your mom had certain ways of doing things does not mean your wife will follow that same path. These are just a few of so many examples.

Many of those with whom we are in relationships will not live up to our desired expectations. This has to be okay with us. Also, we have an obligation to stay committed to our loved ones regardless of their weirdness. Over the years, I have learned to set my expectations low, especially for those I may not be too acquainted with. If they exceed my expectations, excellent! If not, I'm still very much as committed to the relationship as I was from the very onset.

Confession: *Lord Jesus, even at my worse, You love me still. For this, I am thankful. Henceforth, I will be more accommodating of other people's excesses. Give me the strength to achieve this. Amen.*

OCTOBER 13

WORK IT OUT

Let each of you look not only to his own interests,
but also to the interests of others.
Philippians 2:4

Our generation is quickly becoming one whose endurance level dissipates more by the day. We want nothing to do with anything that will inconvenience our perfect lifestyle. If things do not bear any semblance to how we have envisioned them in our minds, we are ready to walk out. If it requires extra effort than planned, we are prepared to cut it off, whether it has a chance of surviving or not. These days, a slight disagreement is enough to crumble relationships that took years to build. Our generation seems to be fast accepting that the only way to get rid of a nagging headache is to cut the whole head off.

Commitment means being dedicated to a cause. Being dedicated sometimes entails fighting for all that we believe in. It involves being tenacious and never accepting mediocrity. Where there is a will, there is a way. Many of the things we run away from find their way back to our lives in different forms. The key is to stay and work with what we have until we see the desired result. To excel at whatever it is we plan to do, we have to be willing to put in the work.

Confession: *Dear Lord, thank You for Your word this day. Please have mercy for when I have given up easily on things You have committed into my hands. I ask for the strength and grace to put extra effort into my relationships and other endeavors. Amen.*

OCTOBER 14

GREENER ON THE OTHER SIDE

But godliness with contentment is great gain.
1 Timothy 6:6

That you married an attractive person does not stop others from being more attractive. That you got a well-paying job doesn't stop other jobs from paying better. That you have a beautiful home doesn't stop others from getting a superior one. The list goes on. The truth is that the grass will always be greener on the other side. Still, this is not enough reason to keep hopping around in search of the so-called "better life." There will always be a more attractive person than your spouse or a better job than yours. Commitment remains the watchword here. We have to stop this habit of flowing with the wind wherever it blows stronger. It's important we develop the attitude of staying rooted in place. We are to discipline ourselves to keep at something, no matter what. We are also to give our very best to all that we set our hearts to do. This is God's expectation of all His children.

Even if things may not look the best for us, we can reassure ourselves that it is most likely God's best for us. If we will be diligent and committed enough, God will see to it that we succeed in all our endeavors. If we will also water and earnestly care for our grass, it will become greener in due season.

Confession: *Dear Jesus, thank you for the great life You have blessed me with. With You, I know things can only get better. If, at any point, I have searched for "better" outside Your will, please forgive me. Henceforth, I will wait on You and all that You have promised. Give me the grace to do this. Amen.*

OCTOBER 15

LOVE WHAT YOU HAVE

Then he said, "Beware! Guard against every kind of greed. Life is not measured by how much you own."
Luke 12:15, NLT

If given the choice, many of us would love to be born into wealthy homes. Also, most of us would like to work in the best places, attend Ivy League schools, or drive expensive cars. Sadly, not all these choices are at our disposal. In assessing all that we do not like about our lives, there is just one question we need to ask ourselves: "Can we in any way change all that we detest about our lives at this moment?" If the answer is yes, then we may begin making changes. But if the answer is no, we may have to make up our minds to start loving and accepting that which we know we cannot change. We may not have all that we love, but we can love all that we have.

No doubt many of us would prefer better lives than we have now. However, we are being urged today to stay devoted and deal with where we are and all we have at the moment. When we are committed to something, it will reflect in our attitude toward it. We will be tenacious.

We may not be able to change certain aspects of our lives, but we can choose what our attitudes will be toward the cards life has handed us. We can be tenacious. We can renew our hopes daily and trust that all things will work for our good eventually. Once we dedicate ourselves to making things work, we will receive great ideas on how to execute them.

Confession: *Dear Lord, I revel in the love You lavish on me. I acknowledge that where I am at the moment is exactly where You need me to be. Give me the grace to accept that which I have no power to change. Help me stay committed to all that You have blessed me with. Amen.*

OCTOBER 16

COMMITMENT TO EXCELLENCE

Whatever you do, do well.
Ecclesiastes 9:10a, NLT

A synonym for "doing things well" is "being excellent." Judging from our reference text, we can conclude that God's standard for all we do is excellence. Today's devotional is dedicated to exploring God's standard for commitment. We will also be examining the extreme case of commitment. This is otherwise known as perfectionism. Excellence and perfection are often mistaken to mean the same thing. This is not true at all. Perfection can be defined as an obsession with being faultless, but excellence is a desire to be outstanding. Perfection breeds fear, dominance, adversity, pressure, criticism, addiction, and anxiety. Excellence breeds optimism, effort, risk, togetherness, satisfaction, and inner peace. Being committed is miles away from being perfect. But being committed without attaching the excellence standard to it is not God's best. This is why today's text insists that whatever is worth doing, we are to "do well." In essence, mediocrity is not acceptable for believers. Commitment to excellence does not connote being flawless. Rather, it entails putting our best into everything we do.

Confession: *Dear God, I marvel at Your excellence. Even the Scriptures describe Your name as excellent. This same character is what You expect from all Your children. Please help me always truly represent You everywhere I go and in everything I do. Amen.*

OCTOBER 17

COMMITMENT TO OUR FAITH

For to me to live is Christ, and to die is gain.
Philippians 1:21

Many people love hanging on to Bible verses that address prosperity. Lots of people also love listening to sermons that focus on living stress free. While all these are beautiful and are part of God's promises for us, there is a lot more. Yes! Christ died that we may be saved. He has also made provisions for our liberation and enjoyment. However, there are certain roles that we need to play in order to enjoy the comfort Jesus has freely given to us. Also, there are a few uncomfortable moments where we will have to persevere before we get our breakthrough. During moments like these, it is incumbent upon us to be dedicated to God.

James 1:3 admonishes us to count it all joy when we face trials because we will always face trials in life. Difficult moments should not be the time when we question God's love or backslide. Instead, they should be times to be joyous and committed. In doing so, wc will obtain the James 1:4 promise: "being perfect and complete and needing nothing."

Confession: *Dear Jesus, thank You for Your death on the cross. You died that I may live. I know that in my journey here on Earth, I will encounter some challenges. But I also know that You will always be with me. Help me find completion in You. Amen.*

OCTOBER 18

LET THEM HAVE A STAKE

For where your treasure is, there your heart will be also.
Matthew 6:21, NIV

The reason why big companies have stakeholders is primarily to grow their businesses. The stakeholders share in almost everything that happens in the company. This includes profit and loss. Stakeholders are always protective of their investments in organizations they invest in.

We also can utilize this knowledge in influencing those around us on how to stay committed. Wherever one's possession lies is where one's heart will be. When we have a stake in something, there will be a clear difference in how we handle it. We may not bother ourselves much with that which we have no commitment to.

To get people to be fully committed to that which we are asking of them, we may have to go beyond telling them. For instance, if you want people to be a part of your proposed project, give them specific roles. That way, they feel included in the decision making. Stakeholders never want to see their investment go down the drain, but anyone who has nothing to lose won't be bothered. Let them begin by having a stake today.

Confession: *Dear Lord, I am thankful for today's word. I ask that You help me come to a deeper understanding of how to partner with others. Amen.*

OCTOBER 19

A PROMISED REWARD

A person who promises a gift but doesn't give it
is like clouds and wind that bring no rain.
Proverbs 25:14, NLT

There are many ways to influence the folks around us into committing. One of these is giving them something worthwhile to look forward to. Having understood this principle, many firms request their staff meet a specific quota. On hitting the set target, they get tangible returns. For instance, some companies request their staff drive the company's truck for some time. The employee then becomes the owner of the truck after meeting some terms and conditions. Many sales firms often grant commissions. This happens when employees meet specific goals, and it usually excludes the basic income. It is what I call "the extra."

A future worth looking forward to can influence one's attitude in the present. A promising future is a good motivating factor that can make people bring their A-game any day, any time. We can begin practicing this with those around us too.

Instead of nagging about our folks' non-committal issue, we could approach things differently. We could give these people something to motivate them. This method has been attested to by many. Please try it today. It works!

Confession: *Dear Jesus, thank You for the gift of another day. A promising future is worth looking forward to. Teach me how to use this to improve my relationships. Help me to be a voice of motivation to those around me. Amen.*

OCTOBER 20

COMMITMENT ALL THE WAY

"But don't begin until you count the cost. For who would begin construction of a building without first calculating the cost to see if there is enough money to finish it?" **Luke 14:28, NLT**

It is better not to begin at all than to begin and quit once we get stretched out of our comfort zone. Getting a notable knowledge of that which we are embarking on before we begin would do us a lot of good. This cuts across every aspect of life, be it marriage, a career path, raising a family, or starting a new business. Our scripture reference encourages us to count the cost of what we intend to do. Part of counting the cost includes doing detailed research on that subject matter. We also need to have a prepared mind toward the venture and check God's stand on the matter. For both short-term or long-term commitments, we are to count the cost first.

No significant achievement comes easily. We will be required to pay certain costs along our path to success. These costs at times may not be pleasant; this is why it is called a cost. Let's be committed to whatever we do. Let's stay faithful to all we have promised to do. As we do this, we will see God manifest Himself mightily. In the end, God will make all our efforts worth it.

Confession: *Lord Jesus, I appreciate all I have been blessed with. Thank You most especially for the blessings I don't see. Your instruction for me today is that I count the cost before beginning an endeavor. Give me the grace to always finish that which I start. Amen.*

OCTOBER 21

THE DECISION TO STAY

This explains why a man leaves his father and mother and is joined to his wife, and the two are united into one.
Genesis 2:24, NLT

"Till death do us part" ends the popular marriage vow. This implies the determination to stay until the very end. Many couples have concluded from the onset that they will be together forever. Their conduct will differ greatly from those in marriages of convenience. They will be ones who exhibit a resolute attitude toward their home as they seek out new methods to add flavor to their marriages. These determined couples are mostly seen engaging in marriage-building activities. These include attending marriage seminars, reading good books, and spending quality family time together. They may even seek counsel when things are not going so well. What we see from these people is a clear commitment to their marriage.

One way to stay committed to anything we set out to do is to make up our minds before starting out. Nothing great comes easily. Many people are uninterested in riding things out or experiencing life's little discomforts. To these people, I say please do not even begin at all.

What is the point of starting things only to quit halfway? This quitter's attitude has a way of affecting one's self-esteem in the long run. It's why many feel like they are failures. We are not failures! We are God's children. We have His strength. By His grace, we can do anything we set out to do.

Confession: *Dear Jesus, despite Your suffering on the cross of Calvary, You persevered. You started and completed Your mission despite all the opposition. Please give me the strength to follow through with all that You have placed on my path. Amen.*

OCTOBER 22

THE MOST COMMITTED OF THEM

For if they fall, one will lift up his fellow. But woe to him who is alone when he falls and has not another to lift him up!
Ecclesiastes 4:10

I had a boss who seemed overbearing upon first meeting him. The reason for this is quite simple. Our workplace was a non-profit, and it was also a volunteer job that didn't promise any incentive. During the selection process, we were made to face a few hurdles. Many presumed this was unnecessary for an unpaid job. When the time came for the boss to select candidates, he did not take the smartest or most qualified of us. Instead, he chose those whose dedication he had tested and could trust. Well, it would seem his approach paid off because, for an unpaid staff, we did well. Many of us who did the job loved what we did. And when the money started coming in eventually, it was only an added bonus. This was our success secret and why we were able to stand out among all others.

Some may not entirely agree with my boss's approach. But those who have had their share of dealing with non-committal people understand the pain that comes with doing so. We would be better off by ourselves than having people who can never be counted on. Not everyone needs to be in our lives.

Do we have people in our lives whose presence or absence does not count for much? Do we have those folks who just enjoy causing us unnecessary pain? This may be an excellent moment to consider letting them go.

Confession: *Dear God, teach me every day to stay committed to all I do. Please surround me with folks that will be sources of help for me during hard times. Also, teach me how to improve my relationships. Show me ways to bring out the best in people. Amen.*

OCTOBER 23

THE MOST COMMITTED OF THEM PART II

...he is a double-minded man, unstable in all his ways.
James 1:8

A speaker at a singles conference some time ago said the following to his audience:

> When settling down, don't just settle with the one that gives you goosebumps. Instead, settle with the one that would be there with you by your sickbed in the hospital. Settle with the one that has been tested and found worthy. Settle not just for the best-looking one but one who is willing to learn and improve. Overall, settle with the one you can always depend on. Good looks and riches may be great attractive features. But when push comes to shove, the commitment to stay and make a marriage is what will sustain a home.

Life is beautiful, but to enjoy it to the fullest, we must be careful whom we permit into our lives. The people that surround us often have an influence on our lives. Those we should be in relationship with are those that are willing to be by our sides through life's ordeals. Indifferent, unconcerned, run-away folks are those we may need to stay far away from. To run life's race and do so successfully, we will need to shield ourselves with a strong support system. Do you have a sound support system?

Confession: *Lord Jesus, please help me stay committed in all my relationships. Help me choose wisely those people that will influence my journey through life. Please keep me far away from those that will derail my destiny. Amen.*

OCTOBER 24

THE OTHER SIDE OF COMMITMENT

The blessing of the LORD makes rich, and he adds no sorrow with it.
Proverbs 10:22

Previously, we established that commitment is a virtue everyone needs to have. Today, we will be discussing the borders of commitment. There are certain times when we may just need to call it quits. Violent relationships, choking jobs, and hazardous situations are good examples. When certain things begin to threaten our lives, sanity, and peace of mind, wisdom dictates that we quit. Walking out on things is not as horrible as many make it seem. Sometimes it may be the only option left on the table.

Anything done in excess seldom ends up well, and commitment is no different. Our constant thought of "Maybe if we tried harder, we could fix it" does not work in every circumstance. Sometimes our best has to be enough. If things still remain the same or become worse after giving our best, we may need to take a bow and exit the stage. After all, our scripture verse today says that God's blessings do not bring sorrow and pain.

Confession: *Dear Lord, You are good. Your thoughts toward me are of good and never of evil. Should there be anything threatening my joy and peace this day, I hand them over to You. Please give me the strength to walk away from harmful situations when I need to. Amen.*

OCTOBER 25

VOLUNTEERING IS ALWAYS A GOOD START

And let us not grow weary of doing good, for in due season we will reap, if we do not give up.
Galatians 6:9

A rich woman, Michelle, was speaking to some of her friends about how out of place she felt. She confided that she felt worthless and depressed. So one of her friends, who volunteered at the homeless shelter, suggested that Michelle tag along for a visit. Michelle only planned to do so once, but upon encountering so much joy and self-worth from the experience, she decided to make it a habit. This is a true story of what the act of volunteering can do. Nearly everyone who volunteers has a similar testimony.

To volunteer means to offer to do something freely. It means to do good while expecting nothing in return. It also means to offer our services at no cost to those who are at the receiving end. But volunteering does not just take away from the volunteer. In return, it gives back plenty.

Volunteering rewards one with experience, joy, optimism, self-confidence, humility, and excellent social skills. It is also a very good antidote for depression. Volunteering teaches us how to stay committed as well. If you have never volunteered before, think about doing so today. Before you know it, you, too, will be a testifier of the blessings that come with that act.

Confession: *Dear Jesus, thank You for being good to me. Your instruction is that I do the same to others. This sometimes is difficult to do. I need Your grace, Lord. As I begin volunteering in my little way, help me. Amen.*

OCTOBER 26

DON'T GIVE UP BEFORE YOU BEGIN

He who observes the wind will not sow,
And he regards the cloud will not reap
Ecclesiastes 11:4, NKJV

Often individuals end up flunking even though they prepared thoroughly. This is because, unknown to them, they gave up on themselves before they started. It's one thing to prepare but another to prepare like a winner. If you have the thoughts and approach of someone who will fail at his or her endeavor, you will probably do so. This may happen regardless of how long you persist.

Fear is powerful. It can keep us under bondage if we permit it to. If you are one who gives up as soon as an unexpected hiccup disturbs your plans, today God is calling you to a better life. If you always have excuses for not doing that which you know you should, God is speaking to you today. There will always be many reasons why you should give in to your fears; the devil can also be counted on to give you a million reasons why you won't succeed at your endeavor. However, decide right now to put your trust in God. Step out in faith. God is all you need. He will come through for you.

When we compare where we are right now to where we still have to go, it can be frightening. But one thing we should never do is start an undertaking with the mindset of a failure. You are not a failure. At least give it a try, especially when you know God is involved. Our aspirations are meant to stretch us.

Confession: *Today I decree that I am not a failure. Lord, when You ask me to go, I will do so with total confidence in Your leading. I will no longer live my life in defeat. Though the journey may be tough, I know You will see me through. In all my endeavors, I will come out a success. Amen.*

THE GOOD LIFE

OCTOBER 27

THE GOOD LIFE

Even though a person sins and gets by with it hundreds of times throughout a long life, I'm still convinced that the good life is reserved for those who fear God, who lives reverently in His presence.
Ecclesiastes 8:12, MSG

Are you someone who loves God with all your heart? Maybe you worship earnestly, keep all scriptural commandments, and serve in church devotedly. Perhaps you do all these things and still feel like the Lord has abandoned you. Maybe you even feel like God's promises are far away and never within reach for you. You may be one who constantly wonders if the Lord will ever grant your long-time desire.

It seems like the season right now when the unrighteous are the ones acquiring the good things of life. It may even appear like the righteous are the ones being punished for being just. The scripture above serves as an encouragement to believers that feel unfairly treated.

Our God does whatever He wants to. The reasons behind His actions are not something He readily reveals. Many biblical characters stuck with God until they received all that God promised them. Solomon was one hundred percent convinced that the good life is reserved for those that fear God and persist. Abraham never stopped believing (Romans 4:20–22), Daniel never stopped trusting (Daniel 1:8–9), and Hannah never stopped asking (1 Samuel 1:10–11). They eventually received their promised inheritance (the good life). In due time, you will receive yours too.

Confession: *Dear Father, sometimes my challenges weigh me down. Many times my problems feel like they will drown me, and Your promises seem so far away. But today I choose to be encouraged by Your promises. You have reserved the good life for me. Sorrow may last through the night, but I know my joy is right around the corner. I will laugh again, and I will testify to Your goodness. My challenges will become my testimonies. Amen.*

OCTOBER 28

TODAY'S DEED

The LORD is slow to anger and abounding in steadfast love, forgiving iniquity and transgression, but he will by no means clear the guilty, visiting the iniquity of the fathers on the children, to the third and fourth generation. **Numbers 14:18**

One day a wealthy man told his children he had no plans to leave them any material inheritances. The only thing he planned to will to them was that which he had fought for all his life—a good name. This came as a huge surprise to his children, who were already banking on their inheritance. Years after this, the wealthy man passed on. His good name and kind deeds to the world paid off tremendously for his offspring. It paved the way for them beyond their expectations.

No one knows what the future holds. This makes our everyday actions important. Some people suffering today are doing so not because God has forsaken them but merely because they are reaping all they have directly or indirectly sown in the past.

Every thought, action, and word matters. They matter because they come back to influence tomorrow. Today's deed can determine a better or worse future. It can also impact the lives of those around us either positively or negatively. Let's endeavor to live each day knowing we did our best. Let's live every day knowing that our daily actions are seeds that will bear fruit in the future. Today's deeds will always come back to either haunt or bless us.

Confession: *A good name is better than gold or silver. Today I pray for the grace to leave the upcoming generation with a reputable name. May I influence my world positively, and may I be known as one who changed my world for the better. May my good deeds pave the way for my children and the generations to come. This I pray through Christ my Lord. Amen.*

OCTOBER 29

WHEN THEY ARE NOT LOOKING

"Beware of practicing your righteousness before other people in order to be seen by them, for then you will have no reward from your Father who is in heaven."
Matthew 6:1

As humans, we tend to be at our best when the spotlight is on us. When the audience is cheering, we are naturally more pleasant. When people we know, or perhaps even strangers, are around us, we have the tendency to appear very gracious. We do this so people will have a good impression of us. The question today is "Who are you when nobody is watching?"

Who are you in the quiet of your own home? What can people who know you well say about you? More importantly, who does God see you as? Answers to these questions will reveal who you really are.

When man is not looking, God is. God sees and knows it all. In the still and quiet, His gaze is intently upon us. We should do the right thing because we fear God, not just for the praise of others. Reverencing God in all our actions is proof that we honor Him. God will then honor and bless us. God loves those who go all out for His sake. Let's endeavor to be such people.

Confession: *Dear Lord. Unlike humans who see only appearances, You see every person's heart. Whether man is looking or not, please grant me the grace to always do right. I long to be right in Your sight. I long to be one whose actions and way of life please You. Please help me that I may live righteously. Amen.*

OCTOBER 30

DO THE RIGHT THING ALWAYS

So whoever knows the right thing to do
and fails to do it, for him it is sin.
James 4:17

At the back of our minds, we all have that great picture of who we would love to be. But who and what is stopping us from being that person? The answer is simple: you and I.

When we don't do that which should be done at the appropriate time, a burden often hangs over our shoulders. Some, as a result, may not be able to sleep well at night. However, when one fully maximizes the day by being diligent, there is an inner joy that often follows. One naturally feels better about himself or herself on these days, no matter how tired.

Doing the right thing doesn't always come easily. Many times we may not get rewarded for doing them. We may even get mocked for always being upright. But do the right thing we must, even if it's just for the sake of doing it for God. Our choices at every moment play a role in determining what our existence will account for. Doing the right thing also brings fulfillment.

Confession: *Dear Jesus, in today's world, living righteously is hardly honored by society. I do not want man's honor but Yours. Today, I pray that I will always be right with You. I will live all my days to honor You. Whether or not my good attitude is celebrated, I will continually live a virtuous life. So help me, God. Amen.*

OCTOBER 31

WHILE YOU WAIT

Even when there was no reason for hope, Abraham kept hoping—believing that he would become the father of many nations. For God had said to him, "That's how many descendants you will have!"
Romans 4:18, NLT

Patience is not just waiting; it is our attitude while we wait. What made the story of Abraham remarkable wasn't just the length of time he had to wait on God. His positive attitude while he did made all the difference (Romans 4:18–21). Several other characters also displayed these attributes in the Scriptures. In essence, anybody can wait. But to wait and keep a good attitude is not within everybody's reach.

What is your response like when you don't get your way? How do you even wait in the first place? What thoughts linger in your mind when you are delayed longer than planned? This says a lot about you as a person. Patience is a fruit of the Spirit that has been made available for everyone through Christ Jesus. Whether or not we utilize it is up to us.

The truth is, we all wait in life, whether in traffic, in the grocery checkout line, or anywhere else. How we wait is all that differs. I suggest we start waiting with a good attitude. Let's determine that nothing will disturb our peace of mind. Also, let's choose to always remain calm until we get our turn. Patience is a secret to a healthier, happier, and more joyous life.

Confession: *Dear Lord, today I repent of all my former foul attitudes during my "waiting" period. Your instruction is that I have a good attitude no matter what. So today I declare that I will not only be patient when I don't get my way but also be graceful in my patience. Henceforth, I will guard my heart diligently so that nothing will steal my joy. Amen.*

NOVEMBER 1

INTEGRITY

But they need not account for the money entrusted to them, because they are honest in their dealings."
2 Kings 22:7, NIV

Imagine a world where everyone trusts each other. Imagine a world where everyone's yes means yes and their no means no. Imagine a world where people treat others exactly as they would love to be treated. Imagine a world where everyone is held accountable for his or her actions. Imagine a world where everyone says what they mean and means what they say. That world is possible, but it begins with you and me.

Integrity is the quality of being honest and having strong moral principles. It's the quality in a person that makes him or her dependable. It's being able to trust and be trusted in return. Integrity doesn't necessarily mean we will not make mistakes. But when we do, we accept complete responsibility and try to make things right again.

We may not be able to change the world, but if we start holding ourselves, families, and those we're responsible for accountable for both the big and little things, then change has begun. Integrity doesn't just jump on people. It's a process of gradual growth. Integrity is passed on through individuals that choose to live exemplary lives. When we all choose integrity, we make the world a better place.

Confession: *Heavenly Father, thank You for today's word. I am to be a good example everywhere I go. To do this, I will need to be a person of integrity. I want to be known as one who is upright and honest. I want to be known as one who stands for righteousness, come what may. I want to be known as one whose actions make the better the world better. Amen.*

NOVEMBER 2

NOTHING SHORT OF HUMILITY

So Bathsheba went to King Solomon to speak to him on behalf of Adonijah. And the king rose to meet her and bowed down to her. Then he sat on his throne and had a seat brought for the king's mother, and she sat on his right. **1 Kings 2:19**

Many successful people, both believers and unbelievers, have something significant in common: humility. "Successful people" in this context does not connote the wealthy and powerful but rather life influencers.

Solomon was an exceptionally humble king. It showed in his dealings with God, his parents, and those around him. No wonder he went far in life. Humble people seldom have problems treating everybody politely and equally. They rarely look down on others regardless of their financial status or class. Truly successful people are never pompous. Many of them are, in fact, some of the most respectful and well-mannered people you'll ever meet.

Let's take a closer look at our lives today and do some reflecting. Like Solomon, who was a humble person, can the same be said about you and me? How well do we treat our parents and other folks? What about our employees and everyone in general? Never forget that God despises the proud and gives grace to the humble (James 4:6).

Confession: *Lord, You favor those who are humble. In all my endeavors, please help me remain submissive to Your instructions. Teach me how to regard others with respect. Help me love and treat my neighbor as I would like to be treated. Amen.*

NOVEMBER 3

•••

HOW DO YOU CARE FOR THEIRS?

"The second is this: 'You shall love your neighbor as yourself.' There is no other commandment greater than these."
Mark 12:31

Today's reference text is not just a statement but a commandment to all God's children. The commandment is simple! Love your neighbor as yourself. It did not say we should only love our neighbors when they are kind to us or if they reciprocate our love. In essence, our place is to love people at their good, bad, and irritating times. To love others also means caring for their possessions as we would ours.

If you wouldn't track dirt into your house, don't do so at a neighbor's. If you wouldn't leave your home without turning out the lights, don't do so at a friend's house you are visiting. The way you would love others to treat your things is exactly how you should treat theirs. Common sense may suggest that being extra nice is unnecessary, but remember, the Bible and all its laid out instructions are miles away from "common sense."

Little things provoke heaven's blessings, and one of them is what we examined today. We would be shocked at how little practices like this can bring about a turnaround of our situations. Always do unto others as you would have them do unto you (Matthew 7:12).

Confession: *Dear Lord, thank You for Your Word. Today I submit to Your instructions to love my neighbor as myself. Help me to be kind to everyone around me. Show me ways I can be a source of blessing to others. Please teach me how to love unconditionally like You, Jesus. Amen.*

NOVEMBER 4

SOWING FOR THE GENERATIONS TO COME.

And David said to him, "Do not fear, for I will show you kindness for the sake of your father Jonathan, and I will restore to you and all the land of Saul your father, and you shall eat at my table always." **2 Samuel 9:7**

People often do evil and get away with it, while others doing good hardly get recognized. But according to today's text, a generation is coming that will reap the fruit of our sown seed. The question is, what seed are we going to sow for the generations to come?

Today's reference chapter takes us into the life of Jonathan's crippled son, Mephibosheth. This man found favor in the eyes of King David. How? While alive, Jonathan was good to David and treated David like he was his brother. Years after Jonathan's death, David searched for Jonathan's son and blessed him. Jonathan's good deeds paved the way for his son. Despite being crippled, Mephibosheth was greatly cared for, all because of his father's kindness.

It's important that we leave beautiful inheritances for our successors. One of the ways to do this is by living righteously at all times. Your act of kindness and selfless deeds w someday be rewarded. Always remember, what you do today, your child may reap in multiples tomorrow. I say we begin planting worthwhile seeds from now on. What do you say?

Confession: *Heavenly Father, I cling to Your throne today and ask for mercy. For those times I have committed hurtful acts, please forgive me. May my generation not become cursed because of my actions. Instead, may they enjoy the blessings of my good works and kind acts. Help me plant good seeds that will bless many generations to come. Amen.*

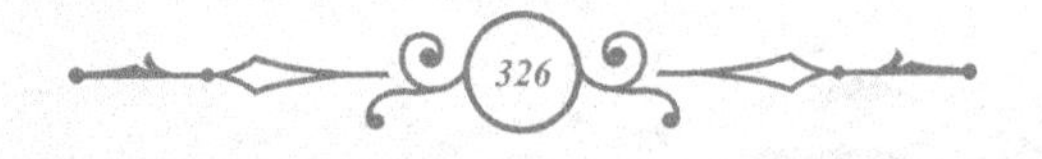

NOVEMBER 5

SPEAK LIFE

Death and life are in the power of the tongue,
and those who love it will eat its fruits.
Proverbs 18:21

Our word choices largely determine the results of our overall life. Words like "I can't," "I am not good enough," "things will never work out," and similar statements tend to negatively affect those who say such things. As small as the tongue is, it carries great power. This is why the Bible often warns about the consequences wrong word choices carry.

The tongue possesses the power of life or death. In the same way, it also possesses the power of healing or harm, prosperity or hardship, breakthrough or stumbling block, and peace or war. Proverbs 21:23 encourages us that "those who guard their mouths and their tongues keep themselves from calamity."

Since the power of life and death lies in the tongue, today I urge to choose life and begin speaking it. As opposed to all the negativity, please confess positivity alone. Instead of pessimism, please speak optimism. Speak this today! Speak this every time! Speak life to your home, your endeavors, and all that is connected to you. With your mouth, begin to resurrect all that has withered. Say what you want to see come to life, and by God's special grace, it will.

Confession: *Dear Lord, you have blessed my tongue with power. I take hold of the power today and call forth change into my situations. I declare increase, promotion, good health, prosperity, and joy into my life today. May all that has dried up and withered away rise in Jesus' name. Amen.*

NOVEMBER 6

MOUNTAINS OUT OF MOLEHILLS

"Catch the foxes for us, the little foxes that spoil the vineyards, for our vineyards are in blossom."
Song of Solomon 2:15

The idiom "make a mountain out of a molehill" means to amplify small things. It could also mean making too much of little matters. Interestingly, what makes an issue complex is not the situation itself but how one responds to it.

The act of making a mountain out of a molehill is responsible for many relationships going sour in today's world. A lot of people enjoy making a big deal out of nothing. Many are also in the habit of dramatizing insignificant issues. However, this kind of life only makes one unhappy, frustrated, and depressed.

Life can be simple if we want it to be. It can also be complex should we make it so. Some issues are temporary, unimportant, and inconsequential. But these same issues can become big problems once blown out of proportion. I suggest today that we choose simplicity by avoiding unnecessary drama. It's not a big deal if we say it's not. So if it's not a big deal, we should desist from taking the bait from anyone who chooses to make it one. Life is too short to spend it fighting irrelevant battles.

Confession: *Dear Lord, I want to be happy and fulfilled. To do this, I know I will have to pick my battles and not engage in every issue that arises. I know I will also have to not complicate simple matters. Help me live a drama-free life. Help me learn how to settle little issues with the attention they deserve. Teach me ways to stay away from those whose aim is to only bait me with unnecessary problems. Amen.*

NOVEMBER 7

SPICE UP YOUR LIFE

The best thing we can do is eat and drink and enjoy what we have earned. And yet, I realized that even this comes from God.
Ecclesiastes 2:24, GNT

What do you do for fun? How excited are you about life? Not everyone would admit it, but many of us live boring lives. The average married Christian works, attends church, cares for the kids, cleans the home, and continues this same cycle all over again. Living a godly life is beautiful, but does this mean we should do so following the same routine? Maybe not.

Christianity should never be associated with boredom. A spicy life alongside a godly one can certainly be achieved. Jesus Himself displayed this while He was on Earth. He was never a routine person. He attended weddings, socialized with friends and strangers, and took time out. He enjoyed life. Jesus did a lot of things differently on many occasions.

Today's scripture encourages us to enjoy life. We can do this by adding creativity and excitement to our lives. Practical examples include taking vacations, socializing with fellow believers, learning new things, stepping out of our comfort zone, and visiting new places. Should we desire to, we can also be "Christ-like spontaneous." Let's endeavor to break old patterns by doing a few unusual things. Marriage, business, and so many aspects of life could be sweetened by using some spice. Routine cages us. Spiciness, however, makes life thrilling.

Confession: *Dear Lord, thank You for today's word of wisdom. I don't want to live a boring life. I long to live life to the fullest and enjoy all Your blessings while on Earth. From time to time, please help me step out of my routine and do things that bring me joy. Teach me how to have godly fun. Amen.*

NOVEMBER 8

SOMETHING TO LOOK FORWARD TO

May the God of hope fill you with all joy and peace in believing, so that by the power of the Holy Spirit you may abound in hope. **Romans 15:13**

Some time ago, a research study was conducted among senior citizens. Two groups were selected for this research. The first group was given a series of activities they could participate in, but the second were not given any particular activity besides their daily routine. Upon being interviewed, the first set expressed joy and excitement they had not had in a long time. The second group was pretty much their usual selves.

There is joy in anticipating a new experience. Boredom can lead to depression, but accomplishing something worthwhile and being adventurous are a good cure for it. Being adventurous also breeds excitement for the future.

Vacations, holidays, and new events are great moments to look forward to. One could even take it a notch higher by breaking from the norm and doing something different. In doing something different, we can choose to change our routine. We can change our hairstyle, cooking style, style of dress, and much more. We can even decide to visit exciting and fun places we have never been to. Let's try to add some spice to our lives by doing things that make every day worth anticipating. Having something to look forward to plays a huge role in our pursuit of happiness.

Confession: *Dear Lord, You always want me to be joyous. I do not want to live a boring life. I want to be happy in You. Holy Spirit, please teach me how to spice up my life. Help me so that I never go in search of excitement in the wrong places. Amen.*

NOVEMBER 9

PEOPLE SEE WHAT THEY WANT TO SEE

He came to his own, and his own people
did not receive him.
John 1:11

Nobody enjoys being rejected. Even the strongest of humans won't mind a little acceptance from others. Being cast aside as irrelevant or not good enough can be emotionally and psychologically painful. Little wonder many would go to any length to get approval, especially from those they care about.

I used to think I was so likable that I almost got addicted to being everyone's favorite. Then I met some people who did not like me. Some of them even went as far as making it obvious that they do not think there was anything special about me. A few of them would practically look down on me like I was insignificant. This started to affect my self-confidence. I would be consumed with thoughts of what I did wrong or how to be liked by these people. After wearing myself out trying to please those who disliked me, some of them came around, but a few of them just never cared. According to them, I was never and would never be good, smart, or classy enough for them. No matter what I did or said, their minds couldn't be changed. Like many others, I had to learn the hard way. Haters will always hate.

Rejection is a serious issue. Not many people know how to handle being rejected. In fact, rejection is one cause of depression. In subsequent days, we will explore how to overcome rejection. We will also discuss how to rise above being called inadequate.

Confession: *Dear Lord, like everyone, I do not like being rejected. It hurts when others disapprove of me. Give me the maturity to be content whether or not others accept me. Help me so that I don't go searching for approval in the wrong places and with the wrong people. Amen.*

NOVEMBER 10

HANDLING REJECTION

As you come to him, a living stone rejected by men
but in the sight of God chosen and precious...
1 Peter 2:4

Who are you? When you think of yourself, what comes to mind? What is your assessment of yourself?

Self-definition is very important, and here is why: No one knows you better than you do. What everyone sees is the side you make obvious to them. No one knows you like you know yourself. Others may claim they know you, but they do not have full, first-hand information about you as a person. The data they have is only half filled in, so they have no right to define you. You shouldn't even give them that power.

Only two definitions of you matter: yours and God's. This doesn't mean living in denial of your own shortcomings. It just means that you've accepted yourself with all your flaws and imperfections. If someone else always insists you are not good enough, then you may need to disregard that person's view of you. Granted, you are not perfect. But if you sincerely know you try your best to live right, then you need to stop caring about other's misguided opinions of you. So long as you know God is pleased with you, then that person who calls you substandard should be ignored. Many times we try too hard to please the wrong people. The good news is that we don't have to anymore. If you say the approval of those who belittle you is irrelevant, then it is.

Confession: *Father, thank you for calling me your own. You love and accept me. I am the apple of your eye. I am special. I am unique. I am beautiful. I am perfect in you. I am relevant. Please, God, let your love be enough for me. Let it satisfy my thirst for acceptance. Amen.*

NOVEMBER 11

HANDLING REJECTION PART II

If the world hates you, know that it
has hated me before it hated you.
John 15:18

Today, we will be doing a brief exercise. This involves taking an inventory of our lives and examining what we spend our energy on. Who are those we go out of our way to please? Are they folks that welcome our love or those that throw it back in our faces? Please take time to answer these questions. In truth, many of us give more credit to those that deserve it less.

Are you one who has folks who genuinely care for you? Today may be a good day to start paying more attention to them. Those that do not approve of you or respond to your affection probably never will. There are certain people you may need to stop chasing after because you may never get their approval. So if some people continue to disregard your respect, maybe they do not deserve you. There may be a few that disapprove of you, but there will always be those that truly care.

Appreciation of those that care for you helps you focus on what is important. It also helps you handle rejection better. Whether it's your spouse, colleagues, friends, or relatives, please appreciate them. Go the extra mile in showing that you are grateful to them for being a part of your life. When you appreciate those that care about you, it makes you worry less about those that don't. It also makes you like yourself better. Finally, it gives you the freedom to enjoy your life to the fullest. Stop bothering about others that can't be bothered about you. Really, life is too short to waste it on those that don't deserve your attention.

Confession: *Dear Lord, thank You for the gift of relationships. I will stop pouring my energy into those that do not care for me. I will not beg for love, because I am already loved. I will focus on and appreciate the love I receive from my friends and family. I will bother less about the love I am not getting and enjoy what I am. Amen.*

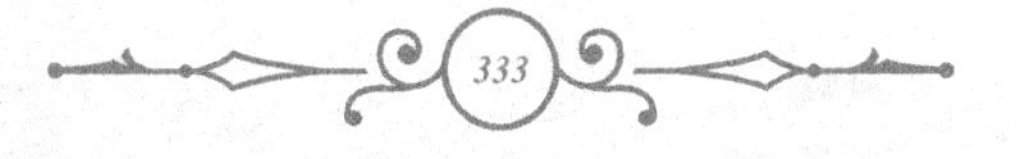

NOVEMBER 12

HANDLING REJECTION PART III

"Woe to you, when all men speak well of you,
for so their fathers did to the false prophets."
Luke 6:26

Not everyone will like you. This is a bitter pill that must be swallowed by everyone. For no particular reason, some people will just not like you no matter how hard you try. Even if you do everything they ask for, they will still find something to complain about. Well, this is life. It's human nature.

We cannot change people. We also cannot force people to like us. While Jesus was on Earth, He was righteous and friendly to all. Yet many people still took offense at the things He did and didn't do. God will purposely make us meet people who disapprove of us to teach us the important principle today's text addresses. Whenever we come across such people, our place is to be as pleasant as we possibly can to them. We can also pray for them. Most importantly, we have to go on living happily with or without their acceptance.

Please never take disapproval personally, especially if you did nothing wrong. It is not your fault, so please do not carry it on your shoulders. You cannot be good enough for everybody. However, you will always be the best for those that cherish you. Those are the people that count.

Confession: *Dear Jesus, while on Earth, You were perfect, yet many hated You. This tells me that no matter how hard I try, some people will still not like me. Help me to be all right with this. My self-worth will no longer be dictated by what others say or think about me. You love and value me. This is enough for me. Amen.*

NOVEMBER 13

TAKE IT AS IT COMES

The blessing of the LORD makes rich,
and he adds no sorrow with it.
Proverbs 10:22

Your endeavor did not work out, but did you do your best? Did you give it your all? If the answer to these questions is "yes," then you did great. The other question is, are you sure that the thing you set out to do was yours to begin with? Please answer this question within yourself. We tend to delve into that which God does not sanction.

Some things are just not meant to be. The earlier we understood this as Christians, the better it will be for us. Many of us spend our lives feeling like if only we did things differently, then a desirable result may have ensued. Some of us even let guilt weigh us down. We burden ourselves with thoughts of "I didn't try hard enough" or "I didn't push far enough." While in some cases doing better may turn events in our favor, this is not true for every situation.

I, for one, have noticed that during those times when I struggle too hard for something, it rarely works as I expect. However, on those days when I do my best and put the rest in God's hands, things turn out well. Today's text lets us know that when God is involved, struggles, sadness, and sorrow have no place. Let's endeavor to always do our best and leave the rest to God. Sometimes things will work out; sometimes things will not. On the occasions when things do not work out as planned, leave it all in God's hands. He's got better plans for you.

Confession: *Heavenly Father, thank You for Your blessings. Today I pray that You will order my steps. I do not want to be involved in anything You do not approve of. Teach me how to discern Your will from my will. I want to enjoy Your grace and not struggle. When things do not work out as planned, give me the strength to move on, trusting You. Amen.*

NOVEMBER 14

FORGIVENESS

Be kind to one another, tenderhearted,
forgiving one another, as God in Christ forgave you.
Ephesians 4:32

To forgive means to let go of grudges and bitterness. Contrary to popular opinion, forgiveness is never really for the other party. Forgiveness is first and foremost for oneself. There is a space in every person's soul that drives powerful emotions, such as love, hate, anger, and bitterness. These emotions are major factors that control an individual's thoughts and actions.

When a person is deeply hurt by another, naturally that person's emotion of hatred is fed. This person may also hold on to resentment. But does resentment bring about any good? No. As a matter of fact, resentment does more harm than good. It is a tool the devil uses to keep people in captivity. Holding grudges imprisons. It keeps one in bondage, turning a person into a victim. Resentment takes away one's happiness. Unforgiveness hardly affects the other party who brought about the hurt. It mostly negatively affects the one who chooses not to forgive.

Yes, it may be hard to forgive, but holding onto a grudge is way harder and consumes a lot of energy. Forgiveness sets a person free. Forgiveness is a gift to yourself. Go ahead and forgive all hurts today. To those that have tried to forgive but could not, our next discussion will provide further information on the matter.

Confession: *Dear Jesus, when I mess up and ask for Your forgiveness, You are quick to forgive. Today I heed Your instruction that says I should forgive. I forgive all those who have wronged me in times past. I lay all my pain at Your feet. Please heal me from every hurt. Unforgiveness will no longer steal my joy. I am free. Amen.*

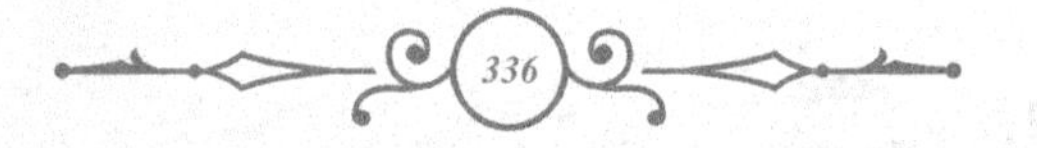

NOVEMBER 15

STEPS TO FORGIVENESS

...forgive, and you will be forgiven.
Luke 6:37

So many people find it very difficult to forgive. This is not always because they do not want to. Most times they just don't know how to. Some have repeatedly tried to forgive. But the more they tried, the more they found themselves resenting those that caused them pain. It may still hurt, but here are some steps that can help in forgiving all wrongs:

- Get closure. For complete healing to occur, deep wounds and intense betrayal need closure. A clear understanding of all that transpired from the beginning to the end helps a lot.
- Pray for the other person. The more you pray for those who hurt you, the more the feeling of hatred subsides and the better you will begin to feel.
- Forgive yourself for making the wrong choice, for trusting the wrong person, and for every other guilty feeling you think you deserve.
- Surround yourself with those that genuinely care about you.
- Give it time; the process of forgiveness may not occur in a day. Forgiveness also doesn't promise we will instantly forget all the painful memories. But with each and every passing day, it gets easier. Total freedom will eventually come.
- Be happy. Move on. Be as successful as you can be.

There is tremendous power in forgiveness. Forgive today, and choose to forgive in the future.

Confession: *Lord, as I take these steps to forgive others today, please grant me Your strength. As I forgive others for their wrongdoings against me, I also forgive myself. I will no longer be weighed down by past events. I lift all these burdens off me. I am delivered from all heaviness. I will begin to enjoy my new freedom found in Christ. Amen.*

NOVEMBER 16

PRAY FOR THEM TOO

"Bless those who curse you.
Pray for those who hurt you..."
Luke 6:28, NLT

When God requires us to do something, it is usually not for Him or for others but for our benefit. When God says to pray for our enemies, it is not so that they will start being better or so that they will stop hating. It is mostly because of what praying for them can do for us both in the physical and spiritual realm.

When you pray for another, especially for those that have hurt you, you will begin to feel less angry about their offenses. You may even begin to develop some tenderness toward them. Here is why: The more you pray for your offenders, the more your spirit sheds some of that heaviness. This in turn rubs off on the physical person.

You don't pray for wrongdoers, just for them. You do so for you too. The more you pray for them, the more you will find relief, peace, and joy again. All they have done will no longer seem as horrible as it used to. I suggest today that you take all your hurts to God. No matter the size of your pain or who is responsible for it, just pray. Pray for the person now, and keep praying for the person. In fact, pray for the person's wellbeing and progress in life. In no time, you will realize the pain inflicted as a result of their actions no longer affects you. You can then once again begin to enjoy that peaceful life Christ died for you to have. Praying for our enemies is good spiritual therapy.

Confession: *Dear Lord, today I overcome evil with good. I pray for all those who have hurt me in times past. I pray that it may be well with them and all that concerns them. I pray that they will find peace and joy again. I pray for myself too, for the strength to keep praying for those who offend me. It's not going to be easy, but I will obey You. Amen.*

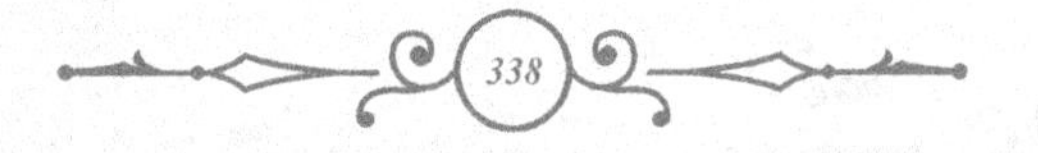

NOVEMBER 17

PARENTS TO CHILDREN

Fathers, do not provoke your children to anger, but bring them up in the discipline and instruction of the Lord.
Ephesians 6:4

To provoke means to annoy, agitate, or irritate. Parents can provoke their children by comparing them to their peers and siblings or constantly finding fault. They can also do so by being overly protective, being overly expectant, or not trusting them. Many kids are unhappy when their parents live vicariously through them. Many are also miserable when their parents are never present during special moments.

There are no perfect parents. No parent has it all figured out when it comes to how best to raise a child. According to today's text, one way parents can raise their children is by first doing their part by not provoking their children to anger. Also, parents are to discipline and instruct their children in the ways of the Lord.

When parents expose their kids to ways of the Lord, godly seeds are sown in their hearts (Psalm 11:3). Also, a solid foundation in Christ is built. This makes the work of the Holy Spirit through them possible. Parents can then be assured that no matter how carried away their children get by life's enticements, they will eventually find their way back to God. Once the God factor is introduced to any situation, positive results can be counted on. The same goes for the child-raising situation.

Confession: *Father, we are to discipline our children and not provoke them to anger. Please teach me how to live by this instruction. Help me love my children and the children around me the way You have ordained for me. May I not be the cause of them making wrong decisions. May my attitude toward them draw them closer to God and not into the world. Amen.*

NOVEMBER 18

CHILDREN TO PARENTS

Children, obey your parents in the Lord, for this is right.
Ephesians 6:1

Every effective system is structured. The family structure is such that parents are the authority over their children. Today's text can be discussed in three ways.

First, children are instructed to obey their parents. They must do this regardless of their feelings. Furthermore, children are expected to "obey in the Lord." This could also be interpreted as doing so out of reverence for God. Lastly, children are asked to obey their parents not necessarily because they will like submitting but because it is the right thing to do.

Charity begins at home. An obedient child at home is an obedient child who submits to authority everywhere. Children are not born obedient or disobedient. The act of obeying begins with parents and their ability to impart this teaching in their kids. Proper discipline is needed in every child's life. It's important for children to obey. Still, it's more important for parents not to fail in the responsibility of teaching their children obedience.

Confession: *Dear Lord, You love an obedient child. You even promised the obedient ones many good things in life. Help me be respectful toward the elderly and my parents. Give me the grace to honor those who are in authority over me. Please teach me how to be gracious to my elders. Amen.*

NOVEMBER 19

THE GOD COMPLEX

When Peter entered, Cornelius met him and fell down at his feet and worshipped him. But Peter lifted him up, saying, "Stand up; I too am a man." **Acts 10:25–26**

It's not uncommon for some with great spiritual authority to, over time, develop a God complex. Before long, their flocks are seen to idolize them. In their defense, just like Peter didn't demand it in today's text, not all of them ask for this. What they do, however, is accept it.

To believe, many people, especially young Christians, need to "see." Since God can't be seen, the next best semblance to Him is His messengers. Messengers of God may include pastors, ministers, and other types of leaders. It takes very little for God's children to embrace and place their leaders in the position meant for God alone. This is common in many churches today.

No one should accept replacing God. It's imperative for God's messengers to always remind God's flock that who they need is God and not them. Overseeing God's children is crucial. Still, this should be at a distance, where people can access God for themselves. It's very important God's flock seeks God and gets to know Him intimately. God's children are obliged to honor those in a place of spiritual authority. However, all worship must be rendered to God alone.

Confession: *Father, I ask for mercy today. If I have in any way unconsciously developed a God complex, forgive me. You alone are God. No one dares share Your glory with You. Henceforth, help me to know my place. Your children need You and not me. Teach me how to direct them to You. Amen.*

NOVEMBER 20

YOUR CHARACTER MATTERS

So let's not get tired of doing what is good. At just the right time we will reap a harvest of blessing if we don't give up.
Galatians 6:9, NLT

Smoke from a fire will eventually be revealed no matter how much one tries to conceal it. The same goes for a person's character. A person's background, location, and life opportunities may be determining factors of whether he or she will succeed, yet while all these other factors are essential, they are not as important as one's character.

It's not enough to climb to the top. It's enough to possess character that will help one maintain that height. The way a man can rapidly climb up is the same way he can come tumbling down. This can happen if he doesn't display the necessary character to stay at the top. That bad attitude, untamed tongue, lack of discipline, and all the other "smoke" characteristics will always come out into the open at some point. No matter how much one tries to hide it, character will speak either for or against a person.

Are you one who does your best to be a good person? Please hang in there. Your integrity will pay off. Yes, it may seem the only people being celebrated are the liars, cheats, and smooth talkers, but please do not give up. Someday you will reap the reward of your labor if you do not give up. Today's text also confirms this. Remain consistent. Your good work will be recognized. It is only a matter of time.

Confession: *Dear Lord, thank You for today's words of encouragement. Sometimes I feel like being a good person does not account for much in today's world. But I have been reassured that in due season, I will reap the reward of my labor. No matter how difficult, please help me to always stay steadfast. I know one day my good character will speak for me. Amen.*

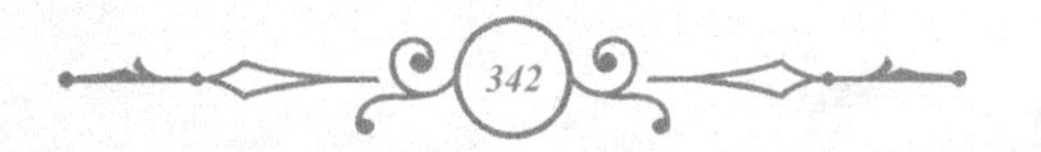

NOVEMBER 21

CHECKING AND BALANCING OUR LIVES THROUGH GOD'S WORD

For no one can lay a foundation other than that which is laid, which is Jesus Christ.
1 Corinthians 3:11

Many people weigh the value of their lives based on their possessions. Many also measure their lives based on what others say about them. Some only judge themselves based on the world's standards. Unfortunately, many of these things are weak and unpredictable.

People change, and the world's standard gets replaced from time to time. Possessions can be taken away at any time. Those that love us today may choose to hate us tomorrow. In essence, nothing in life is constant. This is why many, who only attribute their existence to superficial things, often run into trouble. If things change, they may have no solid foundation to hold on to. Many who appear "put together" often become shattered once all these "things" are taken from them. These "things" include wealth, fame, power, friends, possessions, and more.

Earthly increase wears off, but that of heaven never does. This makes it very important for us to have our roots in Christ and Christ alone. When this is so, our lives and existence become centered on the Word and not the world. When we have our roots in Christ, we are availed of the right to check and balance our lives with God's standard. Our hopes for the future then become renewed daily, regardless of our challenges.

Confession: *Lord Jesus, You are the way, the truth, and the life. From age to age, You remain the same. This day I put my trust in You, the unchanging One. I hold onto You and not material things. So long as I have You, I have everything I need. You are my solid rock. You are my all in all. Amen.*

NOVEMBER 22

MANAGING PEOPLE

But the fruit of the Spirit is love, joy, peace, patience, kindness, goodness, faithfulness, gentleness, self-control; against such things there is no law. **Galatians 5:22–23**

God has made humans in such a way that they will have one or two weaknesses that others find irritating.

It would be nice to only be surrounded by perfect people who love us unconditionally. However, this is not usually the case. There will always be that person that doesn't like us or always assumes the worst of us. We may also be surrounded by those that always pick on our faults and upset us. There is a simple way to handle these people—managing them.

How do we manage people? We do so by first understanding them. We handle people by setting boundaries, taking the high road, and forgiving quickly. Most importantly, we manage others by loving them as Christ loves us. Learning how to tolerate others is crucial to our love-walk. Many people aren't as horrible as we sometimes think they are. When we learn how to manage people, we will find out that we can cope with anybody once we decide to.

Confession: *Dear Father, to enjoy the good life You have blessed me with, I know I will need to learn how to manage people. I no longer want to live frustrated because of other people's irritating habits. Please grant me the wisdom to tolerate and handle others. Teach me to be at peace with everyone. Amen.*

NOVEMBER 23

DEPOSITING INTO OTHERS

"...give, and it will be given to you. Good measure, pressed down, shaken together, running over, will be put into your lap. For with the measure you use it will be measured back to you." **Luke 6:38**

In relationships, three things commonly take place: deposit, withdrawals, or excessive withdrawal. The first two are very common. Excessive withdrawal is also common, but it is not what the Bible teaches. This act is synonymous with using people. It takes place when people request more and give little to none in relationships. Excessively withdrawing is a selfish way to live.

Today's scripture encourages us to do more of one thing: deposit. To deposit means keeping commitments, volunteering, living selflessly, and empowering others. It includes little things like complimenting, listening, and encouraging. When we regularly check up on others and assist them, we show we care. The highest form of depositing comes from praying for those we are in relationships with.

All we do today comes back to haunt or bless us tomorrow. Investing more in people than things eventually pays off. Many can testify to the rewards of depositing into others. When we practice more giving than receiving, we never run out of blessings.

Confession: *Heavenly Father, Your commandment is that I should always be a source of blessing. I am to deposit in others and do things that will make life better for them. Henceforth, I will practice this daily. Holy Spirit, please remind me to always be a giver and not only a taker. I will not be a user. Rather, I will be a depositor. Amen.*

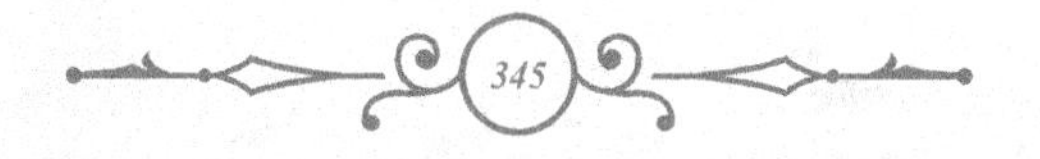

NOVEMBER 24

GOING THE EXTRA MILE

And if anyone forces you to go one mile, go with him two miles. And if anyone would sue you and take your tunic, let him have your cloak as well. **Matthew 5:40–41**

One principle of attaining an extraordinary life is putting in the extra effort. Yes, everybody may be doing it. Everybody may be getting to work late. Everybody may be wasting resources. Everybody may also not be spending time with their family. Everybody may not be exercising. Everybody may not be spending quality time with God. And everybody may be getting away with doing awful stuff. The question now is, do we want the "everybody" kind of life or the extraordinary life in Jesus? Whatever quality of life we desire should inform our decision of whether to follow everybody's footsteps. We can either do what everybody does or do as the Bible commands. The good life will require us to take the high road, be the bigger person, and pass through the fiercer fire. We also have to develop extra discipline, go the extra mile, and be more committed. Every good life in Jesus comes with a price.

The greater the life God plans for a person, the more extra effort that may be required on that person's part. Sometimes it feels unfair that you are often the one asked to give more. I can assure you, it is like that for many of God's anointed children too. He doesn't coddle the ones He's got great plans for coddle. He places heavier tasks on their shoulder, knowing well that they are fully up to the task. If only we would see our lives through heaven's eyes, then we would understand that heaven has many rewards for us.

Confession: *Father, thank You for today's words of wisdom. Because I am ordained, I know greater responsibilities will be demanded of me. I will be required to do more than what "everybody" does. Please help me never to be weary. Help me delight in pleasing You. When "extra" is required, help me do so joyously. Amen.*

UNDERSTANDING GOD'S PRINCIPLES

NOVEMBER 25

CERTAIN BASIC PRINCIPLES OF LIFE

He causes his sun to rise on the evil and the good,
and sends rain on the righteous and the unrighteous.
Matthew 5:45b, NIV

There are certain principles under which the universe has been established. The beautiful thing about these principles is that they hold true for everyone. They affect the rich, poor, young, old, leaders, followers, Christian, and non-Christians. Some of these principles include:

- Time can never be bought or traded. Everybody gets twenty-four hours—no more, no less.
- Life goes on. The earth will never stand still on anybody's account. No matter what event does or doesn't take place, things move on.
- True givers will never lack the good things of life.
- The real and vital things in life are free—air for survival, genuine love for relationships, and salvation for peaceful eternity.

God has structured life in such a way that these principles are within everyone's reach. Ignorance of any of them (even by Christians) won't stop them from taking effect. This is why it sometimes appears that unbelievers are ahead of some Christians. They have studied and mastered how life works. Many unbelievers use these principles mentioned above to their own advantage. For believers, heaven is ultimate. This should actually be our number one priority. Still, we should not be part of the statistics as described in Luke 16:8b: "For the children of this world are in their generation wiser than the children of light." We must work to make our lives here on Earth count. As children of light, we must be wise. Understanding is all that matters.

Confession: *Dear Lord, thank You for today's revelation. You have made many resources available for me. All I have to do is key into them so they can work for me. Please give me the grace to fully utilize Your blessings. Let my life be an inspiration to unbelievers. I want to be a Christian whose life pleases You. Amen.*

NOVEMBER 26

UNDERSTANDING GOD

Just as it is written: "Jacob I loved, but Esau I hated."
What then shall we say? Is God unjust? Not at all!
Romans 9:13–14, NIV

I learned to stop trying to figure God out a long time ago. I learned that I could understand His principles but not how He works. God is diverse, and we just may not get Him. Many times we won't know for sure why He has asked us to do certain things. We may also not understand why He has asked us not to go to a particular place or do that which makes no sense.

Esau I hated; Jacob I loved. From the human perspective, this may not seem fair. The twins were not even born before this declaration was made over their lives. God loved one and hated the other. Period! End of story. We cannot question Him. That is what He decided. It is not our place to understand why He does so. Try as we may, we still will not understand. His ways are not our ways. God is never unjust. God is God.

The Bible records the children of Israel as being God's favorite. Nobody dared mess with them. But some nations did not seem to understand this and were destroyed at the end (2 Chronicles 20:29). The children of Israel were not the holiest or most righteous people in the land. But God loved them. This could also apply to many individuals today. We wonder why God favors some people, especially when we feel He should not. God does as He pleases. No one can dare question Him.

Confession: *Heavenly Father, no one can fathom Your depth. No one knows Your limits. You are the all-knowing, all-seeing God. Who am I to question You? Today I just want to take time to adore You. You are my all in all. Amen.*

NOVEMBER 27

UNFATHOMABLE ARE HIS WAYS

You'll still never figure out the meaning of what God is doing on this earth. Search as hard as you like, you're not going to make sense of it. No matter how smart you are, you won't get to the bottom of it.
Ecclesiastes 8:17b, MSG

It's easy to be an atheist. In reality, God's Word does not make complete sense to the ordinary man. Putting sentiment aside, His ways still do not make absolute sense to me as a believer. If you want to be honest too, there are times when you may have raised your eyebrow at some of the things God has asked you to do. I mean, these things in no way looked close to the solution to that particular problem. Still, in faith, you did them, and things worked out fine at the end for you.

I remember a time when I just wanted to understand the "how," "why," and "where" of God. I sincerely cannot remember a time when I was more miserable. The more I tried to understand Him, the more confused I got. The more I searched, the less I saw. This is because in God's dictionary, two plus two may not always equal four. The more you try to put it together, the more scattered it becomes. For my sanity, the Holy Spirit came to my rescue. I learned the hard way that God's ways are unfathomable and unexplainable. My place as a human is to believe and obey all He says, even when it makes little sense.

Your place as God's child is to put your entire being in His loving hands and trust Him to bring you to a safe landing. Once you start doing all He says, no questions asked, you will begin to experience a tremendous turnaround toward all that concerns you.

Confession: *God, Your ways are not my ways. Your thoughts are not my thoughts. I can never get to the bottom of who You are. Holy Spirit, please help me stay focused on my relationship with God. Father, help me obey You and follow Your instructions. Amen.*

NOVEMBER 28

THE BLESSINGS OF GOD

The blessing of the LORD makes rich,
and he adds no sorrow with it.
Proverbs 10:22

From experience, I have realized that when things begin to look complicated, it is most likely not of God. Many case studies from the Scriptures show God's plan and man's will rarely go hand in hand. And when humans decide to go off God's plan and pursue their desires, God steps aside and lets them please themselves until they are worn out. Such individuals will most likely then begin to struggle. They may also continue to labor hard instead of enjoying God's favor.

God rarely blesses lazy people. Hard work and perseverance will be expected of those whom God chooses to bless. But beyond all these qualities, there is always a place for His special grace.

When a certain thing is of God, we will know it in our hearts. We will also bear a witness in our spirits. When it is of God, there will be a push from within. In God's will, we will find favor and grace. So before we embark on any life journey or make any significant decision, let's seek God first to be sure it's His will.

Confession: *Dear Lord, for those times when I have taken matters into my own hands without consulting You, please have mercy. Help me understand better that it is only Your blessing that can give plenty without adding issues. I do not want to struggle; I want to enjoy Your grace. Teach me how to key into Your divine blessings. Amen.*

NOVEMBER 29

•••

DOES GOD SPEAK?

For God speaks again and again,
though people do not recognize it.
Job 33:14, NLT

Does God speak? I believe this question should be modified to "Do God's children listen?" Yes, God speaks! God has been speaking since the beginning of time. But have His children been hearing Him? Perhaps not.

What could be the reason some of God's children do not hear Him? Maybe it is because they already have preconceived ideas about how God communicates. Some Christians believe God will only talk to them through visions, trances, or dreams. Presumably, some believe God will only reach out to them by first calling their names from their sleep like He did with Samuel (1 Samuel 3). Of course, God uses all these methods for communication. But are these the only ones He uses? No, not so.

God talks to us both directly and indirectly. For instance, He talks via our conscience. This may be why we lose our peace when embarking on something we know God does not support. God also speaks to us through other people—pastors, parents, siblings, friends, or those not even close to us. God sends people into our lives to let us know what His thoughts are concerning specific issues. Most importantly, God talks through His Word. The Bible is the instruction manual for every believer. The only earthly questions the Bible cannot answer are the ones that are of no concern to God's children. God is always finding ways to get through to His children. If we pay attention, we will hear Him loud and clear.

Confession: *Father, I'm grateful for Your Word today. I know You are always trying to get through to me. Sometimes I pay heed to You, but other times I don't. Today I pray that You reveal Yourself more to me. I want to hear from You. Please help me understand the methods You use to communicate with me. Grant me listening ears and a yielding heart. Amen.*

NOVEMBER 30

HEARING FROM GOD

My sheep hear my voice, and I know them, and they follow me. I give them eternal life, and they will never perish, and no one will snatch them out of my hand. ***John 10:27–28***

The way God communicates differs from person to person. It's important that every child of God knows how God talks to him or her. Personally, there are several ways God communicates with me. The most vivid one is through my spirit. As soon as I begin to feel uneasy or restless within myself, I know God is trying to tell me something. Should I heed His instructions, I immediately get my peace back. So when I want to embark on something, I check within. If my inner peace is intact, I know that is my go-ahead sign from heaven. So I go into that thing full force, trusting for grace from heaven. I will admit that it took a while to understand God's method of communicating with me, but every day I keep trusting Him to reveal more of Himself to me.

To hear from God, first we have to be His legitimate heirs. That is, we need to have a personal fellowship with Jesus Christ. We also need to spend time in God's Word. In studying the Bible, we get to know more about God. If we are in need of hearing from God, we can tell Him in our prayers. God listens when we talk to Him. Hearing directly from God is one of the best things that can ever happen to any person. God's direction is the light we need to brighten our pathway through life.

Confession: *Dear Lord, I surrender my heart to You today. Please come into my life. As I study the scriptures, please show me more of You. I want to hear from You, so please speak to me. Speak to my heart, Jesus. Amen.*

DECEMBER 1

CHOICES IN LIFE

Live as people who are free, not using your freedom as a cover-up for evil, but living as servants of God.
1 Peter 2:16

One basic principle of God is that He doesn't interfere with the human's free will. He made this evident through several scriptural examples. Here are a few:

Genesis 3:6 – Free will to eat or not eat of the tree (Adam and Eve)
Genesis 4:4 – Free will to offer a good or lousy offering to God (Cain and Abel)
Genesis 37:50 – Free will to have a good or bad attitude through tribulations (Joseph)

For those of us on the earth, God has given us the free will to be saved or not be saved. He has availed us the freedom to go to heaven or hell. God has given us the ability to do as we please. This is why some people say that every man's destiny is in his own hands.

God never forces, coerces, or manipulates anyone. He rarely conflicts with our choices. For His elect, He is in the habit of giving them a heads-up of the consequences a particular decision will carry. However, He still gives them the free will to do what they want to do (just like in the case of Adam and Eve). God has placed in our hands the power to make our lives whatever we want. The question now is, what will we choose to make of them? I suggest we make our lives count.

Confession: *Father, I love Your lordship. You are the God who neither forces nor manipulates Your children. You have given us the freedom to make our own choices. Today I choose You. I choose Your lordship. You are the one true God, and it's a privilege to be called Your own. Amen.*

DECEMBER 2

THE GOD VACUUM

It is in vain that you rise up early and go late to rest, eating the bread of anxious toil; for he gives to his beloved sleep.
Psalm 127:2

Many celebrities and wealthy people are miserable. This tells us that there is more to life than just attaining a certain class in society.

In search of fulfillment, many have ruthlessly fought their way to the top only to get there and find nothing but emptiness. There is a space in every man called the God vacuum. This vacuum was put there during creation. This vacuum can only be effectively filled when an individual gets in sync with his or her Maker. Any attempts to fill this void with anything or anyone else only results in a wider vacuum.

Contrary to popular belief, true satisfaction doesn't come from accomplishments and relationships alone. Instead, true satisfaction comes from within. It flows from a spring whose source is God. True fulfillment is felt when that connection one should have with his or her Creator hasn't been hindered by fleshly activities. Material things, power, and fame may bring satisfaction, but the joy found in these is usually short lived. Join with God today, and remain in Him. He is everything you need.

Confession: *Dear Jesus, thank You for Your joy. True fulfillment can only come from You. All my attempts to fill my God vacuum with material things have proved futile. Today I humbly ask that You come into my heart. I yield it all to You. Please take Your place in my life. Amen.*

DECEMBER 3

OBEDIENCE

Now when they had departed, behold, an angel of the Lord appeared to Joseph in a dream and said, "Rise, take the child and his mother, and flee to Egypt, and remain there until I tell you, for Herod is about to search for the child, to destroy him." **Matthew 2:13**

Today's text explains an event that took place shortly after Jesus' birth. Two things should be understood here. First, we are discussing God, the One who created the universe and all that is in it. We are also discussing Jesus, God's only begotten Son. According to the text, God instructed an angel to tell Joseph, (Jesus' earthly father), to take Jesus and flee.

After taking a hard look at this story, I figured something wasn't right according to my own human logic. I mean, why would God ask Joseph to flee from a mere man. All God would have had to do was simply destroy Herod and his whole court. That would have saved the day. Also, it wouldn't have cost God anything to do that.

When God talks, it will do us a lot of good to listen. I fear what would have happened to this world if Joseph had disobeyed the angel. If God can tell Joseph to flee with God's own son, then He can tell anyone to do anything. Simple instructions like: Don't go there! Don't eat that! Don't marry that person. Don't travel! Let's endeavor to heed these instructions. When God specifically tells us to do those things, He knows there are alternatives. Still, He always desires that we do what He commands. God loves an obedient child. He even promised blessings to those who honor their parents (Ephesians 6:2–3). Disobedience kills!

Confession: *Lord Jesus, please forgive me. For all those times I turned a deaf ear to Your instructions, please have mercy. You bless those who yield to Your bidding. Holy Spirit, please teach me how to listen. Teach me how to put my human reasoning aside and follow all that God instructs. Amen.*

DECEMBER 4

COMPARISON

Pay careful attention to your own work, for then you will get the satisfaction of a job well done, and you won't need to compare yourself to anyone else. ***Galatians 6:4, NLT***

Knowing our strengths and weaknesses is one of the best things that can happen to us. Once we understand this aspect of our lives, we will better appreciate who we are. We will also comprehend why we do not act like everyone around us and why we may seem different from others.

Do you know who you are? If someone were to ask you to summarize yourself in three sentences, what would they be? One reason folks compare themselves with others is because they don't know who they are. That someone else is better than you in a particular area doesn't make him or her better than you overall. It may just be that the person's field of strength is your own area of weakness. It's high time believers stop beating themselves up because of those things they may not be able to do as well as others.

Take time to find out things about yourself. Consciously study your strengths and weaknesses. Then start focusing more on your capabilities instead of stressing over your limitations. This is the key to a happy and fulfilled life. Stop comparing yourself to others. If you look within, you will find you possess more than you give yourself credit for.

Confession: *Lord Jesus, Your instruction is that I pay attention to my gifts. In doing so, I will not need to compare myself with anyone. Teach me how to focus on my strengths. As I reflect on who I am, please open my eyes of understanding. Please show me how to maximize my potential to the fullest. Amen.*

DECEMBER 5

COMPARISON PART II

But when they measure themselves by one another and compare themselves with one another, they are without understanding.
2 Corinthians 10:12b

God created us for very different purposes. This means we have no business comparing ourselves to others. Also, God deals with us at different levels. For instance, how God blesses Mr. Williams may differ from how He blesses Mr. Smith. The lifestyle He may require from Mr. Davis may differ from the one He requires from Mr. Wilson. As Christians, we need to be especially careful that we don't miss our calling. We all have different destinies. One way to key into God's calling for our lives is to never compare ourselves to others.

It's important we run our individual races. When we run on the track God has set before us and stay focused on our journey, we will get to our destination in due time. But if we let ourselves get distracted by those running beside us, we may end up deviating from our course.

That someone gets to their destination before we do doesn't mean we won't get to ours. God's timing is different for everyone. Today let's decide to stop comparing our lives to other's. God doesn't want us to, so please, let's not. God has different plans for different lives.

Confession: *Heavenly Father, Your instruction is that I follow the path You have set before me. I am to concentrate on my race and not that of my neighbors. I pray that You will order my steps, Lord, and help me stay focused. Amen.*

DECEMBER 6

THE PHYSICAL AND THE SPIRITUAL

Be not overly righteous, and do not make yourself too wise. Why should you destroy yourself?
Ecclesiastes 7:16

Some time ago, I was with a pastor when a church member came complaining about a severe stomach upset. My expectation was that a prayer of healing would be rendered. Much to my surprise, the pastor asked him, "When did you eat last?" The person responded, "I honestly cannot remember." The pastor then told him to go eat. Shortly after doing so, this person became okay again. I picked up a great lesson from this meeting.

In life, there are both spiritual and natural laws. We are to never disregard the natural laws in the hope that the spiritual laws will save us. An overzealous Christian who chooses to jump from a three-story building will likely die. The same goes for the one who intentionally consumes poison. We do not have to act overly spiritual to please God. We are human, and He is aware of this.

God is not a magician. There is that which God will do but also that which we have to do. God will not do what we ought to do for ourselves. As opposed to being overly righteous, we Christians are reminded today to fulfill that which God requires of us. The miracle many people may need is just to fulfill the physical part God has required of them. Wisdom is profitable.

***Confession:** Dear Lord, today You have reminded me that You created me human. Therefore, I am subject to natural laws. Help me so I do not get ahead of myself by trying to be fanatical. Help me play my role as a human, and teach me how to trust You above my human reasoning. Amen.*

DECEMBER 7

HELPING GOD

Can a person do anything to help God?
Can even a wise person be helpful to him?
Job 22:2, NLT

God doesn't need our help to do anything He wants to do. If He chooses us to work for Him at all, it is a privilege. In working for God, it's important that we do not get overzealous to the extent that we begin to go outside of God's will.

A story was told of a church usher who walked a new member out of the church. This woman was sent away because she wasn't dressed according to the church's standard. The usher may have thought she was doing the right thing by cleansing the church of indecent people. She may have even been following the church's protocol. But maybe God was counting on her to show the new lamb God's way. God's way is not rejection and castigation. Rather, it is love and compassion. Of course, churches may choose whatsoever regulations they deem necessary. But how we go about treating people who come seeking God is crucial. Sometimes God purposely puts people in our path so that we will show them the way.

We cannot overstate the importance of the Holy Spirit. We need the Holy Spirit at every point to open our spiritual ears so we can hear what God is asking of us. We also need the Holy Spirit to caution us when we are going outside of God's will.

Confession: *Father, I pray that I will not be overzealous to the extent of incurring Your wrath. While I am to be enthusiastic about Your work, I also know that I should not be too forward. I am to stay in my lane and obey as instructed. Please order my steps. Amen.*

DECEMBER 8

DEFENDING GOD

And when they came to the threshing floor of Chidon, Uzzah put out his hand to take hold of the ark, for the oxen stumbled. And the anger of the LORD was kindled against Uzzah, and he struck him down because he put out his hand to the ark, and he died there before God. **1 Chronicles 13:9–10**

First Chronicles 13 gives us insight as to what happened when the ark of God was being transported. During the transport, the oxen carrying the ark stumbled. All Uzzah tried to do was prevent the ark of the covenant from falling, but he ended up dying for his actions. Now, was Uzzah's intention godly? Absolutely! Was his heart in the right place? I believe it was. Why then would God strike a man for stopping God's own ark from falling? There are so many reasons this may be so, one of which is likely because God did not ask for Uzzah's help. His intentions may have been pure, but his act was not required. Uzzah's story also lets us know that God does not need us to defend Him. He can defend Himself.

We Christians need to be careful so that we stay within our God-mandated boundaries. There are certain works of God that He just does not need our help with. His mandate is that we bring people to Christ, love others, and live righteously. Anything we do that deviates from those specific instructions, all in the name of "defending" God, may lead to an offense before God.

We have not been mandated to condemn others to defend God. Whether their lifestyles sit well with us or not, we are not to judge but love them (Matthew 7:1). This is one example out of God's many simple instructions to His children. Again, it is not our place to defend God. He sees everything. He knows what is going on at every single moment. That He has not done anything about a particular thing yet does not mean He won't. It also doesn't mean that He needs our help with it. May we never incur God's wrath.

Confession: *Holy Spirit, You are my helper. You are also my teacher. Teach me today to follow God's way and not mine. Help me never to engage in any activity that would offend God. I pray that in my excitement to serve, I will not go against heaven. Help me to walk in my lane and follow Your instructions. Amen.*

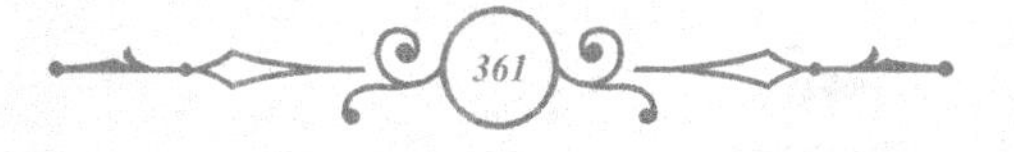

DECEMBER 9

•••

FAMILY PRINCIPLE 101: TO SONS & DAUGHTERS

"Honor your father and mother" (this is the first commandment with a promise), "that it may go well with you and that you may live long in the land."
Ephesians 6:2–3

To honor someone means to hold that person in high regard. It could also mean to celebrate, adore, value, and treasure another.

Today's reference text is one of the most crucial verses in the Scriptures. This is so for three reasons: First, the text is specific. Honor your father and mother, period! Also, it is strategic. It doesn't leave any loopholes. This instruction is for everyone, regardless of what their parents have done or failed to do in the past. So a parent's deeds are not a factor in obeying or disobeying this command. Finally, blessings are attached to this instruction. In essence, failure to carry out this command may lead to the blessing turning to a curse. In summary, honor your parents and get blessed. Dishonor them, and you may get the opposite.

To many, honoring their parents comes naturally as their parents have been amazing. To some, however, maybe not so much. To key into God's blessings of great well-being and long life, we have to do precisely as instructed. This commandment isn't one that gives a person choices. Honoring one's parents is a solid principle that many other blessings are built upon. It is even the first instruction with a promise. In obeying our parents, we automatically qualify for the promises attached to the commandment. Take advantage of it.

Confession: *Heavenly Father, thank You for the revelation of Your Word. I am to honor my parents no matter what. This is Your instruction to me. I pray for the grace to follow this commandment to the letter. Amen.*

DECEMBER 10

FAMILY PRINCIPLE 102: TO SPOUSES

Wives, in the same way submit yourselves to your own husbands so that, if any of them do not believe the word, they may be won over without words by the behavior of their wives... ***1 Peter 3:1, NIV***

In the same way, you husbands must give honor to your wives. Treat your wife with understanding as you live together. She may be weaker than you are, but she is your equal partner in God's gift of new life. Treat her as you should so your prayers will not be hindered ***1 Peter 3:7, NLT***

Contrary to popular opinion, to submit doesn't connote inferiority or being enslaved. Instead, it means to help (Genesis 2:18). To submit to one's husband means to appreciate, respect, and co-operate with him. This could also mean to assist and complement. According to today's first text, a powerful way of winning an unbelieving man over is by being submissive to him.

According to the second text, husbands are to honor, understand, and care for their wives. They are to treat them with respect as equal partners of the gracious gift of life. Failure to do this will result in hindered prayers. This in turn may lead to a frustrated Christian life.

These principles, as well as many others, are mandatory. They cut across everyone. They also come with blessings and repercussions to one's marriage. Should both parties in a relationship choose to comply with them, they will be better for it. Good fruits of marriage, like unity, happiness, fulfillment, and friendship, will be promoted in their home. Should they not, their marriage will likely suffer for it.

Confession: *Dear Jesus, thank you for the gift of relationships. I commit my spouse and all my loved one's marriages to You. Please bless all these marriages. Let good fruit spring forth from our homes. Amen.*

DECEMBER 11

STAYING IN LINE

"For I know the plans I have for you," says the LORD. "They are plans for good and not for disaster, to give you a future and a hope."
Jeremiah 29:11, NLT

One day I was led by the Holy Spirit to go into a particular venture. At first I hesitated because I knew I didn't have the resources for such a big project at that time. Eventually I yielded, and God came through with more provisions than I ever thought possible. On another occasion, I was led to do something else. Since I thought I heard God, I went into it wholeheartedly. Unfortunately, it didn't quite turn out the way I anticipated it would. Today I can look back and understand why God let me go through the good and perhaps not so good.

When we are being led to do something, sometimes the result we get may be what we hoped for. Sometimes it may even be better. But other times the result may not turn out as well as we expected. When God says we should do something, He always has a reason behind it. All God does, He does for a reason. In due time, His purposes will be revealed.

When God speaks through our spirit, it's best we heed His voice. God has great plans for our lives. Also, when God gives us a command, He seldom shows us the "why" behind His request. But if we stick around in faith and follow His lead, we will see for ourselves the reason behind all He does. Our God has everything figured out for our lives. Only when we stay in line will we key into all He has in store for us.

Confession: *Father, thank You for the good and not so good. You know and see all. You see the beginning from the end. When You call, I will listen. When things do not go my way, I will be calm. I know all things will work together for my good. Amen.*

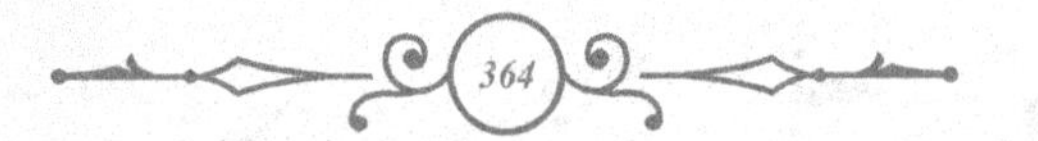

DECEMBER 12

OUR MIRACLES SOMETIMES LIE IN THE "GO"

He looked at them and said, "Go show yourselves to the priests." And as they went, they were cleansed of their leprosy.
Luke 17:14, NLT

Today's scripture reference centers on ten lepers who were seeking healing from Jesus. As soon as Jesus saw them, His instruction was simple: "Go show yourselves to the priests." In essence, all they needed to do was "go." Should they have chosen not to go or questioned whether anything would come out of their going, they may have not received their healing. As they went, they were healed.

Who are those expecting or trusting God for certain things? Are you sure you haven't been given some instructions on what you should do for your part? Are you sure Jesus hasn't asked you to "go" a long time ago?

Many people are in the habit of analyzing and calculating things. They always try to figure out how God would do things. Little do they know that the human, with all his intelligence, can never decipher God's ways. The lepers had not yet received their miracle when they were told to go show themselves to the priests. The priests would supposedly confirm there was healing. Logically, what Jesus asked them to do made no sense. However, they went. And as they did, they were healed. If we hear God say go, it will be in our best interests to do exactly as instructed, no questions asked. Take God's Word and run with it. Go today! Go now.

Confession: *More often than not, I tend to look at situations through my human reasoning. Today I repent of this. Lord, when You ask me to go, I pray that I find the strength to do so. I will never question Your methods or instructions. Even if I don't understand, I will "go," trusting in You. Amen.*

DECEMBER 13

AS MUCH AS YOUR FAITH CAN CARRY

When the vessels were full, she said to her son, "Bring me another vessel." And he said to her, "There is not another." Then the oil stopped flowing.
2 Kings 4:6

Second Kings 4 gives an account of a widow who spoke to Elisha about her debt issues. As soon as she explained her money problems to Elisha, his response to her was "What shall I do for you? Tell me, what do you have in the house?" She replied by saying she had nothing but a jar of oil. He then asked her to go borrow vessels from all her neighbors and urged her to get a lot. Miraculously, all the jars she collected were filled with oil after she did as the man of God instructed. The most intriguing part of this story was that the oil only stopped flowing when there were no more empty jars. In essence, if she had gotten a million containers, they would have all been filled.

Some say if this woman had known the miracle that would take place, she would have gotten more bottles than she did. At least she trusted the prophet's words enough to gather many jars. It was through this miracle that she could settle her debts. What other lessons can be learned from this story? We will discuss these next.

Confession: *Miracle-working God, I adore You. You always make a way where there seems to be none. Just like You did for the widow, I pray that You will help me. Teach me to obey. Open the eyes of my heart that I may never limit Your miracles. Amen.*

DECEMBER 14

AS MUCH AS YOUR FAITH CAN CARRY PART II

"Then go in and shut the door behind yourself and your son and pour into all these vessels. And when one is full, set it aside."
2 Kings 4:4

God performs miracles through various forms. Many times He blesses a person by multiplying whatever He finds in that person's hands. He may also require that the individual being blessed play a role in the miracle process. According to today's reference chapter, Elisha asked the woman, "Tell me, what do you have in the house?" (2 Kings 4:2). Today you and I are being asked the very same question: What do we have in our hands? Better still, what seeds do we have that can be planted to generate many more? What about your own vessels?

When God wants to bless a person, his or her seed may be important. But this does not limit God's blessing. An individual's limiting factor is usually the quality of his or her faith.

How open are you and I to receiving from God? Do we have a surplus of jars for filling? A person will not be blessed beyond his or her faith level. If you believe, you will receive. How much can your faith carry?

Confession: *Jehovah Jireh, You are my provider. Thank You for all that You have blessed me with in times past. Today I hand over my seed to You. I give to You as an offering all You have blessed me with. I do this in faith, trusting that You will multiply my seed to yield a bountiful harvest. Amen.*

DECEMBER 15

NOTHING DISQUALIFIES HIS ELECT

Josiah was eight years old when he began to reign,
and he reigned thirty-one years in Jerusalem.
2 Kings 22:1

When God wants to use a man, his accomplishments, talents, and age are inconsequential. Also, a person could possess abundant "eligible" qualities according to man's standards and still not be used by God.

To God, the vessel is not as important as his or her usability. We become more usable to God the moment we begin to put our hope and trust in Him and rely on Him more than our abilities. We are instrumental to God when, at each juncture, we choose to put our faith solely in Him. We are usable to God if, like Josiah, we long to always walk in righteousness even if our predecessors didn't.

When God is ready to use someone, He makes up for that person's deficiencies. For those still harboring a mindset of inadequacy, please be reassured today. God doesn't use perfect people. Instead, He uses the usable. The question is, are you usable?

Confession: *Lord Jesus, thank You for calling me Your own. Despite my shortcomings, You still see me as eligible. Thank You for making me Your vessel. I give all of myself to You today. Please use me for Your glory. Amen.*

TRUST IS KEY

DECEMBER 16

DEVELOPING A TRUSTING RELATIONSHIP WITH GOD

Some trust in chariots and some in horses,
but we trust in the name of the LORD our God.
Psalm 20:7

When we board a plane, we never ask the pilot to show us his or her license before commencing on the journey. The same holds true when we enter into a vehicle or board a ship on vacation. We just get into that mode of transportation trusting we'll get to our destination safely. In essence, we are comfortable putting our lives in the hands of humans. But do we trust God in the same manner? Do we share that same comfort with God for our overall well-being? Let's take a moment to ponder on this.

Some of us say we trust God. The question is, do we really trust Him or do we just say or think we do? To trust someone means to have one hundred percent confidence in that person's power and ability. To trust God means that we have handed our lives entirely to Him to do as He pleases. So with the way we conduct our lives and affairs, can we say that we wholeheartedly trust God?

In truth, it is easier to trust that which we can see than that which we cannot. This is why trusting God does not come easily. But as with any other relationship, trust grows with time. In the coming days we will discuss in detail how to build a trusting relationship with God.

Confession: *Lord, I know I can always trust You. Today I repent of my unbelief. I am sorry for the ways I have trusted man more than You. Reveal Yourself to me that I may know and trust You more. Amen.*

DECEMBER 17

PASSING THE TRUST TEST

The king was overjoyed and ordered that Daniel be lifted from the den. Not a scratch was found on him, for he had trusted in his God.
Daniel 6:23

In our walk with God, He will grow us to spiritual maturity. How? We will be put through various tests and challenges. If we excel in them, we will move to the next stage of growth. If we don't, we will repeat the tests over and over until we excel in them. How we attain maturity in Christ is usually left to us as individuals, but every person who aspires to grow with God should know that trust is vital.

For any relationship to thrive, trust is crucial. Trust is the foundation upon which any healthy relationship is built. A relationship involving two people who may love but not trust each other is doomed to fail. Love cannot flourish where trust is not present.

We cannot say we love God yet not trust Him. To show that we love God, we must prove that we trust Him, and He will require this proof of us when we are put in situations that may look beyond our strength. At those moments, we will be given the option to either trust God's guidance or try to fix things by our human ability. These moments are defining ones every child of God should be on the lookout for. At some point, every believer will experience this.

Confession: *Dear Lord, Daniel trusted You and was not afraid to be put in the lion's den. You rewarded this trust by making the lions friendly toward him. Lord, please help me be like Daniel. Help me that I may never waver no matter what. I love You, God. I long to prove this daily by trusting You. Amen.*

DECEMBER 18

TRUSTING GOD FOR OUR NEXT MEAL

...and said, "Truly, I say to you, unless you turn and become like children, you will never enter the kingdom of heaven."
Matthew 18:3

Children hardly know where their next meal will come from. All they know is that as soon as they are hungry, food will be provided. This is called "child-like" faith. As adults, many of us do not reason like this. We calculate and analyze things. We mostly depend on our skills and resources. Left to us, our provision is our responsibility. So for food to come, reasoning would have to come into play. Now, from a realistic point of view, the adult's perspective seems more sensible. God's request of us, however, is that we live with a child-like faith. In doing this, we will also enjoy the many benefits that come with trusting God.

There is a certain simplicity that comes with God. This simplicity can only be experienced by those who see through the lens of a child's eyes. They are trusting. They know that most, if not all, of their needs will be met. They worry less than adults do. They have free hearts. They go about life believing everything is fine and will always be okay. Above all, children depend on their parents. They know that their parents will be there for them no matter what. This is the kind of relationship God wants every one of us to have with Him.

God wants us to come simply and openly to Him. Our heavenly Father is always on the lookout for us. The heart of a child is all God requires to manifest Himself mightily in our lives.

Confession: *Lord Jesus, I'm thankful for Your provision. You do not regard human logic, and Your thoughts are not our thoughts. Teach me to trust like a child would. Help me believe in Your simplicity. Amen.*

DECEMBER 19

TRUSTING GOD WITH OUR SAFETY

You can get horses ready for battle,
but it is the LORD who gives victory.
Proverbs 21:31

A person may have all the weapons of defense in the world. They may have several guard dogs to provide protection. But should perpetrators come determined and well prepared, they will get through. Defense weapons become useless when those that can match their strength attack.

Whatever lengths a person may go to secure his or her possessions is entirely up to that person. But even the best of security systems can hardly give their customers a 100% safety guarantee. The best they can do is 99.9%. Only God can deliver absolute protection. While defending our possessions, let's never lose touch with the God factor. After putting measures in place, let's always remember to still ask the Father for preservation.

That which is kept is only kept by God. As a result, God should be the number one factor with all that concerns us most, especially our safety. Do your part, and leave the rest to God. He will always defend you.

Confession: *Some may trust in chariots and others in horses, but I choose to trust in You, O Lord. Please protect me and mine. Amen.*

DECEMBER 20

TRUSTING GOD WITH OUR LOVED ONES

Cast your cares on the LORD and he will sustain you;
he will never let the righteous be shaken.
Psalm 55:22

Those who are parents can agree that a parent's worry list is endless. At the infant stage, a mother may be worried about why her child is not crawling yet. At the toddler stage, she could renew her worries as to why the child is not yet talking. As soon as the child grows, a father may worry that the child is not at the same academic level as his or her peers. At the adult stage, parents may worry about their child's choice of a career or spouse. The list goes on and on. Children are not the only loved ones we tend to worry about. Our worry list may also include our spouses, parents, friends, neighbors, and others.

We have every right to worry about our loved ones. This is only natural. But like every other futile thing in life, worry will not do any good for them or for us.

In place of worrying, we can choose to do something that will be beneficial. We can trust God. When we worry less about our loved ones, we give God free rein to work. Trusting God with our family and friends is like giving Him the job of caretaker over them. God never backs away from His responsibilities. So we can sleep well through the night, knowing that all will be well with those we love. Let's trust God with those we care for. He will protect them.

Confession: *Lord Jesus, today I lift all my concerns to You. Please watch over my family, friends, and other people I know. You are the one true caretaker. Please care for them. Amen.*

DECEMBER 21

PEACE IN THE STORM

Suddenly, a fierce storm struck the lake, with waves breaking into the boat. But Jesus was sleeping.
Matthew 8:24, NLT

Today's text recounts the events that took place while Jesus was traveling with His disciples on a boat. On this day, a storm arose that overwhelmed those on board. The turbulence was so strong that it threw everybody into panic mode. Surprisingly, Jesus slept through it. He probably would have slept through the whole turmoil if He hadn't been awoken. When Jesus got up, His first reaction was astonishment. He was amazed at how those who had been around Him for so long still did not get what it meant to have Jesus on their boat.

In our journey through life, we will encounter different seasons. While some seasons are smooth and without hitches, others may be filled with turmoil. But so long as we are children of God, Jesus is in our boat. Through the turbulent times, He will be present. All He expects from us is what He displayed during the storm—peace.

God will never forsake us. Although surrounding circumstances may look like they will drown us, we will never sink. God is on our side. We need to believe this. His desire for us is that we have peace in the wildest of all storms. We can only do so if our trust is in Him alone.

Confession: *Jesus, thank You for being on my boat. I know You will never desert me. Through life's storms and challenges, I pray that my trust in You will be strengthened more. Amen.*

DECEMBER 22

PEACE IN THE STORM PART II

Even when I walk through the darkest valley, I will not be afraid, for you are close beside me. Your rod and your staff protect and comfort me. **Psalms 23:4, NLT**

Some time ago, a friend desperately wanted to move out of her apartment because she no longer felt safe. But the more she tried to move out, the more roadblocks she encountered. In frustration, she turned to God and asked why she was experiencing such difficulty. She requested to know why something as little as moving into a new place was that tough. God then said to her, "I need you to first learn how to be at peace in the storm." She confessed that it took a while to understand what God's words meant. But as soon as she handed her safety concerns over to God, she said she started experiencing significant changes. Somehow she began sleeping better, as opposed to worrying all night that she might be in danger. She started walking about her environs with confidence she never even knew she had. She said it was as if she had this invisible personal bodyguard watching over her. No matter what was going on around her, she knew she would be okay.

Not everyone will be required to go through this process, but we can learn a few things from her story. To enjoy God thoroughly, we must trust Him wholeheartedly. When we depend on God alone, we can be assured that when we go through the fire, it will not consume us. We can also trust that when we sail through the sea of turmoil, we will not drown. He is the God who uses His wings to guard His beloved. So long as we are under those wings, we can sleep at peace through the night. God, our protector, is on watch over our lives 24/7.

Confession: *Dear Lord, I decree that Your peace that passes all understanding is mine. When I walk through the valley, Your joy is mine. Everywhere I go, I walk in confidence, knowing You are watching over me. Amen.*

DECEMBER 23

WHATEVER IS YOURS WILL BE YOURS

And we know that God causes everything to work together for the good of those who love God and are called according to his purpose for them. **Romans 8:28, NLT**

I once listened to a preacher talk about how God withholds those things that do not belong to His children. I thought I understood this sermon until I was put to the test. On this occasion, I set out to do something. I had all the plans figured out and just needed to get everything in motion. But as soon as I set out, all I got were missed opportunities. One minute I would be very close to getting the resources I needed to achieve my plans. The next minute I would be told that the resources were no longer available. This happened over and over. But being a stubborn person, I persisted until I completely wore myself out. Then I finally turned to God and asked Him the popular question, "Why me, Lord?" Immediately I got the response, "It was never yours to begin with."

God knows what is best for us. We may assume we do, but we don't. No matter how great an opportunity may look, sometimes it is just not for us. If we would be patient enough to let God work out His plans, we would see that everything He does is for our good.

Every time God denies us something, He always gives us something better—maybe not immediately but eventually. One of the best ways to enjoy life is to never get ahead of God's plans for us. Let's choose to rely more on God's blueprint for our lives.

Confession: *Lord, I bless You for the times when You have said yes to me. I also appreciate You for when You have said no. Whatever will be detrimental to me in the long run, please take it away. If it is not mine, then I do not want it, no matter how fancy it may be. I will walk only in the path You have set before me. Amen.*

DECEMBER 24

OUR PLACE IN GOD

This day the LORD will deliver you into my hand, and I will strike you down and cut off your head. And I will give the dead bodies of the host of the Philistines this day to the birds of the air and to the wild beasts of the earth, that all the earth may know that there is a God in Israel! **1 Samuel 17:46**

God will purposely put us in situations where the only things we can depend on are His promises. During these times, all we may have to hang on to are our convictions. It's important we know our place in God. Only then can we enjoy our inheritance in Christ Jesus. According to today's text, David understood his place in God. He looked at the uncircumcised Philistine and told him, "The Lord will deliver you into my hand, and I will strike you down and cut off your head." He didn't say this trembling. Rather, he said it with complete authority.

God never fails those that hold on to Him against all odds. God never abandons those that trust Him in difficult circumstances. He always comes through for those that refuse to let the devil prevail over them. He always compensates those that choose to fear Him. He never deserts them. He ensures their songs end in praise.

Confession: *Dear God, thank You for making me Your heir. I claim my authority in You. I strike down every giant in my life today in Jesus' name. I refuse to let life's challenges get the best of me. I hold on to You. Amen.*

DECEMBER 25

EMULATING ESTHER

Go, gather all the Jews to be found in Susa, and hold a fast on my behalf, and do not eat or drink for three days, night or day. I and my young women will also fast as you do. Then I will go to the king, though it is against the law, and if I perish, I perish. **Esther 4:16**

I remember a particular time in my life when I was left with only two choices. I could either end or continue a mission. The logical thing to do was give up as none of my family were in favor of my pursuit. Many people even cautioned me against the so-called "bad idea." In their defense, they weren't intentionally pessimistic. I believe they meant well. Looking at things from a fair point of view, all odds were against me then.

The more I thought about giving in, the more I thought about Esther and her words, "If I perish, I perish." Esther had nothing going for her but God. She held onto God as she went on a mission some would have termed as impossible or suicidal. Like Esther's decision, mine was a tough choice. After much praying and deliberation, I chose to do that which Esther did. I held on to my God. Today I'm thankful I stood with my decision. It's been one of my best so far.

What's the point of life if all hopes become lost at the slightest discouragement? What is the essence of our Christianity if we cannot exercise our faith when faced with life's issues? God never disappoints. He came through for Esther, and He will do the same for those who choose to depend solely on Him in the most difficult of circumstances.

Confession: *Dear Lord, I hold on to You this day. I know I will encounter times when everyone will be against me. At such times, help me understand that You are all I need. When You tell me to go, please give me the strength to do so. Amen.*

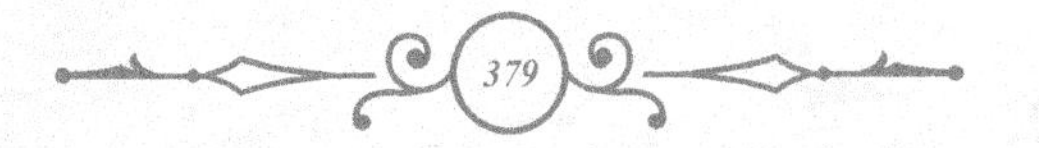

DECEMBER 26

•••

EVEN IF

"If this be so, our God whom we serve is able to deliver us from the burning fiery furnace, and he will deliver us out of your hand, O king. But if not, be it known to you, O king, that we will not serve your gods or worship the golden image that you have set up."
Daniel 3:17–18

And going a little farther he fell on his face and prayed, saying, "My father, if it be possible, let this cup pass from me; nevertheless, not as I will, but as you will."
Matthew 26:39

The first text (Daniel 3:17–18) summarizes the response of the three Hebrew men who refused to bow down to the king's image. The second (Matthew 26:39) tells of the state Jesus was in shortly before His crucifixion. In both scriptures, certain similarities can be seen.

The three Hebrew men went through an ordeal where they needed God to intervene. Yet whether God was going to save them or not, they were determined to only do that which God required. Before His crucifixion, Jesus, at Gethsemane, prayed that the "cup [would] pass from [Him]." Yet He was determined to only do the Father's will. It's worth noting that despite being 100% God and 100% man, Jesus also felt pain and anguish like we all do.

Some key features are worth observing in the lives of Hebrew men and Jesus. These include their absolute trust in God and willingness to lay down their lives, no matter what. What other lessons can be drawn from their stories? We will discuss these next.

Confession: *Lord, those who put their trust in You will have renewed strength. They will rise on wings like eagles. They will run and not get weary. They will walk and not grow weak. I believe You, and I claim all these blessings today. Amen.*

DECEMBER 27

EVEN IF II

He answered and said, "But I see four men unbound, walking in the midst of the fire, and they are not hurt; and the appearance of the fourth is like a son of the gods." **Daniel 3:25**

So then the Lord Jesus, after he had spoken to them, was taken up into heaven and sat down at the right hand of God.
Mark 16:19

The scriptures often reveal how God permits His children to go through challenges. Sometimes He gives the reason behind His actions. Other times He doesn't. Continuing from yesterday, the following can be drawn from the lives Jesus and the three Hebrew men:

- As long as we have God, we have everything and everyone we need.
- We will never run at a disadvantage with God when we put all our hope in Him.
- God often denies us what we want because He has something better and more glorious in store.
- For every challenge faced and conquered through trusting God, promotions follow (Daniel 3:30).
- Trusting God through our actions and lifestyle is crucial. In choosing to do so, others, including our enemies, may become saved in the process (Daniel 3:28–29).

God doesn't want us to merely trust Him. He wants us to rely on Him, especially when confronted with terrible situations. He wants us to depend on Him when we don't understand, because He understands. His thoughts toward us are of good and never of evil, to give us an expected end (Jeremiah 29:11). Let's always be reassured by this.

Confession: *Dear Lord, You are my everything.
Because I have You, I am complete. With You, there are no disadvantages.
I put my absolute trust in You today. I know that for all my troubles, You will bless me with double. Thank you, God, for Your kind thoughts toward me. Amen.*

DECEMBER 28

TRUST NOT IN WORKS AND THINGS THAT CAN BE SEEN ALONE

Jesus asked, "Will you never believe in me unless you see miraculous signs and wonders?"
John 4:48, NLT

Some Christians do not believe their prayers will be answered unless "spiritual materials" are used. These materials may include anointing oil, holy water, and more. Many do not believe God will hear them unless they go through anointed men of God. A lot of believers even unconsciously put more trust in their pastors than God.

As we continue in our spiritual walk with God, trust should also develop. At the babe or beginner's stage, we are permitted to have more of our beliefs in certain spiritual works. However, at some point, growth will be required of us. This is where most Christians encounter problems. Some believers find it is easier to believe in the visible than the unseen.

There is something called the simplicity of God. Until we fully understand this, we may not be able to key into what it means to be complete in God. Hebrews 11:1 says, "Now faith is the assurance of things hoped for, the conviction of things not seen." We do not have to see God to believe. All we have to do is believe. We do not need anything or anyone to help us communicate with God. We have full access to Him at every moment. There is no specific way or method to reach God—none whatsoever. Trust and belief are the keys to accessing heaven.

Confession: *Dear Jesus, today I declare that I believe. Please help my unbelief. I want to understand the simplicity it takes to connect with You more. I do not need any special person or thing to communicate with You. Teach me, Holy Spirit. Amen.*

DECEMBER 29

TRUST NOT IN SPIRITUAL EXERCISES ALONE

Trust in the LORD with all your heart,
and do not lean on your own understanding.
Proverb 3:5

Like the Pharisees in the Bible, many Christians practice religion and not Christianity. This is why some believers measure their connectivity with God by how much they pray or how long they fast. Many even equate their prominent church roles to their spiritual maturity. These days, it is very easy for people to get carried away.

Spiritual exercises like fasting, praying, and more connect us deeper with heaven. But these acts will only be fleshly if that intimate relationship with God hasn't been established first. The Bible encourages us to practice all these exercises without ceasing, but this is not so that we confine God's entirety to these acts alone. Prolonged praying, fasting, working in God's vineyard, and other disciplines are part of connecting with God. But there is more to God than these works. The entirety of God is in God alone and not just performing spiritual activities.

Is our trust more in our prayers? Or is it more in the One who answers the prayers? Where our trust lies is vital. Our one-on-one relationship with God is more important to Him than our doctrine. The state of our hearts matters to the Father. So long as our hearts are in the right place, the Holy Spirit will assist us through God's ordained spiritual walk.

Confession: *Dear Jesus, I thank you for the understanding of Your word today. Have mercy of for the ways I've substituted my spiritual connection with spiritual exercises. My heart is all You require. I don't want to miss You. I pray that You will show me all that You need of me in my walk with You. Amen.*

DECEMBER 30

WHEN WE PRAY

According to the Scriptures, when we pray:

- Time and place are inconsequential – I desire that in every place the men should pray. (1 Timothy 2:8a)
- It should be a private affair – But when you pray, go into your room and shut the door and pray to your Father who is in secret. (Matthew 6:6)
- Our motives should be genuine – And when you pray, you must not be like the hypocrites. For they love to stand and pray in the synagogue and at the street corners that they may be seen by others. (Matthew 6:5a)
- Our focus should be on God and not self – The prayer of a righteous person has great power as it is working. (James 5:16b)
- We should believe God will hear us – Therefore I tell you, whatever you ask in prayer, believe that you have received it and it will be yours. (Mark 11:24)

These are a few prayer guidelines as laid out by Christ and His disciples. These teachings will assist us in building a fulfilling and more effective prayer life. When we pray, let's keep them in mind. Let's also bear in mind some other guidelines as written in the Word of God.

Confession: *Dear Lord, thank You for showing me how to pray Your way. In my daily life, please help me remember this. In the place of prayer, I want to connect deeper with You. Please reveal Yourself to me. Amen.*

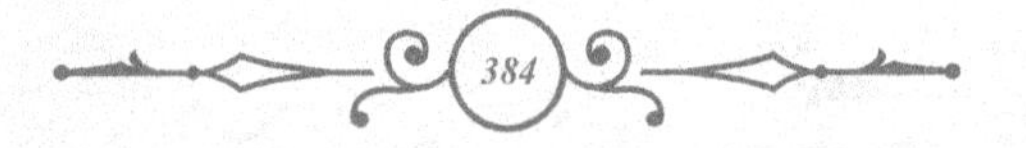

DECEMBER 31

TRUST THE "ME" IN THEM

The king's heart is a stream of water in the hand of the LORD; he turns it wherever he will.
Proverbs 21:1

I heard an unbeliever once say, "I trust everybody; it's just the devil in them I don't trust." At some point, I remember the Holy Spirit telling me something similar. The Holy Spirit said to me, "I am not asking you to trust people. I only ask that you trust the GOD in them."

There is a void in every person. This void can either be filled by God or the devil, depending on the individual's choice. God will never force Himself on people. This is why it is always encouraged that believers engage more with fellow believers. When they misbehave, we can expect that God will deal with them accordingly. There is a part of God in every legitimate child of His. So long as we are dealing with one, we should begin trusting God to take care of things.

Whether it is your spouse, child, friend, boss, or parent, please pray and trust God inside of them. God will do what needs to be done. He will fix all that is required to be fixed in them. He will turn their hearts. God always comes through for every devout child of His.

Confession: *Dear God, You own the hearts of kings. I lift all my loved ones to You today. Please turn their hearts more to You. Help them find You. Reveal Yourself more to them. Amen.*

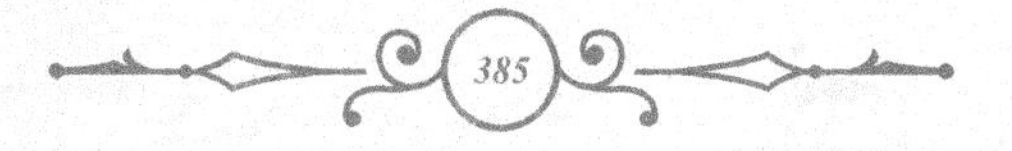

Made in USA - Kendallville, IN
1188914_9781735600307
11.02.2020 1449